C000293027

Cooking with Chillies

Cooking with Chillies

MEG JUMP

THE BODLEY HEAD
LONDON

For Gordon, Matthew, Alan, Ben and Sophie
. . . all of whom are addicted to chilli cooking

A Jill Norman Book

A CIP catalogue record for this book is available from
the British Library

ISBN 0 370 31363 1

Printed in Great Britain for
The Bodley Head Ltd
31 Bedford Square
London WC1B 3SG
by Butler & Tanner Ltd
Frome and London

First published in 1989

Acknowledgments

Many people have generously contributed towards this book. I would like to thank Estelle and Sophie Jump; the staff of the library at Kew Gardens, London; Ron Welsh; Mavis Hadcock; Kath Stevens; Dr Barbara Pickersgill; Dr Janet Long-Solis; Richard and Margot Calder; Bruce Foods Corporation; Graham and Audrey Tunley; Geoffrey and Maureen Davison; Veronica Garbutt; Jakarta Hilton Hotel; Susan Gallagher; Miskiah binte Ali; Rehanna Hameed; Devi Ragoo; Alan Hill; Anne Taylor; Tracey Holden and her mum; Nicole Grosset and Rémy Maurin; India House, London; The South African High Commission, London; The Sri Lankan High Commission, London; The United States Department of Agriculture.

I am particularly indebted to Elisabeth Lambert Ortiz who has allowed me to adapt and reproduce recipes for Caribbean hot pepper sauces, Mexican salsas and South American chilli sauces that have appeared in her authoritative books on Caribbean, Mexican and Latin American cooking. A list of these books is included in the bibliography on page 9. The recipe for Pescado en Almendrada on page 84 is also reproduced with her kind permission.

Jill Norman has edited this book and her help and advice have been invaluable.

My special thanks go to my husband whose support, patience and encouragement made this book possible. He also checked the manuscript, compiled the index and literally ate his way through most of the recipes that appear on the following pages.

Contents

Foreword

The aim of this book is very simple – to introduce the delicious diversity of chilli cooking. Some of the great chilli tastes are, of course, already international favourites – India's heritage of highly-spiced curries; the fiery bean concoctions of the south-western United States; Mexican *tacos* and *tortillas* liberally laced with chillies; racy stir-fried dishes from the Chinese province of Sichuan.

Others remain relatively unknown – the fragrant yet aggressively pungent cooking of South-East Asia; hearty food from North Africa, hot with *harissa*; chilli and peanut sauces from West Africa; spicy stews from the Caribbean and a vast range of hot pepper and tomato dishes from Central and South America.

To the chilli enthusiast, familiar perhaps with only one or two of these, the enormous scope of chilli cooking may come as something of a surprise, for the chilli pepper is extremely versatile. Fresh, dried, pounded, powdered, pickled and sauced, it is an indispensable basic ingredient in most tropical and subtropical national cuisines.

Around the world, chillies, in whatever form, are fried in different oils and fats, simmered in various liquids, blended with locally available herbs and spices, mixed with locally grown fruits and vegetables and served with traditional staple cereals.

The result is an abundance of tastes that often have little in common except the unmistakable piquancy of chillies. This does not mean, however, that all dishes must be stultifyingly hot. Many are, but many more are not. There is a popular misconception that the chilli pepper's main claim to fame is its ability to mask unpleasant flavours and kill all others stone dead! On the contrary. Powerful the chilli might be, but far from overwhelming other ingredients, its culinary magic works to highlight complementary tastes, drawing out their individual characteristics. This unique ability seemingly to predominate at first mouthful but then to mingle on the palate with other flavours and aromas, giving them added zest and vitality, is the genius of the chilli pepper. At its best, it can reach the pinnacle of gastronomic elegance and finesse. At a more mundane level, it makes food taste very, very good.

MEG JUMP, Entrevaux,
June 1987

Bibliography

Africa News Service Inc. The Africa News Cookbook. Viking/Penguin 1985
Andrews, Jean. Peppers. University of Texas Press 1984
Barraclough, Geoffrey (editor). The Times Atlas of World History. Times Books Ltd 1978
Benghiat, Norma. Traditional Jamaican Cookery. Penguin 1985
Bianquis, Laurent. Cuisine Créole. C.I.L. Paris 1988
Booth, George C. The Food and Drink of Mexico. Dover Publications 1979
Brissenden, Rosemary. South East Asian Food. Penguin 1969
Butel, Jane. Chili Madness. Workman Publishing (New York) 1980
Carbet, Marie-Magdeleine. La Cuisine des îles. Marabout (Paris) 1978
Davidson, Alan. Mediterranean Seafood. Penguin 1972
Haroutunian, Arto der. Complete Arab Cookery. Granada 1982
Haroutunian, Arto der. North African Cookery. Century Publishing 1985
Hutton, Wendy. Singapore Food. Ure Smith (Sydney) 1979
Lal, Premila. Meat Dishes. IBH Publishing Co (Bombay) 1969
Long-Solis, Janet. Capsicum y Cultura: la historia del chilli. Fondo de Cultura Económica (Mexico) 1986
Mallos, Tess. The Complete Middle East Cookbook. Lansdowne Press 1979
Mayat, Zuleikha. Indian Delights. Women's Cultural Group (Durban S.A.) 1970
Morichard, Colette (editor). Les Merveilles de la Cuisine Africaine. les éditions j.a. (Paris) 1979
Nguyen, Ngoc Rao. La Cuisine Vietnamienne et Chinoise. Marabout (Paris) 1977
Ominde, Mary. Mary Ominde's African Cookery Book. Heinemann Educational Books (East Africa) 1975
Ortiz, Elisabeth Lambert. Caribbean Cooking. Penguin 1977
Ortiz, Elisabeth Lambert. The Book of Latin American Cooking. Robert Hale 1984
Ortiz, Elisabeth Lambert. The Complete Book of Mexican Cooking. Bantam 1968
Passmore, Jackie. Oriental Snacks and Appetizers. Lansdowne Press 1981
Singh, Dharamjit. Indian Cookery. Penguin 1970
Solomon, Charmaine. The Complete Asian Cookbook. Summit Books 1976

Introduction

When my husband and I returned to Europe after five years of living in the tropics, our eating habits had changed radically and irrevocably. We were hopelessly – but very happily – addicted to chilli.

My early culinary background was bland and English in the extreme. I was born during the Second World War and my childhood was spent in the days of rationing. As I grew up, food became more varied and plentiful. My mother was an able – even adventurous – cook, but her repertoire was basically English. I do not think a clove of garlic ever found its way into her kitchen, nor oil, nor wine and I cannot remember ever seeing a chilli pepper in any form.

My first introduction to foreign food was as a student during the late 50s, when a Chinese restaurant opened in the Midlands town where I lived. A set lunch was served for three shillings and sixpence. My student friend Jenny and I would treat ourselves as often as we possibly could, but a complete meal each was beyond our modest means – so we always ordered one meal and two plates, dividing everything between us. We were young and pretty, and we got away with it for two years!

Then came the Indian restaurant boom in Britain during the early 60s, and the progression from Chinese to Indian cuisine was a natural one. As a keen cook, I began experimenting at home and became reasonably proficient in an amateurish sort of way. This was twenty years ago and there were very few Indian cookbooks, but there was a sizeable ethnic immigrant community in a nearby town, so buying spices did not present a problem.

At that stage, my chilli cooking was almost entirely based on the tastes experienced in Indian restaurants and I was not aware of exactly how limited a selection most of them offered in the context of the Indian subcontinent as a whole. The food was mainly typical of North India and Pakistan, but I did not understand that the cooking of other regions was considerably different. Although I ground my own spices, I barely scratched the surface of the subtle art of spicing, and chilli heat invariably came from chilli powder.

Apart from Indian dishes, I cooked a pretty mean *chili con carne* and was sometimes prompted to add a dash of Tabasco to a spaghetti sauce or a prawn cocktail. That was the sum total of my chilli cooking – and of my chilli eating.

All that changed when my husband was posted overseas. We lived first in Japan, then Singapore and the Middle East. From the beginning it was a gastronomic revelation. Every taste was startlingly new; most were unbelievably delicious; many were breathtakingly hot. Eating this food was not enough; I had to learn to cook it for myself. Many of the ingredients and techniques were unfamiliar. I did not know how to cope with a coconut, clean fresh squid or handle beancurd. I had never seen *lengkuas*, lemon grass, curry leaves, *krupuk* or *blachan*. I could not stir-fry, make up a dry *masala* or grind a wet spice paste.

I discovered, as well, that there was more to chilli than a bright red powder. Fresh chillies came in various shapes, sizes and strengths. They were mixed with soy sauce, fish sauce, palm sugar, yoghurt and coconut milk, or even nibbled raw! Dried chillies were roasted and pounded, soaked and mashed, or fried until black.

In time, I did master these new skills. First-hand instruction came from our cooks at home. They taught me in the same way that their mothers had taught them, and they showed me how to find my way around local markets and ethnic shops. As a journalist, I travelled (and ate) extensively and was grateful to be welcomed into the kitchens of housewives and professional chefs, who were always generous in sharing their knowledge.

When we left Asia to live in France, chilli food had become such a way of life that my husband and I knew we could not willingly do without it. So my kitchen cupboards continued to look much as they had done – a mass of pots and bottles filled with multi-coloured powders and an unlikely assortment of dried leaves, roots, twigs and bits of bark that are the essence of oriental food. I managed to grow a surprising number of tropical plants in my southern French garden, including a fine annual crop of chilli peppers. Compromise was, of course, necessary, and we also ate a great deal of French food, but chilli-hot Asian food played a major part in our daily diet.

My second chilli revelation came with an introduction to North African food. One cannot live in France for long without an awareness of the African connection. The French love affair with the African continent has marked similarities to the British fascination with India during the last century. There is an important African immigrant population in France, and Algerian,

Tunisian – and especially Moroccan – cooking have become popular since the return of the *pieds noirs* (French nationals who lived in North Africa) to France, after Algerian independence.

Chillies are an essential element in North African cooking, so it was not long before we had sampled a few dishes and found that it was very much to our taste. I discovered a new set of ingredient combinations, for chillies are blended with Mediterranean rather than Asian or tropical ingredients. Olive oil (as well as butter and *ghee*, which is called *smen* in Arabic) is the frying medium; the basic vegetables are artichokes, courgettes and sweet peppers, and olives and dates are used profusely. Familiar spices such as cumin, coriander and black pepper play an important part in North African cooking, and the fragrant spices, especially cinnamon, are added in generous quantities. This 'new' cuisine had, therefore, tantalizing echoes of Eastern cooking but offered unknown tastes, many of them involving chillies.

Next came a prolonged stay in Spain, followed soon afterwards by the discovery of Mexican cuisine. A pattern began to emerge, linking the food of Asia with the Middle East, North Africa and Spain via the spread of Islam; and from the New World to Spain with the exploits of Christopher Columbus and the colonization of South America. A distinctive element in this culinary chain was chilli.

From that point on, I was determined to find out everything I could about the chilli pepper – this vegetable-cum-spice that could, seemingly, be combined with almost any other ingredient with delightful results. And so *Cooking with Chillies* was born.

Although the cooking traditions of many lands are discussed in the following pages, this book cannot be – nor is it intended to be – an authority on each or any of them. It is a sampler of chilli dishes; an insight into the national cuisines of which they are a part; and a historical and culinary exploration of the links that connect one with another. It is a voyage of discovery.

Historical Background

The chilli pepper has a dual culinary personality. Fresh, it is a vegetable (or – to be more botanically precise – a fruit). Dried, it is a spice. As a member of the capsicum family, it is the fiery cousin of the sweet bell pepper and the relatively mild paprika pepper. It shares the same name as black pepper but is not, in fact, related.

The chilli pepper has very ancient origins. It is native to Central and South America, where it has been an essential part of the local diet for almost 9,000 years. Excavations at Teoctihuacan in Mexico have revealed evidence that chilli peppers were being eaten there around 7000 BC. These chillies were probably wild but remains of domesticated chillies were found at Huaca Prieta in Peru, dating from about 2500 BC.

Yet before 1492 it was unknown anywhere outside the Americas. When Columbus discovered America his goal was the East Indies, the spice islands of Java, Sumatra, the Moluccas and the Celebes. He was seeking for his royal patrons – Ferdinand and Isabella of Spain – a new sea route to the East, via the West, which would ensure for Spain domination of the lucrative spice trade. In terms of what he set out to achieve, Columbus failed miserably. He did not find a new route to the spice riches of the East; instead, he stumbled upon the New World which offered a bounty of strange new plants and an untasted spice, chilli.

When Columbus anchored off the Caribbean island that he named Hispaniola (now Haiti and the Dominican Republic), he believed he had found the spice islands of South-East Asia. This, perhaps, led him to think that the fiery fruit used by the natives to season their food was pepper. Geographically and botanically he was wrong. His misconceptions caused some consternation to contemporary navigators in the short term; botanists took longer to unravel the truth; but for cooks, chaos still persists.

It seems unlikely that anyone could seriously have mistaken the brightly-coloured fruit that grew so profusely on the Caribbean islands for wizened

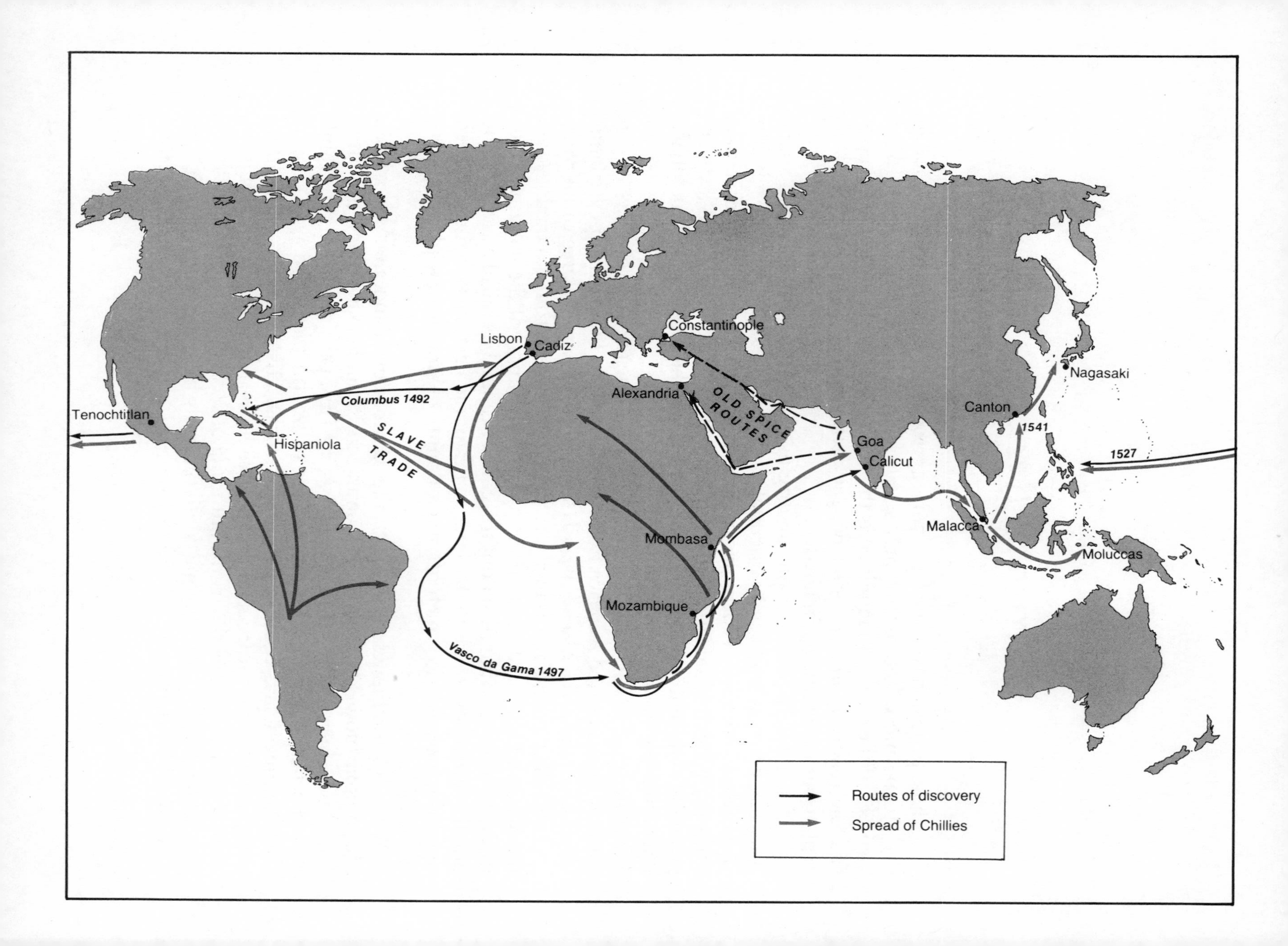
Tenochtitlan
Hispaniola
Columbus 1492
SLAVE TRADE
Lisbon
Cadiz
Constantinople
Alexandria
OLD SPICE ROUTES
Goa
Calicut
Mombasa
Mozambique
Vasco da Gama 1497
Malacca
Canton
1541
Nagasaki
Moluccas
1527
Routes of discovery
Spread of Chillies

black peppercorns, even though they both tasted hot, but this local fruit was christened *pimiento* by the Spaniards, after their word for black pepper – *pimienta*. To add to the confusion, another new berry was also called *pimiento*. This was allspice, which *does* resemble the peppercorn in appearance but does *not* have a hot, peppery taste.

The unsatisfactory result is that the word pepper can refer to all members of the capsicum family, to the peppercorn and to Jamaica pepper (allspice) . . . as can *pimiento* and *pimienta* in Spanish.

For the purposes of this book, the members of the capsicum family will be called chilli peppers or chillies for the hot varieties (and ground chilli in the dried and powdered form); sweet or paprika peppers for the mild varieties (and paprika for the dried and ground form). Jamaica pepper will be referred to as allspice.

The first mention that survives of this 'new' pepper is vague. When Columbus returned to Spain in 1493 he wrote to Ferdinand and Isabella, telling them of the paradise he had found. In his letter he describes native food as 'the food they [the natives] eat with very hot spices'.

More specifically, we know that 'peppers of many kinds and colours' were brought back to Spain on the return voyage, from the writings of Pietro Martyr. He did not visit the New World but was witness to Columbus's arrival at the Spanish court in April 1493. In September of that year, he recorded that 'something may be said about the pepper gathered on the islands and on the continent but it is not pepper, though it has the same strength and flavour, and is just as much esteemed. The natives call it axi.'

Later that year Columbus sailed again for Hispaniola, and in 1494 Dr Diego Chanca – physician to the fleet – wrote about local cooking in a letter he sent back to Spain. He said: 'The principal food consists of a sort of bread made from the root of a herb[1] . . . they use to season it, a vegetable called agi, which they also employ to give a sharp taste to fish and such birds as they can catch . . .'.

This *axi* or *aji* is what we now know as the chilli pepper – *axi* being the word used by the Arawak Indians who inhabited the Caribbean islands at that time. In many parts of South America the chilli pepper is still called *aji* – a Spanish derivation of the Arawak word.

As the Spanish forced their way across mainland South America they heard another word for the colourful vegetable-cum-spice that was equally indispensable in local cooking. In the language of the Aztecs, it was called chilli.

1. Sweet potato.

When Cortes and his conquistadores reached the highlands of Mexico, they discovered at the royal court of the emperor Montezuma a society that was unexpectedly brilliant and sophisticated. The gentle Arawaks and aggressive Caribs of the Caribbean islands were no more than primitive Indian tribes, but here in Montezuma's capital city of Tenochtitlan was a civilization of unsurpassed opulence and splendour.

Bernadino de Sahagun, a priest who accompanied Cortes on that first exploratory trip, has left invaluable detailed information on life at the Aztec court. He described 'the foods that the lords ate', which included 'turkey with a sauce of small chillies, tomatoes and ground marrow seeds; white fish with yellow chilli; grey fish with red chilli; frogs with green chilli; newt with yellow chilli'. His list covers hundreds of items and includes 'hot white doubled tortillas; large tortillas; tortillas formed into rolls; tamales with beans' . . . and 'bright red chocolate; orange-coloured chocolate; black chocolate; white chocolate'.

Sahagun chronicled the lives of the ordinary people too, showing that they also liked their food very hot and chilli-spiced.

The prehistoric South American Indians probably ate their chillies raw and whole, but the early Spanish reporters such as Sahagun state that chillies were – by that time – smoked and dried as well as being used fresh. They were usually pounded to a powder or paste before being simmered to make a sauce. The processing was done in a *molcajete* (from the Aztec words for chilli sauce and bowl), which continued to be the kitchen utensil for chilli preparation until recently, when the electric food processor began to take over the task.

Spain remained all-powerful in South America throughout the sixteenth century but the Portuguese bagged Brazil. Most of the other European nations managed to secure a share of the Caribbean islands and North America. As agriculture and trading became more established, hundreds of thousands of African slaves were shipped in to work on the new coffee plantations in Brazil, the Caribbean sugar plantations and the cotton plantations of the south-eastern states of North America.

Thus there developed in the New World a new civilization peopled by the surviving native Indians, the negro slaves and the white European pioneers. In later centuries, the Asian Indians and the Chinese came too. Each immigrant group brought to the New World ingredients and culinary traditions from its homeland. In time, new cultures and new countries were created, each of which has nurtured a distinctive cuisine in which the chilli pepper plays a greater or lesser role.

Meanwhile the chilli pepper was over-running the rest of the tropical world with incredible speed. Columbus had failed to find an alternative route to the East Indies to secure the spice trade for Spain, but his Portuguese rival, Vasco da Gama, fared better. After leaving Lisbon in 1497, he followed an easterly route via the southern tip of Africa and safely crossed the Indian Ocean, arriving at Calicut on the Malabar Coast in 1498. Retracing this voyage, subsequent Portuguese expeditions reached Malacca on the Malay peninsula in 1509, the Moluccas in 1512 and the Canton River in 1514.

The way was now clear for the Portuguese to take over as main suppliers of spices from the Middle East to Europe. By the mid-sixteenth century a string of more than fifty Portuguese bases stretched from Africa to Nagasaki in Japan, the principal administrative centre and headquarters of the governor-general being at Goa. This network of trading stations provided the stepping stones by which the chilli pepper traversed the world. Spices and other oriental goods were shipped to Europe via these entrepôt depots, but on outward voyages, plants from the New World, including chilli peppers, were sent to the East.

Once the first chillies arrived at Portuguese bases in India, South-East Asia and China, they were dispersed around the region by the many native cargo boats that sailed the Indian Ocean and the South China Sea. Arab traders were also very active along these marine routes and, no doubt, carried the peppers northwards and then along overland routes to the Middle East and the eastern Mediterranean. Paprika peppers are thought to have arrived in the Balkans this way by about 1570.

Sweet peppers were more suited to the Mediterranean climate so their introduction into southern Europe came directly from Spain and Portugal.

Little documentation is available regarding the movement of chillies within Africa but the Portuguese probably took them to West Africa soon after their trade routes were established. Certainly by the early eighteenth century, slave ship captains recorded that the daily diet of their slave cargo included chillies. From the west coast, the chillies might have been taken overland to the interior and the east coast but there was a long tradition of trading between the coastal settlements in East Africa, and India. Chillies could, therefore, have initially come to East Africa from Goa. In addition, Portugal had major bases at Mombasa (1505) and Mozambique (1507).

Ironically, the chilli pepper travelled all around the world before appearing on the doorstep of its original habitat. In pre-Columbian days, chillies had spread to the islands of the Caribbean but not – it seems – as far as the south-east mainland of North America. It was the Europeans who took the chilli pepper to the American states of the deep south – to feed their African slaves.

Botanical Background

The chilli pepper belongs to the Solanaceae family, which also includes tomato, aubergine, potato and tobacco. Peppers generally – i.e. sweet peppers, paprika peppers and chillies – come under the genus *Capsicum.* The capsicum is thought to have originated somewhere around the border between Peru and Bolivia and was one of the first plants to be cultivated by the Mesoamerican Indians, possibly as far back as 8,000 years ago. Because peppers hybridize readily, many strains, both wild and domesticated, had appeared in the Central American isthmus, the Caribbean and the northern half of the South American mainland by the time the Spaniards arrived.

From the twenty-two wild species of capsicum that have now been identified, five domesticated species have evolved. Most of the chillies raised commercially around the world belong to the *Capsicum annuum* species. The notable exception is the *tabasco* chilli pepper, which is grown on a large scale in Louisiana and selected areas of Mexico and Latin America for the production of Tabasco sauce. The *tabasco* pepper belongs to the *Capsicum frutescens* species. Also in this group are many of the tiny potent bird chillies that are grown for local domestic use in tropical regions. The three other species – *Capsicum baccatum* (*pendulum*), *Capsicum pubescens* and *Capsicum chinense* – are found mainly in South America but have been introduced to other parts of the world on a relatively small (or, at least, non-commercial) scale. One of the African cultivars of *Capsicum chinense* is reputed to be the hottest chilli anywhere.

Capsaicin

The heat in chillies comes from a substance known as capsaicin, which is manufactured in the placenta – the central pithy core of the fruit. From here, pungency is transmitted to the attached seeds and, to a lesser extent, to the pericarp or fleshy outer skin. Removing the core and seeds before cooking, therefore, reduces the pungency of a chilli.

The degree of heat in a pepper is solely dependent on the amount of capsaicin present and bears no relationship to the size of the pod. In fact the smaller chillies are usually the hottest, and many of the larger peppers are sweet peppers that contain virtually no capsaicin at all.

Capsaicin is incredibly powerful. Although it has no smell or flavour, its warmth is perceptible in a dilution of 1:1,000,000. It is so highly concentrated and is found in such minute quantities that it is practically impossible to measure scientifically. Human oral testing is the main method used to try and ascertain the capsaicin content in any given chilli pepper.

The Scoville Test, devised by an American pharmacologist in 1920, uses human guinea-pigs as tasters to assess – as objectively as possible – capsaicin heat. The test is carried out with a capsaicin extraction from the cultivar concerned. This is diluted, and a panel of five testers tries to evaluate the strength of the dilution using the Scoville Scale, which expresses pungency in Scoville Heat Units ranging from zero to 60,000+. For example, Mexican dried black chillies may rate around 3,000; *jalapeños* around 8,000; cayennes around 10,000; *tabascos* and bird chillies from 20,000+. A substantial element of subjectivity is inevitable, as the human tastebuds can react very differently to capsaicin. Also, familiarity leads to higher resistance, and testers must not be habitual chilli-eaters.

Various factors can affect the production of capsaicin. As a general rule, if the plant has to struggle during its growth it will reflect that stress by increased capsaicin production. Ideal conditions are a sandy loam soil, moderate daytime heat and slightly cooler night temperatures. So, for example, peppers from poor soil and those that have been subjected to a sudden period of unusually high day or night temperatures may have an unexpectedly high capsaicin content. By the same token, chillies that grow in a tropical climate, with maximum year-round heat, tend to be very hot. Those that grow in the tropics but at a higher altitude may be marginally milder.

The stage of maturity also affects pungency. Capsaicin continues to be produced throughout growth, but in the fully ripe fruit this is balanced by the ripening process, which converts starch in the immature chilli to sugar. Therefore, in the same way that an under-ripe apple tastes tart and a fully ripe apple tastes sweeter, the increased capsaicin in a mature chilli can be tempered by a certain sweetness. This means that it is misleading to assume that a red chilli is hotter than a green one of the same type. A more accurate guide, but by no means infallible, is the shape of the pod. By and large, the slimmer, more pointed and smaller the pepper is, the hotter it will be.

Flavour

In spite of the pungency of chilli peppers, they vary in flavour. Even very hot chillies can have a distinctive and sought-after taste. The flavour of a chilli comes from aromatic compounds located in the outer skin. This explains why some cooks keep very flavoursome chillies whole in the cooking pot, especially if the chilli is also very hot: the capsaicin heat is then contained within the pod and only the aromatic essences in the flesh escape into the simmering sauce.

Colour

Red peppers contain a strong colouring agent called capsanthin (capsanthin is not present in green peppers), which makes up 35 per cent of the pigmentation in a pod. The visual impact this has on dishes containing chillies complements perfectly the effect that chillies have on the tastebuds. When additional intensity of colour is required without extra pungency, many cooks combine chillies with sweet red peppers or paprika powder.

Selected Chilli Peppers

Choosing a representative selection of chilli peppers from the hundreds that exist (no one is quite sure exactly how many there are) is not easy. The types most commonly available will vary enormously in different parts of the world. The following choice covers those chillies that are (a) widely cultivated, (b) essential to certain major chilli cuisines, or (c) distinctively different.

Cayenne

Perhaps the best known chilli pepper in the world. French Guiana with its capital at Cayenne seems to be the likely original habitat, but the name was probably taken long before the town existed from the Cayenne River which flows through the region. However, cayenne chillies are no longer grown in French Guiana and have no modern connection with the town of Cayenne.

To add further confusion, the popular dried chilli condiment called cayenne pepper may – or frequently may not – be made from cayenne chillies. This particular chilli was one of the first to be taken from Latin America at the end of the fifteenth century. Today it is grown extensively in the United States, Africa, India, South-East Asia and the Far East. The cayenne chilli is relatively hardy and easy to grow.

Cayenne chillies are usually about 10 cm/4 in in length (although they can be longer), slender and tapering to a point. They are very hot, with a good flavour, and are picked at both the green and red stages of ripening.

For most of the recipes in this book which call for the use of 'fresh red or green chillies' cayenne chillies have been used. Similarly, the dried red chillies used have usually been dried red cayenne chillies unless otherwise stated.

Scotch Bonnet or Habanero

This is the favourite chilli pepper of the West Indians, and grows all over the islands of the Caribbean. Prettily lantern-shaped, its delicate appearance belies a powerful kick. Scotch Bonnets are very, very hot but this strength is combined with an exquisite fragrance, which explains their popularity. They are largely responsible for the unmistakable flavour of Caribbean dishes.

Scotch Bonnets are about 4 cm/1½ in in diameter and are eaten when yellow, orange and red. Raw, they are finely chopped for fresh chilli relishes. In cooking, they are often used with other chillies, the Scotch Bonnet being left whole so that the flavour permeates the sauce without excessive chilli heat.

Scotch Bonnets are one of the most delightful ingredients for the chilli cook. In season they are widely available in West Indian shops and markets. If unavailable, use a little bottled West Indian sauce, which has an authentic Scotch Bonnet flavour.

Jalapeño

Probably the most popular American chilli, with a passionate following that has reached cult proportions . . . *jalapeño* lollypops, would you believe?

Jalapeño chillies are an attractive rich dark green colour, about 5 cm/2 in long and about half as wide, tapering to a rounded tip. Their fascination undoubtedly lies in the combination of a formidable chilli heat balanced by freshness and sweetness – a blend that makes them irresistible for nibbling raw . . . if you can stand it!

Although found fresh only where they are cultivated – Mexico, Costa Rica and Texas – they are widely available canned (one version features deseeded *jalapeños* for easier eating) and pickled. Try them finely chopped in fresh relishes or as a garnish for *tortillas* and *tacos*, hamburgers and hotdogs, salads and stews. *Jalapeños* also seem to have a special affinity with Cheddar cheese . . . rather as English pickled onions do.

A *jalapeño* cannot be dried, but in Mexico is preserved by smoking, when it becomes a *chipotle*.

Serrano

Serrano chillies are small (4 cm/1½ in), pointed, green and bitingly hot. Used fresh in Mexico, they are widely available elsewhere canned and pickled. These powerful little green devils are popular for uncooked Mexican relishes and for *Guacamole* (p. 50). Fresh green cayenne chillies can be substituted.

Ancho and Mulato (Chiles Poblanos)

In their fresh dark green state, these two similar chillies are known in their native Mexico as *chiles poblanos*. Fresh, they are unlikely to be found outside Mexico and the bordering American states, but they are obtainable canned from Mexican specialist shops. *Chiles poblanos* are traditionally the chillies used for the classic Mexican dish – *Chiles Nogada* (Stuffed Chillies, p. 140). They are similar to the sweet bell pepper in size and shape, usually about 7.5 cm/3 in long; they are mild but spicier than sweet peppers.

When dried, these two similar *chiles poblanos* are called either *ancho* or *mulato* chillies. They both turn almost black and become wrinkled but are distinguishable – the *ancho* (which is probably the most commonly dried chilli in Mexico) is rounder in shape and milder in flavour; the *mulato* is more pointed with a more robust flavour. *Ancho* and *mulato* chillies both need soaking before use (see p. 29). They are then puréed with other ingredients to form the basis of a chilli sauce such as *Mole Poblano de Guajolote* (p. 168).

Pasilla

Pasilla chillies are the dried form of a distinctive Mexican chilli that is almost black in its fresh ripe state. About 15 cm/6 in long and thin, it becomes wrinkled when dried and retains its dark colouring, which is similar to that of *ancho* and *mulato* chillies. Almost all the production goes for drying and – like the *ancho* and *mulato* – *pasilla* chillies need soaking prior to use. They are then puréed with other ingredients and are often combined with *anchos* and *mulatos* to make *moles* (Mexican chilli sauces).

Mirasol

A favourite Peruvian chilli, also found in Mexico. It varies in size from 2.5 cm/1 in to 5 cm/2 in and in strength from fairly mild to fairly hot. Fresh, it is picked at the yellow or red stage of ripening but is never available outside the region. Dried, it is sometimes called *guajillo*. If unavailable, substitute any dried red chilli.

Bird (Birdseye) Chillies

Various kinds of chillies come under this colloquial definition. Tiny fireball chillies appear all around the world and should be treated with respect and caution. Never more than 2 cm/$\frac{3}{4}$ in long, they are all explosively hot.

Ripe red bird chillies mixed with soy or fish sauce are an essential side dish in Thailand, parts of Indonesia and the Malay enclaves on the southern islands of the Philippines. In India they are dried to give impact to curries. In Mexico, dried or fresh, they are known as *chiliquin* or *chitecpin*. In the south-western United States they are *pequin* chillies. Various African varieties exist, and the Japanese *hontaka* is one of the hottest chillies known.

Bird chillies are typical of pre-Columbian wild chillies (some still grow wild) in that they are minuscule, potently hot and often grow erect on the stem in clusters, rather than single and pendulous.

Processing

Except in truly tropical climates, chilli pepper plants produce only one crop a year and, in their fresh state, the fruit is perishable. Preserving and processing, therefore, ensures year-round availability. Many of the most common methods used today were being practised by Amerindian farmers thousands of years ago.

Drying

Natural sun-drying is the oldest and simplest way of preserving chillies. At its most basic, the pods are left on the plant in their fully ripe state until dry. A picturesque development of this is to thread mature chillies on strings, forming brilliant scarlet garlands that festoon local houses as they are hung out to dry.

Bulk drying, however, is usually achieved by spreading the chillies out in the sun either on sand or on wood or concrete floors, or by laying them out on specially prepared mats or beds. The chillies need to be turned frequently and imperfect fruit removed. Pods are sometimes flattened by trampling with bare feet.

The time required for natural sun-drying obviously depends upon weather conditions but can take up to a month. Only fully mature pods can be cured this way and thin-skinned varieties are the most suitable. Moisture loss results in dried chillies weighing approximately 25 per cent of their fresh weight.

Where natural drying is not possible or when a more controlled and/or faster method is required, dehydration by artificial heat is the answer. This method originated in the United States and is the normal system used for all commercial drying in America. It involves ovens, kilns or tunnels through which conveyor belts of chillies pass at predetermined temperatures. Hot air circulates through the chambers so that the fruit dries evenly. Processing can take anything from 24 hours to four days.

Smoking

In Mexico, *jalapeño* chillies – which are too thick-skinned to be dried successfully by either of the two previous methods – are cured by smoking in a pit which consists of an underground fire with a tunnel leading to a smoking chamber. The chillies are placed on bamboo racks and smoked until they become a dark brick red. This smoked *jalapeño* is still called by its original Aztec name – *chipotle*. Today it is likely to be more readily available smoked and then canned, in which case it may be called a *morita*.

Grinding

Almost all dried chillies are destined to be ground – either by the cook or in commercial mills. In the past, most cooks preferred to process dried chillies themselves so that they knew exactly what they were getting. Increasingly, though, commercially produced powders have proved to be more convenient and, therefore, more popular. Ready-made chilli powders can vary considerably in content – see p. 114.

Canning and Bottling

Many American and Mexican chillies are now canned so that they are universally available. Chillies treated this way will not have the crispness of a fresh pepper, but for most culinary purposes they are perfectly adequate.

As Texmex food becomes more and more popular, the wide range of canned, ready-cooked foods steadily increases. Convenience chilli foods account for a substantial amount of American chilli production.

Bottled chilli sauces are popular condiments everywhere.

Chilli Cooking

The chilli pepper does not stand in culinary isolation. It is essentially a great mixer. Its main role is to blend with other ingredients, giving them zest, sparkle and added definition. Chillies can, of course, be nibbled on their own as an adventurous appetizer or a tingling titbit, but the way in which they meld with other ingredients is their great contribution to the art of cooking.

Fresh Chillies

Until relatively recently, fresh chillies were often difficult to obtain outside their natural growing areas. In recent decades mass colonial immigration, improved air freight services and the food demands of a much-travelled public have radically changed the situation. Fresh chillies are today readily available in ethnic shops and increasingly in ordinary markets and supermarkets. The varieties on sale may vary, but the cultivars included in the previous section are among those most likely to be found.

When buying chillies, look for fruit which is fresh, shiny and crisp, not dull, wrinkled and flabby . . . though, if you are desperate, a none-too-fresh chilli is better than none at all! Washed and well dried, chillies will keep in the crisper drawer of a fridge for up to two weeks. If under-ripe, they will mature on a sunny window sill in the same way that green tomatoes will turn red.

The preparation of fresh chillies (and dried chillies, too) can be an unpleasant business, as the capsaicin in the fruit causes a burning sensation. Handling the hottest chillies can result in the hands remaining quite painful for up to two days, and the irritation is transmitted to any part of the body which is touched by the capsaicin-tainted hands. Even mild chillies can cause burning fingers for up to an hour.

Anyone with a sensitive skin is advised to wear protective gloves whenever handling chillies. *Everyone* should wear gloves when handling very hot chillies. Always wash hands in cool soapy water immediately after preparing chillies, and never, *never* touch a baby or young child. If you do inadvertently touch a particularly sensitive area – such as the eyes – rinse with copious amounts of cold water.

All work surfaces and kitchen utensils should be thoroughly washed after use.

Some of the larger chillies – *poblano* and *jalapeño*, for example – have a thickish skin which is protected by an outer membrane. Many cooks prefer to remove this outer layer, though this is not necessary if the chilli is destined to be ground to a purée. The easiest way to peel chillies is by blistering in a hot oven or under a hot grill, until the skin is charred and black. Plunge them immediately into iced water and the blackened skin will peel off quite naturally.

The heat level of a chilli can be decreased by blanching for 3 minutes in boiling water or by soaking in cold salt water for 1 hour before using. The pod may also be left whole (with the stem intact) for cooking – this will make it less potent. Take care not to puncture the pod while stirring, and remove it before serving.

Fresh chillies may be frozen for future use. If they require peeling, blister but do not remove the charred skin. This is best done after thawing out. Other whole chillies (with stems intact) should be blanched for 3 minutes. Allow to cool completely and pack in freezer bags, expelling as much air as possible before sealing. It is a good idea to pack the chillies in individual bags which are geared to the amount you normally use for one meal. Alternatively, wrap the pods separately in foil or film before packaging, so that they can be extracted singly.

When thawed, frozen chillies can be used like fresh chillies. They will, however, be softer than fresh chillies and are not always suitable for eating raw.

Dried Chillies

All dried chillies are intended for further processing – either by grinding to a powder or by soaking and pounding into a purée or paste.

Although commercially ground chilli powders are readily available, many cooks prefer to grind their own dried chillies so that they know exactly what is being ground. The simplest method is to use an electric coffee grinder. The chillies can be ground in bulk for storage up to 3 months, or in individual portions for one dish or one meal.

To grind dried chillies, wash them and allow them to dry completely. Remove the stems and tear the dried skins into pieces. The seeds can either be shaken out of the pod and discarded, or ground with the pod, depending upon the strength of powder required. Grind to a fine powder and store in screwtop jars.

Many Asian cooks prefer to dry roast the dried chillies before grinding. This process is the same as the dry roasting of spices, which is explained on p. 31.

Dried chillies that are to be reduced to a wet paste or purée need soaking before processing. Wash the chillies (there is no need to dry them), remove the stems and shake out the seeds. Tear the pod into pieces and soak in warm water for at least 15 minutes.

Larger, thicker dried chillies, such as the Mexican black chillies, will need to soak for at least 1 hour. Drain and place in the container of an electric blender or food processor with the other ingredients that are to be puréed. Asian pastes prepared in this way are very dry, but Mexican purées have some liquid added before blending. In this case, some of the soaking liquid may be used.

Ground Chilli Powders

Commercially milled ground chillies are available all around the world and are sold simply as 'chilli powder'. However, they may vary considerably in content. American and Mexican chilli powders will almost certainly contain a blend of various types of chillies and may even include other spices such as cumin. Salt may be added too. Close inspection of the packaging may – or may not – reveal just what is contained therein. One thing is certain – it will be very different from an Indian or African chilli powder.

For this reason, the term 'chilli powder' is not used in this book. Ground chilli is called 'ground chilli' and means exactly that – a grinding of dried red chillies of the cayenne type and of the cayenne strength.

The term 'cayenne pepper' is also used, and the two can be substituted for each other in the following recipes.

If an American or Mexican chilli powder is being used for the recipes in this book, the other listed ingredients should be adjusted accordingly.

Cayenne Pepper

See above.

Chilli Flakes

These coarsely ground dried chillies can be used like ground chilli and added directly to the cooking pot. They can also be soaked and used like dried chillies.

Canned and Bottled Chillies

If the actual type of chilli contained in a can or jar is not clearly stated, the only sure way to ascertain the capsaicin strength is by tasting.

Rinse the canned or bottled chillies in fresh water and treat as fresh chillies. If they are being used for an Asian paste, drain them well so that they do not add extra liquid to the paste.

Bottled Chilli Sauces

The most famous bottled chilli sauce is probably Tabasco, a fiery liquid extraction of *tabasco* chillies; but every continent has its own wide selection of chilli sauces, the flavours of which reflect the basic tastes of local cooking. These sauces are essentially condiments intended to be added after cooking for extra heat, or as side dishes and dips. They can also be used in cooking, but will give chilli flavour without the bulk of fresh or dried pods.

A further selection of chilli products appears on pp. 37–44. Instructions are given for their preparation but most of them are also available ready-made.

Spices

Spices are an essential ingredient in all chilli cooking, but it is in the food of the Indian subcontinent and South-East Asia that they reign supreme. In order to capture the full flavour and aroma of the most fragrant spices, it is normal kitchen practice in this part of the world to roast and grind whole spices for each dish.

In chilli cooking outside this area, spices play a vital but more supplementary role. Cooks are therefore not as finnicky and ready-ground spices are more acceptable. It is a fact, though, that ready-ground spices lose their flavour if they have been sitting around for too long on a shop or kitchen shelf. It is also true that pre-packed ground spices are sometimes liable to adulteration with expanders such as rice flour. Many cooks, therefore, prefer to grind their own spices in bulk, if not for individual dishes.

If you have not yet attempted preparing your own spices, I strongly recommend that you give it a try. You will find that it is well worth the extra trouble.

Modern hygiene laws are strict but it is worth picking over the spices and removing any stray twigs, stems and leaves. It is unlikely they will need washing but if they do, rinse them under cold running water and allow them to dry completely, ideally on wicker trays for good air circulation. Drying is best done in the sun or, if this is not practical, in an airing cupboard or cool oven with the door slightly ajar. Redistribute and turn the spices at intervals so that they dry evenly.

Whole spices can be stored in screwtop jars for up to 6 months, or will keep almost indefinitely in airtight containers in the freezer. They do not deteriorate or lose their flavour.

Before grinding, whole spices should be dry roasted by warming them in a heavy frying-pan over medium heat, shaking and stirring all the time so that they roast uniformly and do not burn. This will take 3–4 minutes and releases their aroma. It also makes them easier to grind. Except in Sri Lankan cooking, where spices are roasted to a deep brown giving a very distinctive flavour (see p. 37), the whole spices should change colour only slightly during roasting, to no more than a golden brown.

Grinding is traditionally done with a pestle and mortar or on a grinding stone, but a small electric coffee grinder is a more sensible method for the Western cook. Let the spices cool down for a minute, otherwise condensation will tend to make them a bit damp during grinding in an enclosed container. Do not fill the grinder more than two-thirds full, and work in bursts of no more than 10 seconds. Continue grinding until a fine powder is obtained. This will normally take a maximum of about twelve 'bursts'.

Herbs

The distinctive flavour and aroma of many chilli dishes come not only from spices but from the liberal use of roots, twigs, leaves and grasses, collectively called herbs. Some are so localized that they are not even national. They are plants that grow wild in the jungle or are cultivated in tropical backyard gardens. Many of those that are grown commercially do not thrive in a temperate climate and so may not be available fresh to European cooks. Others are available in dried or powdered form, but all too often are so lacking in vitality that they are hardly worth using. For example, the lovely fragrance of lemon grass cannot be achieved with a powder. In my experience, a small strip of fresh lemon rind makes a far more successful substitute.

Fresh coriander is an essential ingredient in Thai, Indian and Mexican cooking. It is often available from oriental shops, but parsley can be used as a substitute if necessary, although the flavour is very different.

Mint is the mainstay of much Middle Eastern and Indian cooking but, once again, it must be fresh. Rather than dried mint, use fresh parsley or coriander.

Leafy herbs (including basil) can be stored for a surprisingly long time in the fridge. Take freshly picked sprays that have been washed and shaken dry. Put them in a polythene bag and they will remain in good condition for a week or more. Chopped fresh herbs may be kept for about a week in the same way.

Fresh herbs can also be satisfactorily frozen. Wash, chop finely, put into ice-cube trays with a little water, and freeze. Alternatively, put the leaves with a little water into the container of an electric blender or food processor. Blend to a purée and freeze in ice-cube trays. Individual frozen cubes can be dropped directly into the cooking pot but are not suitable for a garnish.

Coconut Milk

The combination of chillies and coconut is basic to cooking throughout the tropics. Coconut milk is extensively used to enrich both savoury and sweet dishes.

There is some confusion about exactly what coconut milk is; it is *not* the watery liquid stored in the centre cavity of the nut. Coconut milk is an extraction obtained from mixing grated coconut flesh with water. Sometimes milk or cream are used instead of water to give a richer blend. In the following recipes, water should be used to make coconut milk unless stated otherwise.

Two strengths are commonly used – (standard) coconut milk and thick coconut milk. The instructions below explain clearly how each is made: recipes specify which should be used.

Happily for European cooks, a supply of fresh coconuts is not necessary in order to make coconut milk. There are cheap alternatives that are perfectly satisfactory and much less trouble.

1 *Desiccated coconut* offers the cheapest substitute. Put 50 g/2 oz desiccated coconut into the container of an electric blender with 250 ml/8 fl oz hot water and blend at high speed for 30 seconds. Strain the mixture through a fine sieve, pressing down with a spoon and scraping off the thick extraction that clings to the underneath of the sieve. Put the same coconut back into the container of the blender and repeat the process with another 250 ml/8 fl oz hot water. The combined yield of these two pressings is standard coconut milk. If a recipe calls for thick coconut milk, use the yield from the first pressing only.

   To make coconut milk from desiccated coconut without a blender, leave the hot water mixture to stand for 10 minutes, press thoroughly for a couple of minutes and then proceed as above.

2 *Creamed coconut* is very easy to use and is closest to the flavour of a fresh coconut. It is sold in 200 g/7 oz blocks and should be kept in the

refrigerator. To make standard coconut milk, dissolve 25 g/1 oz creamed coconut in 250 ml/8 fl oz boiling water. For thick coconut milk, dissolve half a block of creamed coconut in 250 ml/8 fl oz boiling water.

In some instances, I do not bother to dilute the creamed coconut but add it in pieces during cooking. Where I have found this to be particularly appropriate, I have adapted recipes accordingly, and solid coconut cream is listed in the ingredients.

3 *Canned coconut milk and coconut cream* can be bought but I find them lacking in flavour. However, it can be handy to keep a can or two in reserve. Use coconut milk straight from the can after stirring well. Dilute coconut cream to the required strength.

With this choice of relatively cheap, trouble-free substitutes, only the most enthusiastic of European cooks is likely to tackle a real coconut. If you do have a fresh coconut to hand, this is the way to deal with it.

A coconut is opened round its 'belly', not from top to bottom. Hold the coconut in one hand with the 'belly' uppermost. Tap it sharply in the centre with the back of a heavy cleaver. Keep turning and tapping around the 'belly' until the shell cracks and eventually splits. If necessary, assist the splitting by prising open the crack with the blade of a knife. The liquid inside a coconut has few culinary uses, so save it for drinking.

Put the two halves of the coconut in a slow oven (120°C/250°F/gas 1) for 15–20 minutes, when the flesh will start to come away from the shell. Prise out the flesh and cut away the brown skin.

The flesh now has to be grated. In countries where coconuts are everyday food, a specially-designed sturdy grater is standard kitchen equipment. An ordinary grater is not really tough enough for the job and it is all too easy to end up with scraped knuckles in addition to grated coconut. An electric blender is the answer. Reckoning on 250 ml/8 fl oz of water to each half coconut, cut the coconut flesh into manageable chunks and blend with the water until reduced to a purée. Now repeat as for desiccated coconut but, because fresh coconut is more moist, a third pressing is often possible.

Please note that coconut milk – however it is made – deteriorates quickly and should always be kept in the refrigerator. A pinch of salt will prevent it turning sour too quickly in hot weather. Coconut milk can also be deep-frozen but the solid, oily part will separate. As long as the milk is going to be cooked, this does not matter. It will reintegrate when heated.

When coconut milk is heated curdling is a constant potential hazard. When it is added to other hot ingredients, it should be stirred all the time while it is coming to the boil. Never cover a pan that contains coconut milk during cooking, as the condensation can cause curdling. For this reason coconut milk is added towards the end in all dishes that require long, slow simmering. Such extended cooking is best done in a covered pan to avoid too much evaporation, and this would not be possible if the simmering liquid included coconut milk.

In dishes that require shorter cooking, it is more usual for coconut milk to be added with any other liquids, after frying the main ingredients and seasonings. Thick coconut milk, on the other hand, is more commonly stirred in just before serving so that it gives body and retains all its rich flavour.

As coconut milk cooks it releases its natural oil, which takes on the colour of the chillies and other spices and floats on the surface of the sauce. A brightly coloured, oily film is, therefore, quite normal – even desirable – and does not indicate that the dish is too greasy.

Oils

A variety of oils are used in chilli cooking around the world, each giving a distinctive flavour – mustard oil, coconut oil, palm oil, dende oil. Many of these are not well known in Europe and others have a taste that is sometimes unpleasant to western palates. Although it may not always produce a truly authentic taste, the selection of oils incorporated in recipes in this book has been simplified to use one of the following:

1. Where a recipe specifies 'oil', a *polyunsaturated oil* with no pronounced taste, such as corn oil, peanut oil or sunflower seed oil, is preferable.
2. *Olive oil* is widely used in Latin American, North African and Middle Eastern cooking. Best-quality oil from the first pressing is rich and thick, with a full-bodied flavour that gives an unmistakable taste and texture to sauces and vegetable dressings. If preferred, substitute half olive oil and half one of the above oils, for a lighter (and cheaper) dish.
3. *Sesame oil* is the thick, golden extraction from sesame seeds that is indispensable for some Chinese dishes, where it is used as a final flavouring rather than as a frying medium. Sesame oil is also an essential ingredient in Korean cooking.

Fats

Modern attitudes to healthy eating discourage excessive use of solid fats. Some chilli cooking, however, traditionally incorporates alarming amounts of butter, *ghee* (clarified butter) and lard or rendered pork fat. The taste of the finished dish may be superb but some cooks (and I am one) cannot bring themselves to put that much potential cholesterol in the cooking pot! Where it seems appropriate, therefore, I have reduced the quantities of fats commonly used. If the fat content is still unacceptable, substitute oil for part of the fat specified but use enough butter, *ghee* or lard for flavouring.

Onions

Onions are an essential ingredient in almost all chilli cooking. Shallots are particularly favoured by South-East Asian cooks for their distinctive flavour. Spring onions are popular in Chinese and Indo-Chinese cooking.

The preparation – coarsely chopped, finely chopped, finely sliced, etc. – is often an element in producing the desired texture for the finished dish, as is the degree of frying, which affects the colour, taste and texture.

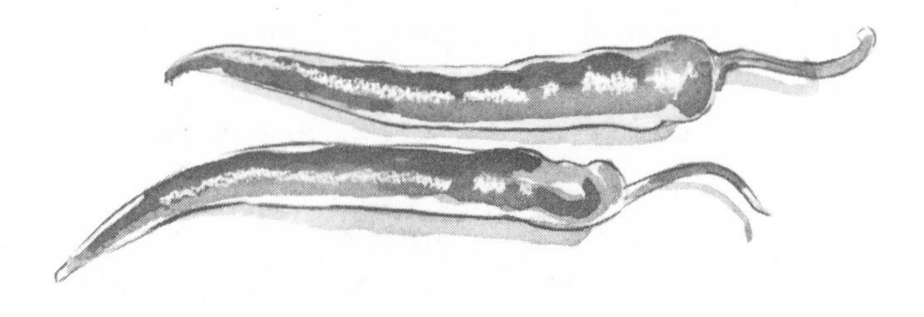

Dry Spice Preparation

Curry Powders

Popular opinion suggests that there is no place for curry powders in Indian cooking. I do not believe this is strictly true. It is a fact that the ubiquitous turmeric-tinted, general-purpose, commercially produced curry powder is rarely seen in kitchens where curries are cooked regularly. The art of spicing is sophisticated and complex, so no single powder can conceivably satisfy the subtle and diverse demands of meat, fowl, fish, vegetables and eggs.

However, there are definite patterns to classic spice combinations, many of which use the same basic spices in similar proportions. These spices can be mixed to make a ready-made ground powder that will provide the body of the seasoning in certain dishes. Extra character and individuality comes from additional spices – often whole spices – which are chosen according to the main ingredient.

Even so, curry powders offer only limited scope to the creative cook and the majority of recipes in this book are spiced with freshly ground whole spices.

I do not put any chilli in my curry powders. I find it more practical to adapt chilli content to my mood or to the palate of my guests at the time of cooking. It is easy enough to make food hotter but not so easy to take away unwelcome fire power! I have, however, included a token amount of chilli in the following recipes in the form of ground chilli or dried red chillies. Remember that dried chillies destined to be ground do *not* need soaking.

Spices for curry powders should be dry roasted and ground according to the instructions on p. 31. After grinding, mix the spices together thoroughly, including any ready-ground spices such as turmeric. Allow to cool completely and store in screwtop jars. Label clearly.

Curry powder will keep fresh for up to 3 months. Alternatively, it can be stored in airtight containers in the freezer. It will remain fresh almost indefinitely and will not set solid.

Meat Curry Powder*

6 tablespoons coriander seeds
2 tablespoons cumin seeds
1 tablespoon fennel seeds*
12 black peppercorns
4 cardamom pods*
4 cloves
5 cm/2 in cinnamon stick
10 dried red chillies or 1 teaspoon ground chilli
1 tablespoon ground turmeric

Fish Curry Powder

6 tablespoons coriander seeds
2 tablespoons fennel seeds*
1 tablespoon cumin seeds
1 teaspoon fenugreek seeds*
10 black peppercorns
10 dried red chillies or 1 teaspoon ground chilli
1 tablespoon ground turmeric

Sri Lankan Curry Powder

Sri Lankan curries have a distinctive flavour and colour, due to the special roasting of spices. Before grinding, the spices are roasted until they are a rich dark brown which gives them – and the actual curry – an aroma and taste that is quite different from Indian curries. When preparing Sri Lankan spices, it is important that each spice is dry roasted separately, as some reach the correct stage of roasting faster than others, and will very easily burn.

Although Sri Lankan curries can be excessively hot, this curry powder contains relatively little chilli. Individual recipes specify the addition of extra ground chilli or fresh green chillies, which are popular with Sri Lankan cooks.

4 tablespoons coriander seeds
2 tablespoons cumin seeds
½ tablespoon fennel seeds*
1 teaspoon fenugreek seeds*
2.5 cm/1 in cinnamon stick
5 cloves
4 cardamom pods*
1 tablespoon dried curry leaves* (if available)
10 dried red chillies or 1 teaspoon ground chilli

* Notes on items marked with an asterisk can be found in the Glossary, p. 279.

South African Curry Powder

South African curry powders are conspicuous by their emphasis on the fragrant spices and their high turmeric content. They have perhaps evolved to complement the sweetness of some popular meat dishes, which feature dried and fresh fruits, chutneys and jams among their ingredients.

- 3 tablespoons coriander seeds
- 2 tablespoons cumin seeds
- 2 teaspoons fennel seeds*
- 1 tablespoon fenugreek seeds*
- 1 teaspoon cloves
- 1 teaspoon black or white peppercorns
- 1 tablespoon cardamom pods*
- 3 teaspoons chilli
- 3 tablespoons ground turmeric
- 1 teaspoon ground ginger

Caribbean Curry Powder

During the last century Hindu Indians migrated to the Caribbean, settling mainly in Trinidad, where ethnic Indians today make up about one-third of the population. Their curries have undergone some changes but are still essentially Indian. It is interesting to note that as fresh red chillies are so widely used in Caribbean cooking, dried or ground chilli is not necessarily included in curry powders.

VERSION 1

- 3 tablespoons coriander seeds
- 4 tablespoons cumin seeds
- 1 tablespoon poppy seeds
- 1 tablespoon cloves
- 1 tablespoon black mustard seeds*
- 1 teaspoon black peppercorns
- 2 teaspoons ground ginger
- 4 tablespoons ground turmeric

VERSION 2

- 4 tablespoons coriander seeds
- 1 tablespoon cumin seeds
- 1 tablespoon fenugreek seeds*
- 2 teaspoons black peppercorns
- 1 tablespoon cardamom seeds*
- 7.5 cm/3 in cinnamon stick
- 1 tablespoon ground ginger
- 4 tablespoons ground turmeric

Garam Masala

Like curry powder, *garam masala* is a mixture of ground spices but it is used in a very different way. In practice, curry powder provides the basic body of seasoning for a dish. In contrast, *garam masala* gives additional spice finesse.

It is used in much smaller quantities and is dominated by the fragrant spices. It may be added at the early frying stage but is more likely to be sprinkled on during the last few minutes of cooking.

There are as many versions of *garam masala* as there are cooks. Mix and match and make your own!

Garam Masala 1

4 tablespoons cumin seeds
1 teaspoon black peppercorns
2 teaspoons cloves
1 tablespoon cardamom pods*
10 cm/4 in cinnamon stick
¼ nutmeg

Garam Masala 2

2 tablespoons coriander seeds
1 tablespoon cumin seeds
2 teaspoons black peppercorns
1 teaspoon cardamom seeds* (husks removed)
1 teaspoon cloves
5 cm/2 in cinnamon stick

Fragrant Garam Masala

1 teaspoon cloves
1 teaspoon mace blades
1 teaspoon cardamom seeds* (husks removed)
10 cm/4 in cinnamon stick

Other Dry Spice Preparations

Ras-el-Hanout

A spice mixture widely used in North African cooking. The better-quality bought mixtures are supposed to include a couple of dozen or more spices, but this recipe is adequate. Alternatively substitute *Baharat* (next recipe).

To make *Ras-el-Hanout*, mix together the following ground spices in equal quantities:

Fragrant Garam Masala

cinnamon
cardamom
cloves
allspice
ginger
ground chilli
black pepper

Baharat

In the cooking of the Arabian Gulf, this blend of spices is the equivalent of the Indian *garam masala*.

Ingredients	
1 tablespoon black peppercorns	ground together
1 tablespoon coriander seeds	
1 tablespoon cumin seeds	
1 tablespoon cloves	
5 cm/2 in cinamon stick	
½ whole nutmeg	
6 cardamom pods,* husks discarded	
2 tablespoons paprika	
1 teaspoon ground chilli	

Berber

A fiery ground chilli and spice mixture that seasons Ethiopian cooking. Definitely not for the faint-hearted!

- 4 tablespoons ground chilli
- 2 tablespoons paprika
- ½ teaspoon ground black pepper
- ½ teaspoon ground ginger
- ¼ teaspoon each ground cardamom,* coriander, fenugreek,* nutmeg, cloves, cinnamon and allspice*

Wet Spice Preparation

Making a Wet Spice Paste

Grinding 'wet' spices – i.e. onions, garlic, ginger and chillies – to a paste is the first stage in preparing many Asian dishes. Although recipes are included here for spice pastes that can be made in bulk and stored for use when required (Curry Paste see below and *Sambalan* on p. 42), this processing is usually done individually for each dish. Traditionally the wet spices are pounded manually, but the obvious alternative for the Western cook (and, increasingly, for any Asian housewife who has electricity) is an electric blender or food processor. With these machines the operation is completed in seconds, but there is one point that needs mentioning.

When wet spices are pounded manually, no liquid is added. In order to facilitate the proper blade action of a blender or food processor, extra liquid may be necessary. If the paste is going to be fried, add some of the oil that will be the frying medium. If the paste is going to be boiled, add water, stock or coconut milk – whatever seems appropriate.

Inevitably the additional liquid will produce a softer, wetter paste. This will not affect subsequent boiling but does require attention if the paste is to be fried. To fry the spice paste, heat the remaining oil in a heavy frying-pan or wok until fairly hot. If no oil remains, this is not a problem – simply heat the dry pan. Add the spice paste and fry over a gentle heat for 5–15 minutes (depending on the moisture content), stirring constantly to prevent burning. Initially the paste may appear to be simmering rather than frying. Don't worry – eventually the excess liquid will evaporate, the oil will surface and frying will begin. Continue frying until the paste smells 'cooked'. It will also reduce in quantity and take on a richer, darker colour.

Curry Paste

Keep a jar of this home-made paste in stock for quick curry-making. Simply fry the onions specified in the recipe you are using and then add 1 tablespoon of the paste for each 500 g/1 lb of meat or fish, in place of the usual ginger, garlic and spices. To make a sauce, add yoghurt or coconut milk. This is a fairly hot paste.

- 10 cloves garlic
- 2 tablespoons chopped fresh ginger
- 6 tablespoons ground cumin
- 1 tablespoon ground black pepper
- 1 tablespoon black mustard seed*
- 1 tablespoon ground chilli
- 1 tablespoon ground turmeric
- 1 teacup closely packed coriander leaves
- 2 tablespoons vinegar
- 200 ml/7 fl oz oil

Put all the ingredients except the oil into the container of an electric blender. Blend to a purée, adding a little of the oil if necessary to make the blades work properly. Heat the remaining oil in a heavy frying-pan. When fairly hot, add the spice paste and reduce the heat. Fry the paste, stirring constantly, until the oil separates. This will take about 10 minutes. Cool and bottle.

Hilba

A chilli-hot fenugreek paste from the Gulf.

- 2 teaspoons fenugreek seeds,* soaked in water for 24 hours
- 3 cloves garlic
- 1 teacup closely packed coriander leaves
- ½ teaspoon salt
- 2 teaspoons lemon juice
- 2 fresh red chillies, deseeded and chopped

Soaking the fenugreek seeds will produce a jelly-like coating. Drain them (reserving the liquid) and put with all the other ingredients into the container of an electric blender. Blend to a smooth purée. If more liquid is necessary to make the blades work properly, add a little extra lemon juice or the reserved fenugreek soaking water. Store in a screwtop jar in the fridge.

Sambalan

Used in the same way as the curry paste recipe on p. 41, this Indonesian paste features the typical combination of chillies, dried shrimp paste and palm sugar. To make a quick, easy, complete dish, fry meat or fish in oil and add the *sambalan* – 2 tablespoons for each 500 g/1 lb of main ingredient – for the last 5 minutes cooking. If a sauce is required, add coconut milk (p. 32).

- 20 dried red chillies, stems and seeds removed

- 3 large onions, chopped
- 10 cloves garlic, peeled and chopped
- 2 tablespoons chopped fresh ginger
- 2 teaspoons dried shrimp paste*
- 150 ml/¼ pint oil
- juice of 1 lemon, made up to 250 ml/8 fl oz with water
- 2 tablespoons palm sugar* or dark brown sugar
- 2 teaspoons salt

Soak the dried chillies in warm water for 30 minutes. Drain and tear them into pieces. Put into the container of an electric blender with the onions, garlic, ginger, dried shrimp paste and oil. Blend to a purée, using a little extra oil if necessary.

Heat a heavy frying-pan or wok and cook the chilli paste over a medium heat for 5–10 minutes until the oil has separated and the paste has turned dark red. Stir constantly to prevent sticking. Add the remaining ingredients and simmer for 2 minutes. When cool, store in a screwtop jar in the fridge. *Sambalan* will keep for a month.

Sambal Ulek

Originally an Indonesian preparation, this is ideal for using instead of fresh chillies in any dish, as it contains no other flavourings than salt and vinegar. Make it when you have a good supply of fresh red chillies. When cooking, use 1 teaspoon of *sambal ulek* in place of 2–3 fresh chillies.

- 25 fresh red chillies, stems removed
- vinegar
- 1 teaspoon salt

Put the chillies with their seeds in the container of an electric blender. Add just enough vinegar to allow the blades to work properly, and blend to a coarse paste. Add the salt. Put in sterilized jars and store in the fridge.

Aji

A South American chilli paste that can be used instead of fresh chillies in many recipes.

- 50 g/2 oz dried red chillies, stems (and seeds if preferred) removed
- 3 tablespoons olive oil
- 4 cloves garlic, peeled and crushed
- ½ teaspoon salt
- 125 ml/4 fl oz water

Soak the dried chillies in warm water for 30 minutes. Break each chilli into 3 or 4 pieces and put in the container of an electric blender with all the other ingredients. Blend to a smooth purée, adding a little more water if necessary. Store in a screwtop jar in the refrigerator for up to 1 month.

Harissa

This is the classic chilli sauce of North Africa. It is used instead of fresh chillies but is also served as a condiment, when it is usually diluted with water. I mix a little with commercially bottled tomato ketchup . . . kids love it!

- 100 g/4 oz dried red chillies, stems and seeds removed
- 4 cloves garlic, peeled and crushed
- 2 teaspoons ground coriander
- ½ teaspoon ground caraway
- 1 teaspoon salt
- water

Soak the chillies in warm water for 30 minutes. Tear them into pieces and put them into the container of an electric blender with all the other ingredients. Add enough water to allow the blades to work properly, and blend to a purée. Store in a screwtop jar in the refrigerator for up to 3 months.

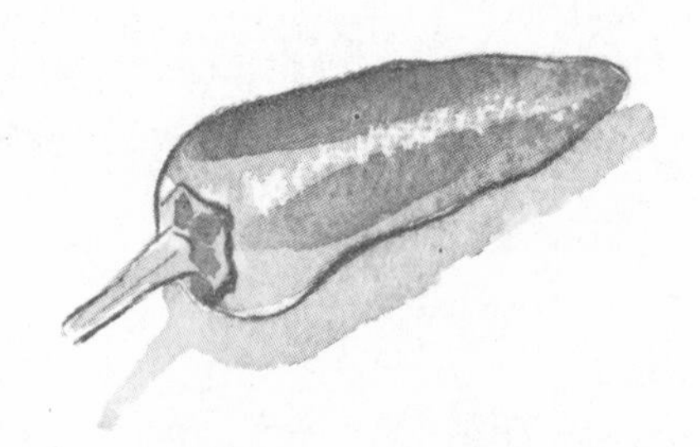

Equipment

Food Processor

The extensive and varied amount of food preparation commonly involved in chilli cooking is exactly the kind of kitchen work that the food processor has been developed to take over. Its great virtue is the number of jobs it will perform – chopping vegetables, mincing meat, blending and grinding, etc. These are all food preparation techniques that occur with monotonous regularity in the recipes in this book. A food processor is, therefore, of immense value in chilli cooking, but it is not essential. If you do not possess a food processor, there are two pieces of equipment that I would suggest *are* almost indispensable – an electric blender and a coffee grinder.

Electric Blender

Reducing chilli (in some form or other) and additional raw ingredients to either a paste or a thinner purée, prior to cooking, is a basic starting point for many chilli dishes. It takes considerable skill, time and energy to pound these raw ingredients into a smooth paste using the traditional pestle and mortar or a coarse, heavy stone rolling pin and stone rolling board. A blender or food processor is a far more practical proposition for most modern cooks. It may be necessary to add a little extra oil or water in order to make the blades turn properly, thus giving a slightly runnier consistency than is produced by manual pounding, but the results are quite satisfactory.

Electric Grinder

In all curry-based cuisines, whole spices are generally freshly roasted and ground before cooking. Traditionally the grinding is done with a pestle and mortar or a grinding stone, but a small electric coffee grinder is ideal for the job. Please note, though, that frequent spice-grinding does little for the flavour of coffee beans, so it is a good idea to keep a grinder exclusively for spices if you intend using it regularly for this purpose.

I also use my grinder for nuts, dry cereals and pulses – ground rice flour and chickpea flour, for example. It tends to be a noisy operation in the initial stages, but the machine copes satisfactorily with something as tough as a chickpea.

The grinder is also useful for making breadcrumbs and for grinding tiny dried prawns into dried prawn powder.

Mini-hachoir

While this little machine is certainly not essential, it is one of my favourite gadgets. It will finely chop leafy herbs like mint, parsley and coriander in seconds (a chore which I hate). It deals equally efficiently with chopping fresh chillies, sweet peppers, garlic, ginger and onion. I like it specially for the way it deals with onions – no more running eyes, which is good news for any *aficionado* of Mexican food, in which finely chopped onion is an indispensable topping for every *tortilla*-based dish.

Pestle and Mortar

Modern electrical equipment almost makes the old-fashioned pestle and mortar redundant, but I believe it has a place in every kitchen for coping with small quantities. A few allspice berries, a couple of cloves, a pinch of cinnamon are all much nicer freshly ground; the fiery *sambals* of South-East Asia are so pungent that only tiny amounts are needed. Mini-quantities like this are easily pounded manually.

If a pestle and mortar is being used permanently instead of an electric blender or processor, choose a large size, but if – as is more likely – the bulk of your pounding is going to be delegated to a machine, opt for a smaller mortar about 10 cm/4 in in diameter, and the heavier the better. Pretty olive-wood models, and those in painted pine, might look very attractive sitting on a kitchen shelf but they cannot really stand up to heavy duty. I prefer the primitive ones made of coarse-textured stone but these are not generally available in Europe. Marble or alabaster are probably the best buy.

Pots and Pans

The standard saucepans and earthenware dishes of European cooking, preferably supplemented by a wok, will be quite adequate for most of the dishes in this book. A few purpose-designed utensils are discussed in the recipe section – griddles for cooking unleavened bread, *fondue*-type cooking pots, *couscous* steamers, *tortilla* presses, etc., but none of these can be considered as basic equipment.

HORS D'OEUVRE, SNACKS AND APPETIZERS

Today in the Western world, *hors d'oeuvre* are usually incorporated in the meal as a first course served at the table, but in many societies, such small dishes play the role of snacks and in-between-meal treats to be enjoyed any time, anywhere. This is particularly true in parts of the world where meals are not served in courses but all the dishes are placed on the table together.

Call them snacks, appetizers or *hors d'oeuvre* . . . the following recipes are for spicy, chillied titbits, nibbles and slightly more substantial dishes, all of which will stir the tastebuds and whet the appetite. None of them is aggressively chilli-hot (though many are served with a fiery sauce as an optional side dish), as the hotter seasonings are more appropriate later in the meal, but all have a hint of heat that is a perfect introduction to the courses to come, whether or not they contain chilli.

The Mezzeh Table

The *mezzeh* table – which is, in fact, a selection of *hors d'oeuvre* dishes – is a symbol of Arab hospitality and is found, in various forms, throughout the Middle East and North Africa. No visit into an Arab home, no matter how informal the visit, nor how lowly the home, is conceivable without the offer of refreshment. This will probably include coffee and a choice of dishes which may simply be two or three bowls containing, perhaps, olives, nuts and dates. On a grander scale, a cloth is laid and a spread of cooked dishes and cold salads displayed upon it.

The dishes on the *mezzeh* table are the classic *hors d'oeuvre* – offerings outside the main course.

Puréed Chickpeas with Sesame Paste
Hummus-bi-Tahina

An essential element in a *mezzeh* spread, *Hummus* is also an excellent starter to any meal, eaten with warm *pitta* bread which is used as a scoop for the chickpea dip. Serve *Hummus* on its own or – even better – with *Mutabbal* (see below). With a bowl of olives and one of salad, the four dishes make up a mini-*mezzeh* table. The salad could be coarsely chopped tomatoes and cucumber with thinly sliced onion, dressed with lemon juice and sprinkled with finely chopped mint.

For other *mezzeh* dishes consult the index.

SERVES 8–10

- 250 g/8 oz chickpeas, soaked 8–24 hours
- 3 cloves garlic, finely chopped
- juice of 2 lemons
- ½ teaspoon ground chilli
- 1 teaspoon cumin (optional)
- 150 ml/¼ pint *tahina* paste*
- salt to taste (start with 1–1½ teaspoons)

Drain the chickpeas and put them in a large heavy saucepan with fresh water to cover. Bring to the boil, cover the pan, and simmer until they are soft. This will take 1½–2½ hours. Check occasionally, adding hot water if necessary and removing any scum. Drain the chickpeas and rinse well.

The chickpeas now need to be puréed in an electric blender or food processor. Do this in batches, adding the garlic and lemon juice. If more liquid is required to make the blades work properly, add a small amount of water but do not let the purée get too runny. When all the chickpeas have been processed, put them in a large bowl and beat in the remaining ingredients.

Serve in a large bowl or in individual bowls. Smooth the surface, dribble a little olive oil over, and sprinkle with ground chilli. A little ground cumin and/or finely chopped parsley are also sometimes sprinkled on.

Puréed Aubergine with Sesame Paste
Mutabbal

Although the *tahina* paste gives this dip a similar flavour to *Hummus*, *Mutabbal* has a distinctive smoky taste resulting from the charring of the aubergines.

SERVES 8–10

- 2 large aubergines
- 3 cloves garlic, finely chopped
- juice of 2 lemons
- ½–1 teaspoon ground chilli
- 1 teaspoon ground cumin
- 125 ml/4 fl oz *tahina* paste*
- 1 tablespoon olive oil
- salt to taste

Make 2 slits in each aubergine and place them in a hot oven or under a medium grill for about 30 minutes, turning often. During this time the skins will turn dry and black and the flesh will become soft. Allow them to cool, then peel off the skin. Remove the stems. Chop the aubergine flesh and blend to a purée, proceeding as for the previous recipe.

To serve, pour a little olive oil on top, sprinkle with finely chopped parsley and garnish with black olives.

Dips

Dips like *Hummus* and *Mutabbal* make easy and interesting appetizers. Serve them with flat bread such as *pitta*, commercially produced crackers and biscuits, or home-made pastries, for example Devilled Cheese Sticks (p. 53) and Chillied Ham Straws (p. 52). *Crudités* (raw vegetables) are also popular because of their freshness and crunchiness. Choose from carrot and cucumber sticks, spring onions, cauliflower florets and strips of red or green sweet pepper. Leave the vegetables in iced water in the refrigerator for 30 minutes before serving, so that they are really crisp.

Aubergine Purée

This is the Tunisian version of the Middle Eastern *Mutabbal.*

SERVES 8

- 2 large aubergines, peeled and cut into large cubes
- 2 sweet red peppers, cut in half and deseeded
- 1 tablespoon lemon juice
- 1 teaspoon *harissa** or ground chilli
- 3 cloves garlic, very finely chopped
- ½ teaspoon ground caraway seeds
- 2 tablespoons oil
- salt and black pepper to taste

Put the aubergines in a large saucepan of water and boil until they are soft – about 20 minutes. Add the sweet red peppers for the last 5 minutes. Drain and chop the sweet pepper finely. Set aside.

Gently squeeze the aubergines to extract any excess liquid. Put them in a bowl and mash them. Stir in the remaining ingredients and the chopped peppers. Spread in a shallow dish and sprinkle with a little ground chilli or paprika. Serve with warm *pitta* bread and a bowl of black olives.

VARIATIONS

A similar dish can be made with courgettes. Omit the sweet peppers and add ½ teaspoon each of ground coriander and cumin. Do not peel the courgettes.

Another version substitutes a generous 500 g/ 1 lb of peeled, cubed pumpkin for the aubergines and is garnished with chopped mint.

Guacamole

Guacamole is a classic Mexican dish that is both a sauce and a dip.

SERVES 3

- 1 very ripe avocado
- 1 tomato, finely chopped
- 1 fresh green chilli, deseeded and

Cut the avocado in half and remove the stone. Carefully scoop out the flesh, including the green flesh near the skin. Mash the avocado flesh and gently stir in the other ingredients, using enough

- finely chopped
- 1 tablespoon finely chopped mild onion
- 1 teaspoon finely chopped parsley or coriander leaves
- lime or lemon juice
- salt and freshly ground black pepper to taste

lime or lemon juice to give it a tang but not enough to make it sloppy. Remember that avocado discolours when exposed to the air for too long, so do not prepare *Guacamole* until immediately before serving.

For an *hors d'oeuvre, Guacamole* is usually served as a dip accompanied by *totopos*, which are deep-fried *tortilla* triangles. Make them yourself in advance, or use any bought crackers or crisps.

VARIATIONS

Make *Guacamole* without the tomato and serve in tomato shells that have been scooped out, salted and left upside down to drain for 10 minutes.

Serve *Guacamole* as a dressing for cauliflower that has been cut into florets and boiled for just a few minutes so that it is still slightly crisp. Put the cauliflower on a bed of lettuce, spoon on the sauce and top with grated cheese.

Chilli and Pineapple Dip

This looks great in a scooped-out fresh pineapple. Use it as the centrepiece on a large round tray, surrounded with *crudités* and crackers or crisps.

- 500 g/1 lb cream cheese
- 2 teaspoons French mustard
- 125 g/4 oz yoghurt
- 25 g/1 oz finely chopped walnuts
- 2 fresh red or green chillies, deseeded and finely chopped
- 1 fresh or canned pineapple ring, finely chopped
- salt and pepper to taste

Put the first 3 ingredients in a bowl and beat until well mixed. Stir in the walnuts, chillies and pineapple and season to taste.

Chilli Crab Dip

a 200 g/7 oz can crabmeat, drained, picked over and flaked
2 teaspoons finely chopped capers
2 hard-boiled eggs, quartered
2 tablespoons lemon juice
2 teaspoons mild French mustard
3 tablespoons dark rum
¼ teaspoon salt
¼ teaspoon ground black pepper
¼ teaspoon ground allspice*
¼ teaspoon cayenne pepper or Tabasco sauce*

Blend all the ingredients until smooth, using an electric blender or food processor.

Mexican Bean Dip

a 250 g/8 oz can red kidney beans, drained and rinsed
2 cloves garlic, chopped
2 teaspoons cumin
1 tablespoon mayonnaise
1 tablespoon tomato ketchup
1 tablespoon lemon juice
Tabasco sauce* to taste
1 teaspoon finely chopped chives

Blend all the ingredients except the chives until smooth using an electric blender or food processor. Put into a bowl and sprinkle with the chives.

Chillied Ham Straws

2 egg yolks
3 tablespoons water
½ teaspoon Tabasco sauce*
250 g/8 oz flour
½ teaspoon salt
¼ teaspoon cayenne pepper
½ teaspoon dry mustard powder
125 g/4 oz butter or margarine
125 g/4 oz cooked ham, finely chopped

Put the egg yolks, water and Tabasco sauce in a small bowl and beat together. Sieve the flour, salt, cayenne pepper and mustard powder into a separate bowl, and rub in the butter or margarine until the mixture resembles fine breadcrumbs. Stir in the ham. Add the egg mixture and mix to a stiff dough. Knead lightly for a couple of minutes, then roll out thinly on a floured board. Cut out about 12 circles 5 cm/2 in across. Cut a smaller circle (about 3 cm/1¼ in) out of the centre of each to form 12 rings. Cut the remaining dough into straws about 8 × 3 cm/7 × 1¼ in. Place on greased baking trays and bake for 15 minutes in a moderate oven, 220°C/425°F/gas 7. Cool on a wire tray.

Serve by placing some straws in a small tumbler and putting bundles of straws through the rings.

Devilled Cheese Sticks

MAKES ABOUT 48

- 1 egg yolk
- 2 tablespoons water
- ½ teaspoon Worcester sauce
- ½ teaspoon cayenne pepper
- 75 g/3 oz butter
- 125 g/4 oz plain flour
- ½ teaspoon salt
- ½ teaspoon ground ginger
- ½ teaspoon sugar
- 1 tablespoon caraway seeds
- 125 g/4 oz grated cheese

Put the egg yolk in a bowl large enough to hold all the ingredients and beat in the water, Worcester sauce and cayenne pepper. Melt the butter in a small saucepan and add to the egg mixture. Sift in the flour, salt and ground ginger. Stir in the remaining ingredients and form into a soft dough. Chill for 10 minutes.

Divide the dough into two balls. Roll one out between two sheets of waxed paper until it is about 1 cm/¼ in thick. (Do not use extra flour.) Cut into strips 8 ×2 cm/7 ×¾ in. Repeat with the second ball of dough. Place the sticks on a greased baking tray and bake for 8 minutes in a moderate oven, 200°C/400°F/gas 6. Cool on a wire tray.

Savoury Packets

Wrapping chilli-spiced fillings in pastry or pancake packets is a favourite way of creating appetizers in many countries. In miniature they make popular and unusual cocktail accompaniments, while served with a salad they are a meal in themselves. Certainly they are eaten everywhere as in-between-meal snacks. As a main meal starter course, however, they are perfect for whetting the taste buds, especially if there is more spicy food to come.

All the following recipes are suitable for freezing. Freeze after assembling the packets. It is not necessary to thaw them before cooking, but you may need to allow a little longer than the cooking times stated.

Singapore Curry Puffs

I was taught to make curry puffs by an elderly Chinese gentleman in Singapore, who was reputed to make the best curry puffs on the island. He was quite prepared to divulge the secrets of his art to anyone – even to other aspiring professional curry puff makers – all the secrets except one. He would not tell anyone the formula for his spice mixture.

He also used to roll his pastry out with a beer bottle. Younger members of his family had tried to persuade him to use a rolling pin but, in typical Chinese philosophical fashion, he said that as he made the best curry puffs in Singapore with a beer bottle, he was not prepared to risk changing his technique at all. Change the beer bottle and it might somehow affect the taste, or even worse his luck.

FILLING

- 3 tablespoons oil
- 1 small onion, finely chopped
- 2 teaspoons finely chopped fresh ginger
- 250 g/8 oz minced beef or lamb
- 2 tablespoons meat curry powder (p. 36)
- ½ teaspoon ground chilli
- 1 tomato, peeled and chopped
- ½ teaspoon salt
- ¼ teaspoon ground black pepper
- 1 large potato, boiled and diced
- 1 teacup cooked peas

Heat the oil in a heavy frying-pan and fry the onion and ginger for 5 minutes. Add the meat and fry for a further 5 minutes. Add the curry powder and the ground chilli. Fry for 2 minutes, stirring constantly to prevent burning. Add the tomato, salt and black pepper with 5 tablespoons of water. Simmer, covered, for 20 minutes. Stir in the potato and peas. Leave to cool.

TO ASSEMBLE

Roll out 250 g/8 oz shortcrust pastry and cut into circles around a saucer (approx. 10 cm/4 in). Place a spoonful of filling on one half, dampen the edges, fold over and press with a fork to seal. Deep-fry in medium hot oil for about 8 minutes until golden. Serve warm.

VARIATIONS

Make the filling with shredded cooked chicken instead of minced meat, and place a segment of hard-boiled egg (my teacher insisted it had to be a one-fifth segment) in the centre of the filling. Use flaky pastry and bake the puffs in a pre-heated oven at 200°C/400°F/gas 6 for 10 minutes.

Jamaican Meat Patties

Use either flaky pastry or shortcrust pastry, cut into 10 cm/4 in circles and then folded in half over the filling. 2 teaspoons of curry powder or ground turmeric can be added to the flour if making shortcrust pastry.

MAKES APPROX 20

- 750 g/1½ lb pastry

FILLING

- 2 tablespoons oil

Heat the oil in a heavy frying-pan and fry the minced beef for 5 minutes, breaking up any

- 500 g/1 lb minced beef
- 1 small onion, finely chopped
- 3 spring onions, finely chopped
- 1 clove garlic, finely chopped
- 1 tomato, peeled and chopped
- 1 tablespoon curry powder
- ½ teaspoon thyme
- 1 fresh red chilli, deseeded and finely chopped, or West Indian pepper sauce* to taste
- salt and freshly ground black pepper to taste

lumps with a fork. Add the onion, spring onions and garlic and fry for a further 5 minutes. Add all the other ingredients and 4 tablespoons of water. Simmer, covered, for about 20 minutes, by which time the meat should be tender and the liquid absorbed. If necessary, cook for a few minutes without a lid so that any excess liquid will evaporate.

Allow to cool and use about 1½ tablespoons of filling for each patty.

Bake for 30 minutes in a pre-heated oven at 200°C/400°F/gas 6.

Samosas

These triangular-shaped Indian turnovers are made from paper-thin pastry, but an easy alternative is to use Chinese spring roll wrappers (large size), which are now widely available fresh or frozen.

Because of the dietary restrictions of the main Indian religions, *samosa* fillings can be made from beef, lamb, chicken or vegetables. If making a selection, it is a good idea to put a tiny dot of food colouring on one corner of the *samosas*, in order to differentiate between the fillings.

For each type of filling – 12 large size spring roll wrappers.

MEAT FILLING

- 2 tablespoons oil, butter or *ghee**
- 1 large onion, finely chopped
- 2 cloves garlic, finely chopped
- 1 teaspoon finely chopped fresh ginger
- 1 tablespoon meat curry powder (p. 37)
- ½ teaspoon ground chilli
- 250 g/8 oz minced beef or lamb, or shredded cooked chicken
- 1 tablespoon lemon juice
- ½ teaspoon salt
- 1 tablespoon finely chopped parsley, coriander or mint leaves
- 1 teaspoon *garam masala**

Heat the oil, butter or *ghee* in a heavy frying-pan and gently fry the onion, garlic and ginger until golden. Stir in the curry powder and ground chilli and fry for 1 minute. Stir in the meat or chicken and fry for 2 minutes. Add the lemon juice, salt, chopped herbs and 3 tablespoons of water. Bring to the boil and simmer, covered, for about 20 minutes until the meat is tender and the liquid has been absorbed. (If using cooked chicken, add 1 tablespoon of water and simmer for 10 minutes.) Stir in the *garam masala* and allow to cool.

VEGETABLE FILLING

3 tablespoons oil, butter or *ghee**
1 medium onion, finely chopped
2 cloves garlic, finely chopped
1 teaspoon finely chopped fresh ginger
2 fresh green chillies, deseeded and finely chopped
1 teaspoon *garam masala**
1 large potato, boiled and chopped
25 g/1 oz cooked cauliflower, chopped
1 tablespoon finely chopped parsley, coriander or mint leaves
½ teaspoon salt
1 tablespoon lemon juice
25 g/1 oz cooked peas

Heat the oil, butter or *ghee* in a heavy frying-pan. Gently fry the onion, garlic, ginger and chillies until golden, then stir in the *garam masala*. Add all the other ingredients, leaving the peas till last so that they do not get too mashed up. Mix well. Allow to cool.

TO ASSEMBLE

Thaw out the spring roll wrappers, if frozen, and cover them with a damp cloth until needed. Working with strips approximately 5 × 15 cm/ 2 × 6 in, fold the top of a strip over to form a triangular flap. Place a spoonful of filling under this flap and fold again so that a rectangular shape remains. Fold again diagonally, and again so that a triangular flap remains. Brush this with beaten egg and fold over, pressing the edges gently to seal.

Deep-fry in moderately hot oil until crisp and golden. Serve warm with Fresh Mint or Coriander Chutney (p. 250) or with Chilli Sauce (p. 274).

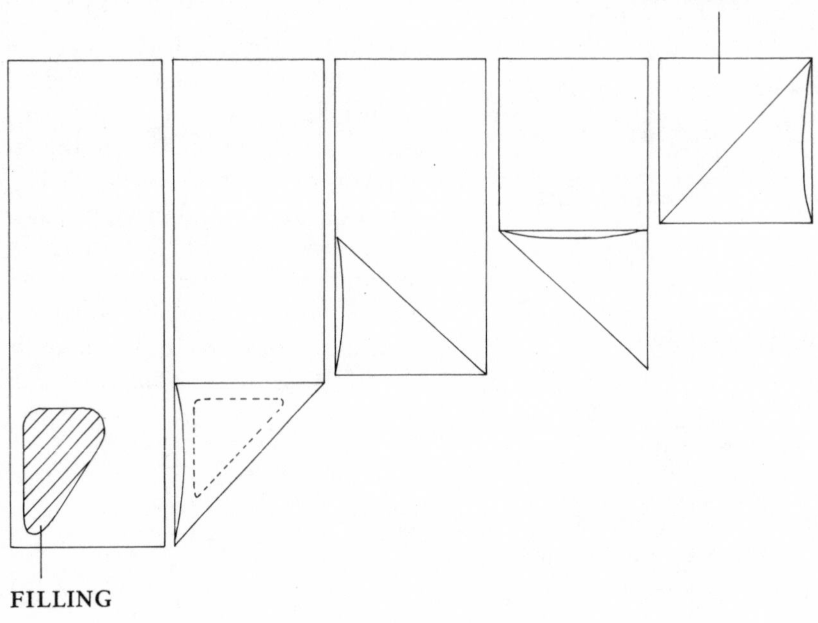

Popiah Goreng

An example of the strong Chinese influence on Malay cooking, these Malaysian-style spring rolls are filled with beansprouts, chicken, prawns and chillies. For convenience, use ready-made spring roll wrappers (large size). There is enough filling for 12 spring roll wrappers.

FILLING
1 tablespoon oil
125 g/4 oz boneless chicken breast or pork, shredded, cut into small dice or minced
125 g/4 oz peeled prawns, chopped
1 clove garlic, finely chopped
5 spring onions, finely sliced
2 fresh red chillies, deseeded and finely chopped, or 1 teaspoon *sambal ulek**
200 g/7 oz beansprouts, washed and picked over
1 tablespoon light soy sauce*

ADDITIONAL FILLINGS
hoisin sauce*
washed and dried lettuce leaves
cucumber, peeled and diced

Heat the oil in a heavy frying-pan or wok and stir-fry the chicken or pork over a high heat for 1 minute. Add the prawns, garlic, spring onions and chillies and stir-fry for 30 seconds. Add the beansprouts and soy sauce and stir-fry for 1 minute. Transfer to a bowl and allow to cool.

TO ASSEMBLE

Lay out a spring roll wrapper and spread with ¼ teaspoon of *hoisin* sauce, leaving 2 cm/¾ in clear all round. Place a lettuce leaf in the centre with a generous portion of filling and a little diced cucumber. Fold the long edges in 2 cm/¾ in, and roll up firmly. Secure the end by dampening with a little water and pressing firmly. Leave the roll with the seam underneath so that it is sealed by its own weight.

Deep-fry in moderately hot oil until crisp and golden. Serve immediately with the following sauce.

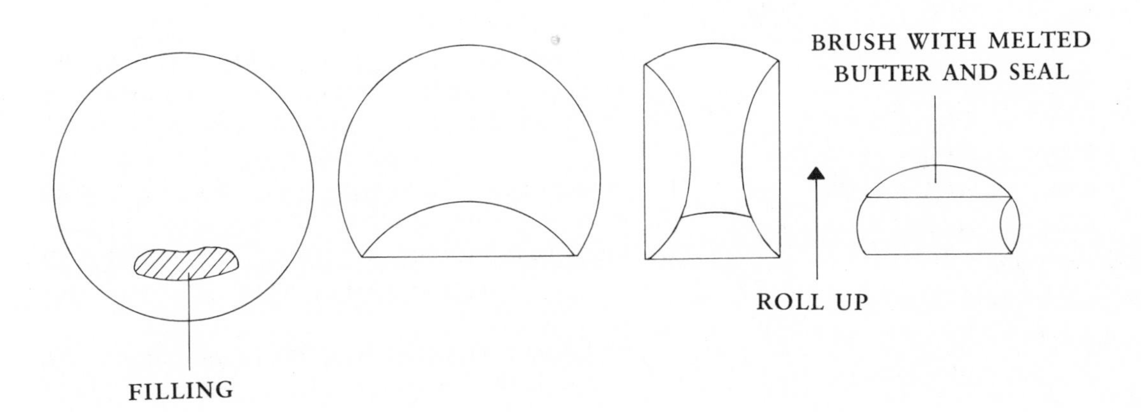

DIPPING SAUCE

- 2 spring onions, chopped
- 3 cloves garlic, chopped
- ½ teaspoon chopped fresh ginger
- 2 fresh red chillies, deseeded and chopped, or 1 teaspoon *sambal ulek**
- 3 tablespoons light soy sauce*
- 3 tablespoons vinegar
- ½ teaspoon sugar

Use a pestle and mortar to pound the spring onions, garlic, ginger and chillies to a paste. If using *sambal ulek*, add this towards the end of the pounding. Stir in the other ingredients. Taste and adjust the seasonings if necessary. Serve in small individual bowls.

Middle Eastern Lamb Pies

Little pies filled with minced lamb and nuts are an essential part of any *mezzeh* table and appear all over the Near and Middle East in various shapes – round like jam tarts, open triangles, closed triangles, cylinders, or cigar-shaped. The pies can be made from a choice of pastry bases – yeast pastry, shortcrust, or paper-thin *filo* pastry, and come under an assortment of names – *fatayer, lahm bi'ajeen, sambousek, sfeeha*. The one thing that they all have in common is that they are irresistibly delicious.

1 kg/2 lb pastry or 24 sheets of filo pastry (30/20 cm/12 × 8 in)
makes 24

FILLING

- 2 tablespoons olive oil
- 4 tablespoons pine nuts
- 1 large onion, finely chopped
- 1 kg/2 lb minced lamb or beef
- 2 canned tomatoes, mashed with 4 tablespoons juice
- ¼ teaspoon ground allspice*
- ¼ teaspoon ground cinnamon
- ½ teaspoon ground chilli
- ¼ teaspoon ground black pepper
- 1 teaspoon salt
- 1 tablespoon lemon juice
- 2 tablespoons finely chopped parsley or coriander leaves

Heat 1 tablespoon of olive oil in a heavy frying-pan and gently fry the pine nuts until golden. Do not allow them to get too brown. Remove the nuts with a slotted spoon and set aside.

Add the remaining olive oil to the pan and gently fry the onion and meat for 10 minutes. Add all the other ingredients and simmer, covered, for about 15 minutes until the meat is tender. Stir in the pine nuts and leave to cool.

TO ASSEMBLE

Roll shortcrust pastry out thinly and cut into 10 cm/4 in circles. Put a generous portion of filling in the centre of each, and dampen the edges. Fold the edges to the top, forming a triangle. Leave a small hole – the size of a fingernail – in the centre and smooth the pastry out. Brush with oil or beaten egg and bake for 10 minutes in a pre-heated oven at 200°C/400°F/gas 6.

Alternatively, use ready-made *filo* pastry and cut each sheet in half to give a piece about 30m/

20 cm/12 × 8 in. Brush lightly with melted butter and fold in half lengthwise. Brush again and put about 2 tablespoons of filling near one of the short ends. Fold the long edges in a little, and roll up to form a cylinder about 7.5 cm/3 in long. Place on an oiled baking tray, with the seam underneath. Brush with butter and bake for about 20 minutes in a pre-heated oven at 190°C/ 375°F/gas 5.

Serve warm.

NOTE

As *filo* pastry tends to be quite greasy, cut down the olive oil used in the filling to 1 tablespoon.

Breiks

Breiks are the North African version of savoury packets, sharing obvious culinary origins with the *samosas* of India and the Middle Eastern pies. They vary slightly throughout the region and are also known as *briouat* in Morocco, and *bourek* in Algeria.

Breik pastry is sometimes available in specialist shops and is sold in large circles about 25 cm/10 in in diameter. The pastry is paper-thin and is folded into a multi-layered packet. *Filo* pastry can be used instead, but is sold in rectangular shapes. If using *filo* pastry, shape packets as described in the previous recipe or make into triangles like *samosas* (p. 55). The circular sheets of *breik* pastry should be folded according to the instructions on p. 55. Seal the edges with a little melted butter or oil, pressing with the prongs of a fork if necessary.

Breiks can either be deep-fried in medium hot oil until golden, or brushed with beaten egg and baked in a pre-heated oven at 200°C/400°F/gas 6 for 10–15 minutes.

Serve with lemon wedges, and a dipping sauce of *harissa** diluted with water.

MAKES 12

Each type of filling – 12 circular *breik* wrappers or 12 sheets of filo pastry (30 × 20 cm/12 × 8 in)

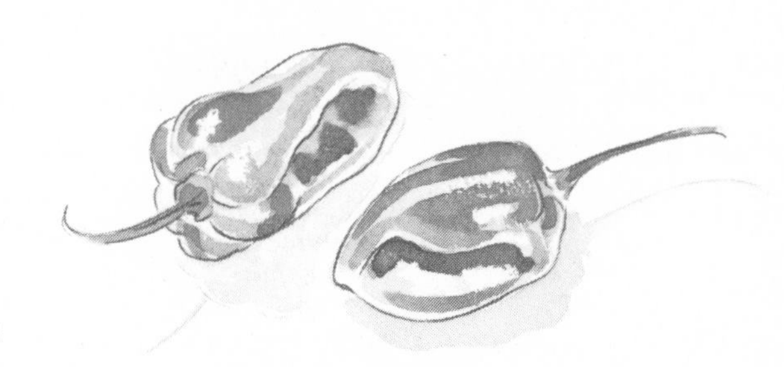

MEAT FILLING

- 500 g/1 lb minced lamb
- 1 small onion, grated
- 1 teaspoon paprika
- ½ teaspoon ground chilli
- 1 teaspoon ground cumin
- 4 tablespoons finely chopped parsley or coriander leaves
- 4 tablespoons oil or butter
- ½ teaspoon salt
- ¼ teaspoon ground black pepper
- 4 eggs, beaten
- ½ teaspoon ground cinnamon

Mix together the first 6 ingredients. Heat the oil or butter in a large heavy frying-pan and gently fry the meat mixture for 15–20 minutes until the meat is tender and all the liquid has evaporated. Stir in the salt, pepper and beaten eggs, and stir well to distribute the eggs. Sprinkle in the ground cinnamon and cook for 1 minute. Remove from the heat and allow to cool.

CHICKEN FILLING

- 2 boneless chicken breasts
- 1 medium onion, finely chopped
- 1 teaspoon oil or butter
- 2 medium potatoes, boiled and roughly mashed
- 3 tablespoons finely chopped parsley or coriander leaves
- 1 teaspoon *harissa**
- ½ teaspoon salt
- ½ teaspoon ground black pepper
- 1 tablespoon lemon juice
- 1 hard-boiled egg, shelled and finely chopped
- 2 eggs, beaten

Gently poach the chicken breasts for about 15 minutes until tender. When cool enough to handle, shred or chop them finely. Gently fry the grated onion in oil or butter until soft. Mix the chicken, onion and all other ingredients together well.

FISH FILLING

- 1 tablespoon oil
- 1 medium onion, finely chopped
- 2 cloves garlic, finely chopped
- 2 fresh green chillies, deseeded and finely chopped
- 2 tomatoes, peeled and chopped
- a 250 g/8 oz can tuna, drained, bones and skin removed, and flaked
- 6 tablespoons cooked rice

Heat the oil in a heavy frying-pan and gently fry the onion, garlic and chillies until the onion is soft. Add the tomatoes and simmer, uncovered, until thick and pulpy. Transfer to a bowl and add all the other ingredients. Mix well.

4 tablespoons finely chopped parsley or coriander leaves
¼ teaspoon ground black pepper
salt to taste
1 hard-boiled egg, shelled and chopped
1 tablespoon lemon juice

MERGUEZ FILLING

Gently fry some *Merguez* sausages (p. 134) until tender. Drain on kitchen towels and wrap in *breik* or *filo* pastry.

Empañadas

These are the Latin American adaptation of savoury packets, introduced by the Spanish. Every country has its own variation. Make *empañadas* – or *empañaditas* (little *empañadas*) – with shortcrust pastry, which can be either baked or fried, as in the recipe for Singapore Curry Puffs on p. 53. Make pastry circles 12.5 cm/5 in in diameter for *empañadas*, and circles 7.5 cm/3 in in diameter for *empañaditas*. Fold in half over the filling, to form semi-circles, dampen edges and seal.

MEAT FILLING

Use the *Picadillo* recipe on p. 140. Add extra finely chopped chillies if liked, and put a segment of hard-boiled egg in each pastry packet with the meat.

750 g/1½ lb pastry and 500 g/1 lb *picadillo* makes approx. 18 *empañadas* or 40 *empañaditas*

Miscellaneous Hors d'Oeuvre

Spiced Fruit

Although it needs a little experimenting to get the balance of flavour right – hot, sweet, sour and refreshing – this makes an intriguing starter to a really hot curry meal.

Use a selection of fresh fruit cut into small cubes – banana, pineapple, red and green apples (do not peel them), melon, mango. Put into a glass bowl, to display the pretty colours, and squeeze on plenty of lime or lemon juice. In a separate bowl, mix together ground ginger, ground chilli and sugar. As a start, try ¼ teaspoon each of ginger and chilli, with 1 teaspoon of sugar to season enough fruit for 4–6 servings. Sprinkle over the fruit and stir in about 2 teaspoons of finely chopped mint. Chill for 30 minutes and serve with a bowl of well-beaten and chilled yoghurt.

I like thinly sliced brown bread and butter with my spiced fruit, but this is highly irregular!

Orange Salad

This Moroccan salad may seem a bit strange at first, but it makes a superb appetizer before a *couscous* dish or a *tajine*.

SERVES 4–6
3 large oranges
a handful of stoned black olives, halved
1 tablespoon lemon juice
2 teaspoons orange blossom water*
½ teaspoon cumin
a pinch of ground cinnamon
½ teaspoon *harissa**
½ teaspoon salt, or to taste

Peel the oranges, carefully removing all the stringy pith and the pips. Divide into segments and cut in half. Mix all the ingredients together in a glass bowl. Chill for 30 minutes, then stir to distribute the juices and serve.

Mango and Prawn Salad

Both mangoes and prawns are expensive in Europe, so this is a bit of a luxury . . . but rather special. The amount of ground chilli may seem excessive, but the mixture of coconut cream and salad cream seems to soak up its pungency. Try and use lime juice for sprinkling on the mangoes, but if it is not available, lemon juice will do.

SERVES 6
3 large firm ripe mangoes
350 g/11 oz cooked prawns
1 tablespoon fresh lime juice
125 ml/4 fl oz coconut cream (p. 33)

To remove the flesh from the mangoes, cut them in half horizontally and lift out the stone. Cut the flesh in a diagonal criss-cross pattern, taking great care not to cut into the skin. Turn inside out so that the flesh stands up in diamonds. Trim off, put in a bowl with the prawns and sprinkle with the lime juice.

- 50 ml/2 fl oz salad cream or mayonnaise
- ½–2 teaspoons ground chilli
- 1–2 teaspoons sugar
- lettuce leaves and mint sprigs to garnish

Return the mango skins to a boat shape and carefully scrape out any remaining flesh. Mix together the coconut cream, salad cream or mayonnaise, ground chilli and sugar. Stir in the scraped mango flesh.

Place each mango skin on a bed of lettuce, and fill with prawns and mango. Top with a spoonful of the cream mixture and a mint sprig. Chill for 30 minutes before serving.

Chilli-avocado Dressing

This is a most delicious and versatile dressing, which can be combined with various ingredients to make unusual *hors d'oeuvre.* One avocado makes enough for 3 generous servings.

- 1 ripe avocado
- 1 tablespoon finely chopped onion
- 1 clove garlic
- 1 fresh green chilli, deseeded and chopped
- 3 tablespoons oil
- 3 tablespoons lemon juice
- 3 tablespoons water
- 2 tablespoons mayonnaise (ready-made is all right)
- Tabasco sauce,* salt and pepper to taste

Cut the avocado in half, remove the stone and scoop out the flesh, including the green flesh near the shell. Put into the container of an electric blender with the onion, garlic, chilli, oil, lemon juice and water, and blend to a purée. Transfer to a bowl and beat in the mayonnaise. Season to taste. If it is too thick (it should be quite thick), dilute with a little milk or single cream.

Use the dressing with hard-boiled eggs, rather like egg mayonnaise; with sliced hard-boiled egg and tomato slices; spooned over a mixed salad; mixed with seafood and then piled back into the empty avocado shells.

A garnish of red chilli flowers (p. 223) makes a colourful contrast to the pale green sauce.

Tuna with Tomato

Drain a small can of tuna in oil. Remove the skin and flake the fish. Gently mix with 1 quantity of *Salsa Cruda* (p. 268). Arrange on a bed of crisp lettuce leaves on individual plates and garnish with lemon wedges and segments of hard-boiled egg. Serve with brown bread and butter.

Lemon Sardines

This is so simple but looks terrific – chillied sardines in a lemon cup.

SERVES 6

- 6 perfect lemons with unmarked skins
- 250 g/8 oz cream cheese
- 1 small onion, chopped
- 1 teaspoon chopped parsley
- 1 tablespoon lemon juice
- two 125 g/4 oz cans sardines in oil, drained and bones removed
- ½ teaspoon cayenne pepper or Tabasco sauce*
- sliced cucumber and a little extra chopped parsley to garnish

Cut a slice off the stem end of each lemon about one-third of the way down. Cut the tip off the opposite end so that the lemon will stand firm. Carefully scoop out the lemon flesh from the larger portion to form an empty shell. Reserve 1 tablespoon of juice from the discarded lemon slice.

Put the cream cheese, onion, parsley, lemon juice, sardines and cayenne or Tabasco sauce into the container of an electric blender or food processor, and blend until smooth. Pile the mixture into the lemon shells and sprinkle with chopped parsley.

The lemons look crisp and fresh served on a bed of shredded lettuce, topped by a few paper-thin cucumber slices.

Cold Sichuan Chicken and Beansprouts

If you want to serve a Chinese meal in courses, Western-style, rather than placing all the dishes on the table together, this is ideal as a first course or, even better, as a cold course after the soup and before the main dish. The chicken is pre-cooked but should be moist and not at all over-cooked. For a special occasion, lightly roast or poach a fresh chicken and use the breasts soon after they have cooled. For a simple family meal, use left-over roast chicken (at room temperature, though, and not straight from the fridge). Pork can be substituted for the chicken.

SERVES 6

[Sichuan Sauce p. 275]
500 g/11 lb fresh beansprouts
250–300 g/8 10 oz cooked chicken

Make Sichuan Sauce according to the recipe on p. 275, but omit the sesame paste* and add 1 tablespoon of sesame seeds.*

Wash and pick over 500 g/1 lb of fresh beansprouts, and plunge them into a large saucepan of boiling, lightly salted water for 1 minute. Tip the beansprouts into a colander and rinse them under cold water. Drain.

To assemble, spread the beansprouts on a large serving platter. Arrange the sliced chicken on top. Pour the sauce over and garnish with a few coriander leaves.

SOUPS

Although in the West soups are traditionally served at the beginning of a meal, this is not their accepted role in other parts of the world. In many less sophisticated societies, soup is still a nourishing one-pot stew which is served as a meal in itself.

Indian soups perform another role. It is normal practice over much of the subcontinent for food to be eaten with the hands and so some dishes tend to be rather dry, particularly if they are intended to be scooped up with flat bread. Highly spiced watery soups are served on the side, either to be sipped in between mouthfuls of food, or to be used to moisten plain boiled rice.

In the Far East, soups are more likely to be offered at the end of a meal in order to refresh the palate.

The 'dry soups' of Mexico are not even soups at all, in the generally accepted sense of the word. Served after the 'wet soup' course and before the main course of a typical Mexican meal, they are usually rice-, pasta- or *tortilla*-based and have, therefore, been included in other sections of this book.

The soups featured here cover a wide chilli taste spectrum – hot and sour, mild and creamy, robust and full-flavoured, fragrant and subtle. Some are authentic native dishes, others are adaptations that make them ideal for incorporating in Western-style 3–4 course meals.

Vegetable Chorba

During the winter, this is the soup that I make without fail at least once a week. Simple, cheap, nourishing and spicy, it is a culinary cross between the classic vegetable soup that is still the evening meal for country families all over France and the *chorbat* (soups) of North Africa, laced with *harissa* and paprika.

SERVES 4

- 1 large leek, cleaned and thinly sliced
- 1 large potato, peeled and diced
- 2 carrots, peeled and diced
- 1 small turnip, peeled and diced
- 1 celery stick (with leaves), diced

Put all the ingredients into a large saucepan and simmer for about 40 minutes until the vegetables are tender. Remove the bay leaf before serving.

VARIATIONS

Add a tin of baked beans in tomato sauce or a tin of ready-cooked chickpeas, or – for a real cosmopolitan mish-mash – 3 tablespoons fast-cooking

- 1 tomato, peeled and chopped, or 1 canned tomato, chopped
- 1.5 litres/3 pints water
- 1 chicken stock cube
- ½–1 teaspoon *harissa**
- 1 teaspoon paprika
- 1 teaspoon cumin
- ¼ teaspoon ground caraway seeds (optional)
- ¼ teaspoon ground black pepper
- bay leaf
- 2 teaspoons finely chopped parsley or coriander leaves
- salt to taste

Indian lentils, e.g. black gram* or split yellow *moong dahl.*

Mulligatawny Soup

There are many variations of this famous Anglo-Indian soup, both in England and India. The name is derived from the Tamil word for pepper water – *milakutanni* – and the soup became a favourite with the British in India during the eighteenth century. This is an Indian version.

SERVES 6–8

- 1 small chicken
- 1 kg/2 lb beef bones
- 1 large onion, coarsely chopped
- 6 cloves garlic
- 1 thumb-sized piece fresh ginger, peeled but left whole
- 2 tablespoons coriander seeds
- 1 tablespoon cumin seeds
- 1 teaspoon ground turmeric
- 1 teaspoon ground chilli
- 6 black peppercorns
- 6 cloves
- 6 cardamom pods,* bruised
- 1 teaspoon concentrated tamarind extract*
- 1½ teaspoons salt
- 6 curry leaves* or 1 bay leaf
- 600 ml/1 pint coconut milk (p. 32)

Put all the ingredients except the coconut milk into a large heavy saucepan with 2 litres/3½ pints of water. Bring to boil and simmer for 1 hour. Remove the chicken and strip the meat from the bones. Discard the carcass and shred the meat. Set aside. Boil the stock vigorously, uncovered, for a few minutes to concentrate the flavour, then strain. There should be about 900 ml/1½ pints. Rinse out the pan and put back the stock. Add the coconut milk and bring to the boil, stirring constantly to prevent curdling. Add the shredded chicken meat and simmer, uncovered, for 5 minutes.

A tasty garnish for the soup can be made by frying 1 large onion, finely sliced, and 1 teaspoon of black mustard seeds* in 1 tablespoon of oil, butter or *ghee** until dark golden brown. Do not allow to burn. Stir into the soup immediately before serving.

Harira

During the Moslem fasting month of Ramadan, no food or drink is taken during the hours between sunrise and sunset. In North Africa the fast is traditionally broken every evening with *Harira* – a thick, nourishing soup that is eaten with dates and honey pastries. The soup appears in many forms but is essentially robust and filling, containing a selection of vegetables, pulses and sometimes meat or chicken. *Harira* is usually thickened with a little flour, and this version contains beaten eggs for extra body.

SERVES 6–8

- 25 g/1 oz butter or *ghee**
- 1 chicken portion, halved
- 1 large onion, coarsely chopped
- 1 celery stick (with leaves), chopped
- 6 tablespoons finely chopped parsley or coriander leaves
- ½ teaspoon ground turmeric or ¼ teaspoon ground saffron*
- ½ teaspoon ground black pepper
- ½ teaspoon ground chilli
- 1 teaspoon ground cinnamon
- 1 teaspoon salt
- 2 fresh chillies, deseeded and finely chopped
- 1 tablespoon tomato purée
- a 400 g/13 oz can chickpeas, drained
- 125 g/4 oz long grain rice
- 2 tablespoons flour mixed with 150 ml/¼ pint water
- 2 eggs, beaten

Put the first 12 ingredients into a large heavy saucepan with 2 litres/3½ pints of water. Simmer, covered, for 30 minutes. Remove the chicken and the meat from the bones. Shred the chicken meat and return it to the pan, discarding the bones. Add the chickpeas and rice and simmer, covered, for 15 minutes. Add the flour and water mixture, stirring constantly to prevent lumps. Simmer for 5 minutes, adding a little extra water if the soup is too thick or a little extra flour (mixed with water) if it is too thin. Remove the pan from the heat and gently stir in the eggs immediately before serving.

Serve with lemon wedges so that lemon juice can be squeezed over the soup to individual taste, pitta bread and dates.

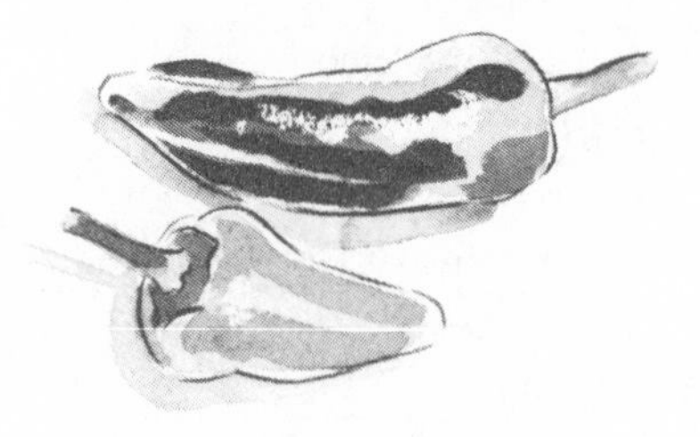

Spiced Cauliflower Soup

Serve this at any dinner party and I can guarantee it will be a show-stopper! Delicately spiced, prettily coloured, rich and creamy, it tastes like no other soup. It is, however, quick, easy and cheap to make. After the classic French soup process of sweating the vegetables in butter, they are simmered in a stock which is thickened with ground lentils. Any lentils are suitable – split peas will give a light green soup and yellow lentils will produce a golden soup. (Avoid brown lentils if you want a colourful dish.) Yoghurt and *garam masala* hint at Indian origins. Finely chopped herbs add freshness and flavour. As a final touch, try serving warm *chapatis* instead of bread with the soup.

SERVES 4

- 2 tablespoons lentils or split peas
- ½ small cauliflower, cut into tiny florets
- 1 large onion, finely chopped
- 1 small sweet green pepper, deseeded and coarsely chopped
- 1 stick celery, coarsely chopped
- 50 g/2 oz butter
- 1 teaspoon ground turmeric
- ½ teaspoon ground chilli
- 550 ml/18 fl oz water
- 2 chicken stock cubes
- 150 ml/5 fl oz milk
- 150 ml/5 fl oz yoghurt
- 1 teaspoon *garam masala**
- salt to taste
- 2 tablespoons finely chopped parsley or coriander leaves

Grind the lentils to a fine powder in an electric grinder, and set aside.

Put the cauliflower, onion, green pepper and celery into a large heavy saucepan with the butter. Cook for 10 minutes over a low heat, stirring constantly so that the vegetables are coated in butter but do not brown. Stir in the turmeric and ground chilli. Add the water and the stock cubes. Bring to the boil and simmer, covered, for about 10 minutes until the cauliflower is tender but not too soft.

Mix the ground lentils to a smooth cream with the milk. Add to the soup, stirring to prevent lumps. Add a little of the hot liquid to the yoghurt. Take the pan off the heat and add the warm yoghurt, stirring constantly. Add the *garam masala* and salt. Simmer, uncovered, for 2 minutes. Stir in the herbs and serve.

Pepper Water

Traditionally pepper water is served in a small bowl or cup and sipped or used to moisten rice. It is also thought to aid the digestion.

SERVES 4–6

- 25 g/1 oz butter or *ghee**
- ½ teaspoon black mustard seeds*
- 1 small onion, finely sliced
- 5 cloves garlic, finely sliced
- 6 curry leaves*
- 1 teaspoon ground cumin
- ½ teaspoon turmeric
- 10 black peppercorns, crushed
- pinch of fenugreek seeds*
- 2–4 fresh or dried chillies, deseeded and finely chopped
- 1 litre/1½ pints water or stock
- 1 teaspoon instant tamarind pulp*
- salt to taste

Heat the butter or *ghee* in a large heavy saucepan and fry the mustard seeds until they jump and pop. Add the onion, garlic and curry leaves and fry gently until golden. Add all the other ingredients, bring to the boil and simmer, covered, for 30 minutes. Strain and serve.

Sothi

Sothi is a spiced coconut milk soup from Sri Lanka which is spooned over rice. The original version uses ground dried prawns, but fresh prawns make an interesting Western-style soup.

SERVES 6

- 1 tablespoon oil
- 2 medium onions, finely sliced
- 2 fresh red or green chillies, deseeded and finely sliced
- ½ teaspoon fennel seeds*
- 6 curry leaves*
- 600 ml/1 pint coconut milk
- ½ teaspoon ground turmeric
- ½ teaspoon salt or more to taste
- 150 g/5 oz small raw prawns
- 125 ml/4 fl oz thick coconut milk (p. 32)
- lime or lemon juice to taste

Heat the oil in a large heavy saucepan and gently fry the onions, chillies, fennel seeds and curry leaves until the onion is golden. Add the coconut milk, turmeric and salt, stirring constantly to prevent curdling. Simmer uncovered for 10 minutes, then add the prawns and simmer for 3 minutes more. Add the thick coconut milk, stirring constantly, and simmer very gently for a few minutes until the soup thickens. Check the seasoning, and stir in the lime or lemon juice just before serving.

Laksa Lemak

Popular in Malaysia and Singapore, *Laksa Lemak* is a delicious combination of noodles, beansprouts, seafood and a chilli-hot soup. Fresh *laksa* noodles are traditionally used, but Chinese egg noodles or – as a last resort – spaghetti make satisfactory substitutes.

SERVES 6

TO MAKE THE SOUP
6 dried red chillies, soaked in warm water for 30 minutes
1 medium onion, chopped
1 teaspoon *laos* powder*
1 teaspoon ground turmeric
½ teaspoon *blachan**
1 teaspoon chopped lemon rind
4 candlenuts* or 1 teaspoon flaked almonds
2 tablespoons dried prawns,* soaked in warm water for 30 minutes
1½ teaspoons ground coriander
4 tablespoons oil
750 ml/1¼ pints coconut milk (p. 32)
4 tablespoons thick coconut milk (p. 32)
salt to taste

Put the first 9 ingredients into the container of an electric blender or food processor. Add enough of the oil to allow the blades to work properly, and blend to a paste. Heat the remaining oil in a heavy saucepan and gently fry the paste for 5 minutes, stirring constantly to prevent sticking. Pour in the coconut milk, continuing to stir constantly to prevent curdling. Bring to the boil and simmer, uncovered, for 5 minutes. Stir in the thick coconut milk and salt. Simmer for a few minutes longer until the soup thickens.

TO ASSEMBLE
250 g/8 oz Chinese dried egg noodles
250 g/8 oz beansprouts
300 g/10 oz cooked prawns

Bring a large pan of water to the boil, add the noodles, and boil for about 5 minutes or until tender. Break up any tangles with a fork. Drain, and add a dash of oil to prevent sticking. Keep them warm.

Bring a large pan of salted water to the boil, add the beansprouts, and boil for 30 seconds. Drain and rinse in cold water.

To serve, put a few noodles in 6 deep bowls. Add the beansprouts and prawns, and pour the hot soup over.

Sichuan Hot Sour Soup

Sour, hot, thick and rich, this is a soup for winter.

SERVES 4–6

- 75 g/3 oz lean raw pork, shredded (or use half pork and half chicken)
- 2 teaspoons oil
- 4 large dried black mushrooms,* soaked, squeezed and shredded
- 150 g/5 oz fresh beancurd,* diced
- 750 ml/1¼ pints chicken stock
- 2 teaspoons light soy sauce*
- 1 teaspoon rice wine or dry sherry
- 1 tablespoon vinegar
- ½ teaspoon sugar
- 1 tablespoon cornflour, mixed with 3 tablespoons water
- 1 egg, beaten
- 1 teaspoon sesame oil*
- ½–1 teaspoon chilli oil*
- 2 spring onions, finely sliced
- 1 tablespoon finely chopped coriander leaves
- white pepper to taste

Fry the pork (or pork and chicken) gently in oil for a minute or two until it changes colour. Add the mushrooms, beancurd and stock, and simmer for 10 minutes. Add the soy sauce, rice wine or sherry, vinegar, sugar and cornflour, and stir until thickened. Just before serving, take off the heat and stir in the beaten egg so that it forms threads. Add the remaining ingredients and serve immediately in a tureen or individual Chinese soup bowls.

Tom Yam

This classic Thai soup is deliciously thin, hot, sour and fragrant. For the best results, it really has to be made with fresh, raw prawns in their shells. Fresh lemon grass is also almost essential, but lemon rind will do at a pinch.

SERVES 6

- 1 kg/2 lb raw prawns
- 2 stalks lemon grass,* bruised, or rind (yellow zest only) of ½ lemon
- 1 teaspoon *laos* powder* (optional)
- ½ teaspoon salt
- 3 fresh chillies, whole
- 2 litres/3½ pints of water

Shell and devein the prawns. Put the heads and shells into a large heavy saucepan with the lemon grass, *laos* powder, salt, whole chillies and water. Bring to the boil and simmer, covered, for 20 minutes. Strain, and return the stock to the rinsed-out saucepan. Add the raw prawns and simmer for 3 minutes. Stir in the fish sauce and the lemon juice. Pour into a large heated soup tureen and sprinkle with the sliced chillies, coriander and spring onions.

- 1 tablespoon fish sauce*
- 2 tablespoons lemon juice, or more to taste
- 1 fresh red chilli or 2 fresh birdseye chillies, very finely sliced
- 2 tablespoons finely chopped coriander leaves
- 4 spring onions (including some green), finely sliced

You may like to serve a small jug of lemon juice separately so that everyone can adjust the amount of acidity to their own taste. Remember, too, that as the soup stands it becomes progressively hotter from the chillies scattered on before serving.

Callaloo

In some form or other, this famous West Indian soup is found on many Caribbean islands. It is basically a brew of leafy vegetables, chilli and crab. The authentic vegetables are rarely available outside the region, but other greens can satisfactorily be substituted.

In Jamaica this soup is also called pepperpot and should not be confused with the stew that is known as pepperpot on other islands. A recipe for Pepperpot appears on p. 161.

SERVES 6

- 500 g/1 lb spinach or Swiss chard, washed and coarsely shredded
- 2 litres/3 pints water, or chicken stock, or water+stock cube
- 250 g/8 oz salt pork or beef
- 2 cloves garlic, finely chopped
- 4 spring onions, chopped
- 3 fresh green chillies, deseeded and finely chopped
- 1 whole Scotch Bonnet chilli (optional)
- 12 young okras
- 250 ml/8 fl oz coconut milk (p. 32)
- 250 g/8 oz canned or frozen (and thawed) crabmeat
- ¼ teaspoon ground black pepper
- salt

Put the first 8 ingredients into a large heavy saucepan and bring to the boil. Simmer, covered, for about 1½ hours or until the meat is tender. Remove the meat, cut it into pieces, then return it to the pan. Add the coconut milk and bring to the boil, stirring constantly to prevent curdling. Add the crabmeat and ground pepper, and simmer, uncovered, for 10 minutes. Check the seasoning, and add salt if necessary, depending upon the saltiness of the salt pork or beef.

Sopa de Elote

A simple Mexican soup that can be made with canned sweetcorn.

SERVES 4

- 25 g/1 oz butter
- 1 small onion, finely chopped
- 1 or 2 fresh red chillies, deseeded and chopped
- a 300 g/10 oz can sweetcorn, drained
- 4 tablespoons tomato juice
- 1 litre/1¾ pints chicken stock, or water+stock cube
- 125 g/4 oz diced cooked chicken
- salt and freshly ground black pepper to taste

Heat the butter in a large heavy saucepan and gently fry the onion until soft. Add all the other ingredients and simmer for 10 minutes.

VARIATIONS

Stir in 150 ml/¼ pint of cream immediately before serving.

Reserve the chicken and 3 tablespoons of sweetcorn, then liquidize the soup and return the chicken and reserved sweetcorn as a garnish.

Argentinian Beef Soup
Chupi

SERVES 6

- 3 tablespoons oil
- 1 large onion, finely chopped
- 1 clove garlic, finely chopped
- 1 medium sweet red pepper, deseeded and finely chopped
- 2 fresh red chillies, deseeded and finely chopped
- 3 tomatoes, peeled and chopped
- 500 g/1 lb finely minced beef
- 1 large potato, peeled and diced
- 2 carrots, peeled and diced
- 1.2 litres/2 pints water
- 2 beef stock cubes
- 1 tablespoon finely chopped parsley
- salt and freshly ground black pepper to taste

Heat the oil in a large heavy pan and gently fry the onion and garlic until golden. Add the pepper, chillies and tomatoes and simmer for 5 minutes until pulpy. Stir in the beef, breaking up the lumps with a fork. Add all the other ingredients and bring to the boil. Simmer, covered, for 20 minutes.

Serve with a hot chilli sauce (pp. 268–72) and grated cheese in side dishes.

FISH AND SEAFOOD

There is a very special affinity between the chilli pepper and fish – a relationship that often comes as a surprise to cooks from northerly climes, who tend to associate seafood generally with the blandest of dishes. In temperate zones, the delicacy of fish is considered to be best suited to the simplest of treatments – frying in butter or simmering in a mild *bouillon*. Accompanying sauces are pale and creamy.

This is not the case in the tropics, where fish is seen as the perfect partner for pungent and complex seasoning that frequently includes daunting amounts of chillies. In the Caribbean, for example, cooking fish without chillies is almost unthinkable. Every fish dish begins with a marinade or stock involving chillies. In the coastal areas of the Indian subcontinent and South-East Asia, too, fish curries are famous for their potency and searingly hot gravies. For dry dishes, vicious chilli and spice pastes are smeared over whole fish or steaks before grilling or frying. In Louisiana, Tabasco sauce is reputed to have been created to pep up the local oysters.

However, the actual species of fish that are available in different parts of the world vary considerably, and creatures that thrive in warm tropical waters rarely relish the icy depths of colder seas and oceans. The recipes in this book, therefore, are not always specific about the kind of fish to use, except if the seasoning is more suitable for strongly-flavoured oily fish such as mackerel. For the majority of the recipes, any white fish can be used.

There is also considerable choice in the form the fish should take – whole, steaks or fillets. Although most fish-lovers will agree that as a general rule fish is better cooked whole on the bone, many people find it unpleasant to eat fish this way and prefer the convenience of steaks or fillets. Some of the recipes included here demand whole fish but others can be adapted.

If frozen fish is being used, allow it to thaw out completely before marinating or cooking. The only recipes that are not suitable for frozen fish are the raw fish dishes.

Raw Fish

Raw fish is considered a great delicacy in many parts of the world. The classic Japanese *sashimi* is, perhaps, the ultimate example of fish that is subjected to no other culinary treatment than skilful slicing and stylish presentation, though any *aficionado* of the oyster may argue the point.

The Scandinavianses have long been masters of the art of creating delicious dishes that rely on salt, brine and pickling processes for fish, rather than actual cooking. Smoking is often used for oily fish, from herring to salmon.

In chilli-based cuisines, however, the most usual guise for raw fish is in a marinade of lemon and/or lime juice. Similar dishes appear in Latin America, Africa, South-East Asia and the Pacific. Complementary ingredients vary but the general format is the same – the freshest of white fish fillets are cut into bite-size pieces and steeped in citric juice for anything up to 24 hours. The fish is then drained and mixed with finely chopped or shredded chillies plus any other locally favoured seasonings. The resulting dish is colourful, with an interesting contrast in taste and textures. During the marination the juice turns the fish opaque, with a texture not unlike that of cooked fish and a soft sourness that is the perfect foil for fresh chillies.

The choice of fish varies around the world. I prefer flat fish. Sole and turbot are superb but very expensive; plaice is good; cheaper flat fish such as flounder or dab may not have quite the same delicacy but give satisfactory results. Almost any firm-fleshed white fish can be used. Of prime importance is that the fish is absolutely fresh and that there are no hidden bones.

Use freshly squeezed lime or lemon juice. There must be sufficient juice to cover the fish completely.

Ceviche

Ceviche appears in similar forms all over Latin America. Although usually eaten as an *hors d'oeuvre*, the typical Peruvian version is served with boiled potatoes and sweetcorn, making it a fairly substantial meal in itself.

SERVES 6

- 500 g/1 lb white fish fillets
- 200 ml/7 fl oz fresh lemon juice
- 1 fresh red chilli, deseeded and finely chopped
- 1 medium onion, very finely sliced and separated into rings
- 2 cloves garlic, sliced
- salt and pepper to taste
- lettuce leaves
- 2 fresh red chillies, deseeded and cut into ribbons

Cut the fish into 2 cm/$\frac{3}{4}$ in chunks and put into a glass or ceramic bowl. Mix the lemon juice, chilli, onion rings, garlic, salt and pepper together. Pour over the fish to cover completely, adding more juice if necessary. Cover and chill for at least 4 hours or overnight.

To serve, arrange lettuce leaves on 6 plates. Drain the fish and spoon a portion on to each lettuce bed. Decorate with chilli ribbons. If serving the *Ceviche* Peruvian-style, place half a freshly boiled sweetcorn cob and a freshly boiled potato or sweet potato on each plate too.

Mexican Ceviche with Avocado

Avocados are cheap and plentiful in Mexico, but their price in Europe puts them more in the luxury class. Teamed with *Ceviche*, the smooth creaminess of the avocado contrasts well with the chilli tang of marinated fish.

SERVES 6

- 500 g/1 lb white fish fillets
- 200 ml/7 fl oz lime or lemon juice
- 4 tablespoons olive oil
- salt and freshly ground black pepper to taste
- 1 tomato, finely chopped
- 1 small sweet red pepper, deseeded and finely chopped
- 2 fresh green chillies, deseeded and finely chopped
- 3 spring onions, finely sliced
- 1 tablespoon finely chopped parsley or coriander leaves
- 3 avocados

Cut the fish into 1.5 cm/½ in dice. Put in a glass or ceramic bowl and pour the juice over to cover completely. Cover and chill for at least 4 hours or overnight.

Drain the fish and toss in the olive oil. Season with salt and pepper. Gently mix in the tomato, sweet pepper, chillies, spring onions and herbs.

Cut the avocados in half, discarding the stones, and carefully scoop out the flesh. Chop the avocado flesh and mix with the fish. Check the seasoning and add more salt if necessary. Pile the mixture back into the avocado shells and serve immediately.

Marinated Fish Thai Style

This South-East Asian version of marinated fish is mixed with chillies and creamy thick coconut milk.

SERVES 6 AS A STARTER OR 3 AS A MAIN COURSE WITH SALAD

- 500 g/1 lb white fish fillets
- 200 ml/7 fl oz lime or lemon juice
- salt and pepper to taste
- ½ teaspoon sugar
- 3 tomatoes, diced
- 1 small cucumber, peeled and diced
- 1 tablespoon chopped chives
- 1 fresh red chilli, deseeded and finely chopped

Cut the fish into narrow strips and put into a glass or ceramic bowl. Pour over the juice to cover and add the salt, pepper and sugar. Cover and chill for at least 4 hours or overnight.

Drain the fish and mix with the tomatoes, cucumber, chives and chilli. Carefully stir in the thick coconut milk and adjust the seasoning if necessary.

Arrange lettuce leaves in a large bowl or in individual dishes. Pile the fish mixture on top and garnish with chilli flowers.

2 tablespoons thick coconut milk (p. 32)
lettuce leaves
chilli flowers to garnish (p. 223)

Marinated Fish Salad from Indo-China
Koy Pa

Traditionally *Koy Pa* is served with a bowl of crisp lettuce leaves and another of fresh mint leaves. A mint leaf is placed in the centre of a lettuce leaf with a small portion of fish. The lettuce is then rolled up, dipped in a chilli sauce or *Nuoc Mam* (p. 275), and popped in the mouth.

SERVES 6

500 g/1 lb fish marinated with juice, salt, pepper and sugar as in the previous recipe
3 spring onions, finely sliced
1 clove garlic, very finely chopped
1 fresh red chilli, deseeded and finely chopped
6 young green beans, thinly sliced diagonally and blanched
1 tablespoon fish sauce*

Mix the fish with the remaining ingredients and serve.

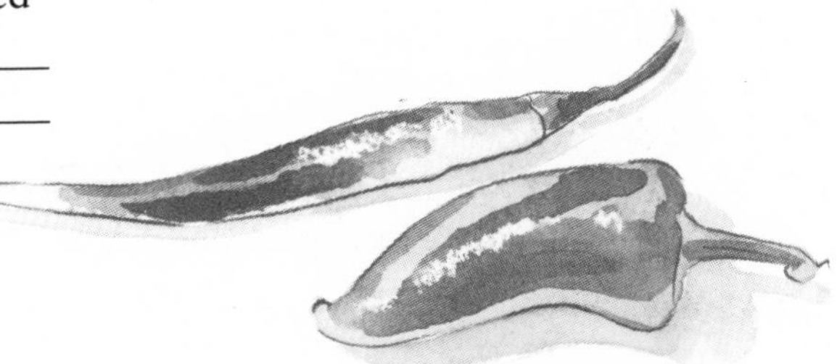

Pickled Fish

In the days before refrigeration, pickling fish by first cooking it lightly (usually by frying) and then steeping it in an oil and vinegar mixture was a common method of food preservation. Not only would the fish remain edible for a few days but the pickling liquid – which was invariably highly seasoned – matured and imparted its flavour to the fish. In tropical regions, chillies were an obvious ingredient to be incorporated in pickled fish dishes and many variations exist around the world, each combining chillies with local herbs and spices.

Escabeche

In Central and Latin America, pickled fish is credited with Spanish origins and is known by derivations of the Spanish word for this dish – *escabeche*. There are many, many versions; two are given here, one suitable for white fish fillets and one for oily fish.

SERVES 6 AS A MAIN DISH OR 12 AS A STARTER

- 1 kg/2 lb white fish fillets
- flour seasoned with salt, pepper and ground chilli, for dredging
- olive oil for frying
- 1 medium onion, cut into thin rings
- 1 clove garlic, finely chopped
- 2 fresh green chillies, deseeded and shredded
- 150 ml/¼ pint olive oil
- 150 ml/¼ pint white wine vinegar
- 1 tablespoon finely chopped parsley
- ½ teaspoon salt
- ¼ teaspoon ground black pepper
- 2 tablespoons capers, chopped
- 2 tablespoons stoneless olives, chopped

Wash and dry the fish, and dredge it in seasoned flour, shaking off the excess. Fry the fish in hot oil until the fillets are golden on both sides and just cooked through. Remove them from the pan with a slotted spoon and arrange them in a large shallow dish. Scatter with the onion, garlic and chillies.

Mix the remaining ingredients together and pour over the fish. Cover with foil and chill for 12–36 hours. Serve at room temperature, on lettuce leaves.

Escabeche of Mackerel

SERVES 6 AS A STARTER OR 3 AS A MAIN COURSE

- 3 mackerel, weighing about 250 g/ 8 oz each, cleaned, with heads and tails removed
- seasoned flour (see previous recipe)
- oil for frying
- 4 spring onions, cut in half horizontally and then shredded vertically
- 3 cloves garlic, thinly sliced

Dredge the mackerel with the seasoned flour and fry them in moderately hot oil for 5 minutes on each side. Remove with a slotted spoon to a chopping board. Carefully remove two fillets from each fish (with skin) and place in a single layer in a shallow dish. Scatter with the spring onions, garlic and chillies.

Mix all the remaining ingredients except the orange slices together and pour over the fish. Chill for 12–36 hours. Serve at room temperature, garnished with orange rings.

3 fresh red chillies, deseeded and shredded
4 cloves
6 peppercorns
2 bay leaves
5 cm/2 in cinnamon stick
½ teaspoon coriander seeds, coarsely crushed
¼ teaspoon oregano or marjoram
½ teaspoon salt
125 ml/4 fl oz oil
50 ml/2 fl oz dry white wine
50 ml/2 fl oz white wine vinegar
2 tablespoons fresh orange juice
50 g/2 oz pimento-stuffed olives
4 gherkins, chopped
thinly cut orange slices for garnish

South African Pickled Fish

A favourite South African dish, pickled fish is believed to have been brought from the East Indies by Malay slaves during the seventeenth century. Serve it as a first course or with a salad as a light main course.

SERVES 4–6
500 g/1 lb fish fillets
flour
1 large onion, thinly sliced
2 bay leaves
2 fresh red or green chillies, deseeded and cut into shreds
½ teaspoon black peppercorns
½ teaspoon allspice berries*
1 tablespoon brown sugar
250 ml/8 fl oz vinegar
2 teaspoons curry powder
½ teaspoon ground turmeric
½ teaspoon salt

Cut the fish into serving portions and dredge them in flour, shaking off the excess.

Put a layer of onions in the bottom of an ovenproof baking dish, lay the fish on top, and cover with the remaining onions. Add all the remaining ingredients and cover with kitchen foil. Bake in a pre-heated oven at 180°C/350°F/gas 4 for 30 minutes. Remove the foil and allow to cool. Re-cover and leave in the refrigerator for 2 days. Serve at room temperature.

Vinegar Fish
Acar Ikan

Acar Ikan is found in Malaysia and Indonesia. It is probably the type of dish that the previous recipe was originally based on.

SERVES 4

- 1 large onion
- 2 fresh red chillies, chopped, or 1 teaspoon *sambal ulek**
- 2 tablespoons flaked almonds
- 1 teaspoon chopped ginger
- 3 cloves garlic
- ½ teaspoon salt
- ½ teaspoon ground turmeric
- 500 g/1 lb oily fish stakes, e.g. tuna, mackerel or mullet, or a whole fish, cleaned and scaled
- 3 tablespoons oil
- 3 tablespoons vinegar
- 1 tablespoon lemon juice
- 125 ml/4 fl oz water
- chilli flowers for garnish (p. 223)

Peel the onion and cut it in half. Thinly slice one half and set aside. Chop the remainder and put in the container of an electric blender or food processor. Add the chillies, almonds, ginger and garlic, and the minimum amount of water needed to allow the blades to operate. Blend to a paste and set aside.

Rub the salt and turmeric into the fish.

Heat 2 tablespoons of the oil in a large, heavy frying-pan and fry the fish until it is nicely browned on both sides. Remove with a slotted spoon. Add the remaining oil and gently fry the sliced onion until golden. Add the chilli paste from the blender and fry for 3 minutes, stirring constantly to prevent sticking. Return the fish to the pan with all the remaining ingredients (except the garnish). Bring to the boil and simmer, uncovered, for about 5 minutes until the fish is cooked and the sauce has reduced and thickened. Check the seasoning and add more salt if necessary.

Serve at room temperature, decorated with chilli flowers (p. 223). Plain rice and an assortment of *sambals* (p. 262) are the usual accompaniments.

Poached and Braised Dishes

Poisson en Blaff

A superb method of poaching fish, which comes from the French Caribbean islands of Guadeloupe and Martinique. The unusual name is said to come from the sound made as the fish is dropped into boiling stock . . . *blaff*.

SERVES 4

1 kg/2 lb very fresh firm-fleshed fish (can be 4 individual fish weighing about 250 g/8 oz each, or 2 larger fish weighing about 500 g/1 lb each), gutted, scaled and washed, with heads and tails left on

FOR THE MARINADE

- juice of 1 lemon or 2 limes
- 3 cloves garlic, crushed
- 1 spring onion, halved lengthwise
- 1 fresh chilli, deseeded and halved
- ½ teaspoon salt

FOR THE HOT PEPPER SAUCE

- juice of 1 lemon or 2 limes
- 3 tablespoons olive oil
- 1 tablespoon finely chopped parsley or coriander leaves
- 1 spring onion, finely chopped
- 1 clove garlic, finely chopped
- 1 fresh chilli, deseeded and finely chopped
- salt and pepper to taste

FOR THE BOUILLON

- 250 ml/8 fl oz dry white wine
- 500 ml/17 fl oz water
- 2 spring onions, halved lengthwise
- 1 clove garlic, whole
- 1 whole fresh chilli, preferably a Scotch Bonnet
- 1 bay leaf
- 1 bouquet garni
- 2 cloves
- 2 allspice berries*
- 4 black peppercorns
- ½ teaspoon salt

Place the fish in a shallow dish and add the marinade ingredients together with enough water just to cover. Leave in the refrigerator for 1 hour then drain the fish and discard the marinade.

The sauce is best made at least 1 hour before so that the flavours blend. Stir all the ingredients together and serve in a separate bowl. The sauce will keep in a screwtop jar in the refrigerator for up to 1 week.

Just before the marinading time is up, put the *bouillon* ingredients in a heavy saucepan large enough to hold the fish comfortably. Bring to the boil and simmer, covered, for 15 minutes. Add the fish (and a little extra water if there is insufficient to cover it). Simmer on a very low heat for 5–10 minutes depending upon the size of the fish, so that the flesh is cooked but still very soft and tender.

Transfer to a warm platter and serve immediately with rice.

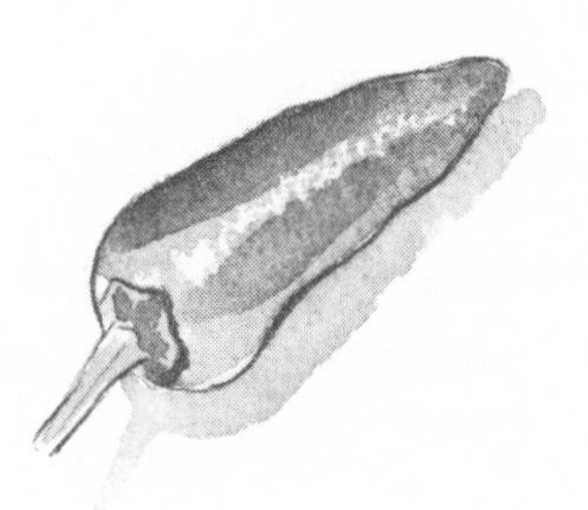

Fish in a Green Almond Sauce
Pescado en Almendrada Verde

A delicately flavoured Mexican fish dish that can be made with any white fish fillets but is especially nice with flat fish such as plaice or sole.

SERVES 6

1 kg/2 lb white fish fillets

FOR THE BOUILLON

1 small onion, halved
1 clove garlic, halved
1 tablespoon lemon juice
1 glass dry white wine
1 whole fresh green chilli
1 bay leaf
½ teaspoon salt
¼ teaspoon ground white pepper

FOR THE SAUCE

1 slice crustless bread, lightly toasted
75 g/3 oz blanched almonds
3 fresh green chillies, deseeded and chopped
4 tablespoons chopped coriander or parsley leaves
1 clove garlic, chopped

Put the *bouillon* ingredients in a saucepan with 450 ml/¾ pint of water. Bring to the boil and simmer, covered, for 15 minutes. Drain, reserving the liquid and discarding the seasonings. Return the *bouillon* to the pan, bring to the boil and very gently poach the fish fillets until cooked but not falling apart. This will take 4–10 minutes depending upon thickness. Remove the fish with a slotted spoon and keep warm on a serving dish.

Combine the *bouillon* and all the sauce ingredients in the container of an electric blender or food processor and blend to a purée. Transfer to a saucepan, bring to the boil, and simmer, uncovered, for a few minutes until the sauce thickens. Pour the sauce over the fish and serve immediately, garnished with a few coriander sprigs.

The pale green sauce of this dish looks very pretty served with rice that has been cooked with a little saffron* and garnished with toasted flaked almonds.

Vatapá

A fish and coconut milk stew from Brazil that is typical of the African cooking of Bahia province. Authentically dende oil would give the brilliant orange colouring to the dish, but paprika and turmeric have been substituted here.

SERVES 6–8

4 tablespoons dried prawns*
4 tablespoons olive oil
1 medium onion, finely chopped
½ teaspoon finely chopped fresh ginger

Soak the dried prawns in warm water for 20 minutes, then drain, reserving the liquid. Reduce the dried prawns to a purée, using a minimum amount of soaking liquid. Set aside.

Heat 2 tablespoons of the olive oil in a large heavy frying-pan. Gently fry the onion, garlic,

- 2 cloves garlic, finely chopped
- 3 fresh red chillies, deseeded and finely chopped
- ½ teaspoon paprika
- ¼ teaspoon ground turmeric
- 3 tablespoons ground almonds
- 3 tablespoons ground roasted peanuts (not salted)
- 450 ml/¾ pint coconut milk (p. 32)
- salt and pepper to taste
- 500 g/1 lb white fish fillets, cut into 2.5 cm/1 in chunks
- 500 g/1 lb peeled raw prawns

ginger and chillies until the onion is just turning gold, then stir in the paprika and turmeric. Add the puréed dried prawns and cook for 3 minutes, stirring constantly. Stir in the nuts and cook for 1 minute. Add the coconut milk, salt and pepper. Bring to the boil, stirring constantly to prevent curdling. Simmer, uncovered, for about 10 minutes until the sauce has thickened. Set aside.

In another pan, heat the remaining 2 tablespoons of olive oil and gently fry the fish chunks until they are golden on both sides and just cooked through. Remove with a slotted spoon and add to the sauce. Put the prawns in the pan, cook for about 2 minutes until they are turning pink, and add to the sauce. Return sauce and fish to the heat. Simmer for 5 minutes.

Serve with rice, a salad or green vegetable and a chilli sauce (pp. 266–73).

Fish in Red Sauce

A much-loved Algerian fish dish with a flamboyant hot red sauce. Grouper or sea bass are most frequently used in North Africa, but any fish steaks can be substituted.

SERVES 6

- 4 large tomatoes, peeled and sliced
- 6 fish steaks, washed
- 5 tablespoons olive oil
- 5 tablespoons water
- 1 teaspoon *harissa** or ground chilli
- 1 teaspoon paprika
- ¼ teaspoon ground black pepper
- ½ teaspoon ground cumin
- ½ teaspoon salt
- 1 tablespoon finely chopped coriander or parsley leaves

Lay half the tomato slices in the base of a large heavy frying-pan. Place the fish on top and cover with the remaining tomatoes. Mix all the remaining ingredients together and pour over the fish. Bring to the boil and simmer, covered, for 25 minutes. Serve with rice or *couscous* and a salad.

Thai Fish Curry

A chilli paste made from fresh green chillies and coriander leaves, plus stems and roots, provides the seasoning for this fragrant curry.

SERVES 6

FOR THE CHILLI PASTE

- 5 fresh green chillies, chopped
- 1 small onion, chopped
- 4 cloves garlic, chopped
- 3 tablespoons chopped coriander leaves, plus roots
- rind of ½ lemon, chopped
- 1 teaspoon *blachan**
- 1 teaspoon *laos* powder*
- 1 teaspoon *serai* powder*
- ½ teaspoon ground turmeric
- ½ teaspoon ground cumin
- 2 teaspoons ground coriander
- ¼ teaspoon ground black pepper
- 2 tablespoons oil

FOR THE CURRY

- 600 ml/1 pint coconut milk (p. 32)
- 1 fresh green chilli, deseeded and finely chopped
- a handful fresh basil leaves, finely chopped
- ½ teaspoon salt
- 1 tablespoon fish sauce*
- 750 g/1½ lb white fish fillets

Put all the ingredients for the paste into the container of an electric blender or food processor and blend to a paste. Put the chilli paste and the coconut milk in a heavy saucepan and bring to the boil, stirring constantly to prevent curdling. Add all the remaining ingredients and bring back to the boil. Simmer, uncovered, for 10–15 minutes until the fish is cooked. Serve with boiled rice.

Fish Head Curry

This favourite Singaporean dish can present a daunting sight to the uninitiated – a great fish head proudly placed in the centre of a serving bowl, swimming in lots of very hot, thin, red gravy. There is, in fact, a surprising amount of edible flesh on a giant fish head, which is highly regarded for its sweetness and succulence. However, for cooks who really cannot face the idea of a fish head, this excellent sauce could be used with any white fish fillets.

SERVES 6

- 1 very large fish head
- 2 tablespoons lemon juice
- 2 teaspoons salt
- 15 dried red chillies, torn into pieces and soaked for 15 minutes
- 1 medium onion, chopped
- 5 cloves garlic, chopped
- 2 teaspoons chopped fresh ginger
- 4 tablespoons oil
- 2 tablespoons coriander seeds
- 1 tablespoon cumin seeds
- 1 teaspoon fennel seeds
- 1 teaspoon fenugreek seeds
- ½ teaspoon black peppercorns
- 1 teaspoon ground turmeric
- 1 teaspoon black mustard seeds
- 5 cm/2 in cinnamon stick
- 2 bay leaves
- 1 litre/1¾ pints coconut milk
- 1 teaspoon sugar
- 1 teaspoon concentrated tamarind extract
- 125 g/4 oz small okra, stems removed
- 3 medium tomatoes, quartered

Rub the fish head with lemon juice and sprinkle on 1 teaspoon of salt. Set aside.

Drain the chillies and put them in the container of an electric blender or food processor with the onion, garlic and ginger. Add enough of the oil to allow the blades to operate properly. Blend to a paste. Set aside.

Dry roast and grind the coriander seeds, cumin seeds, fennel seeds, fenugreek seeds and peppercorns according to instructions on page 31. Mix well with the ground turmeric and stir in a very little water to make a stiff paste. Set aside.

Heat the remaining oil in a large saucepan or deep frying-pan and fry the mustard seeds until they pop and jump. Add the cinnamon stick and bay leaves. Cook for 30 seconds and add chilli paste. Fry gently for 4 minutes, stirring constantly to prevent burning. Add the spice paste and fry for 3 minutes, still stirring. If there seems to be too little oil to fry the spices, add 1 tablespoon more. Add the coconut milk slowly, stirring constantly to prevent curdling. Add the remaining salt, sugar and tamarind extract. Bring to the boil and simmer, uncovered, for 5 minutes.

Rinse the fish head and add it to the pan with the okra. Simmer for about 15 minutes until the fish head is cooked through. Add the tomatoes for the last 2 or 3 minutes of cooking time.

Serve with boiled rice.

Baked and Fried Fish Dishes

Fish with Sesame Paste Sauce
Samak Harrah

Most often associated with Lebanon but found all over the Middle East, this rich fish dish is baked with a delicious sesame paste sauce. Traditionally the dish is garnished with bright red pomegranate seeds and sprigs of green coriander leaves, which contrast nicely with the pale creamy sauce.

SERVES 4

- 4 tablespoons olive oil
- 1 medium onion, chopped
- 6 cloves garlic, chopped
- 250 ml/8 fl oz *tahina* paste*
- 150 ml/¼ pint water
- 75 ml/3 fl oz lemon juice
- ½ teaspoon salt or more to taste
- 2 fresh green chillies, deseeded and chopped
- 2 tablespoons chopped parsley
- a whole firm-fleshed fish, weighing 1.5–2 kg/3–4 lb, cleaned and scaled
- 2 tablespoons pine nuts, lightly fried until golden
- 2 tablespoons pomegranate seeds (optional)
- sprigs of parsley and lemon wedges to garnish

Heat 1 tablespoon of oil in a frying-pan and gently fry the onion and garlic until soft. Transfer to the container of an electric blender or food processor. Add the *tahina* paste, water, lemon juice, salt, chillies and parsley and blend to a purée. Set aside.

Heat the remaining oil in a large frying-pan that will hold the fish comfortably. Fry the fish until it is lightly browned on both sides but not cooked through. Transfer to an ovenproof dish and pour the sauce over. Cover with foil. Bake in a moderate pre-heated oven at 180°C/350°F/gas 4 for 35 minutes. Remove the foil and decorate with pine nuts, pomegranate seeds and parsley. Lay lemon wedges around the edge of the dish.

Serve with rice and/or *pitta* bread. A side salad also makes a refreshing accompaniment.

Fish Veracruz Style in Tomato Sauce
Pescado a la Veracruzana

An unusual blend of fish and orange juice from the Mexican sea port of Veracruz. Red snapper is the locally preferred fish for this dish, but any firm-fleshed white fish fillets can be substituted.

SERVES 6

- 1 kg/2 lb white fish fillets
- juice of 1 lemon

Sprinkle the fish with the lemon juice. Spread half the tomatoes over the base of an ovenproof baking dish large enough to hold the fish fillets in

3 large tomatoes, peeled, deseeded and finely chopped
1 large onion, finely sliced
2 cloves garlic, finely chopped
3 fresh green chillies, deseeded and shredded
juice of 1 orange
pinch ground cinnamon
pinch ground cloves
salt and freshly ground black pepper to taste
1 bay leaf
1 tablespoon capers
18 stuffed olives
thinly sliced orange and lemon to garnish

a single layer. Add half the sliced onion, garlic and chillies. Place the fish on top, then the remaining tomatoes, onion, garlic and chillies. Add all the other ingredients except the garnish. Cover with foil and bake in a moderate oven pre-heated to 180°C/350°F/gas 4 for 40 minutes. Remove the foil and garnish with orange and lemon slices.

Serve with rice or new potatoes.

Fish with Peanut Stuffing

Any large fish can be filled with this tasty peanut and chilli stuffing, which is typical of many coastal areas of West Africa.

SERVES 4

2 slices crustless bread, soaked in water and squeezed dry
6 tablespoons ground roasted peanuts (not salted)
2 cloves garlic, finely chopped
1 fresh red or green chilli, deseeded and finely chopped
1 tablespoon tomato purée
½ teaspoon salt
¼ teaspoon ground black pepper
1 large fish weighing about 1 kg/2 lb, gutted, scaled and washed
2 tablespoons oil
juice of 1 lemon
⅛ teaspoon ground chilli
⅛ teaspoon ground ginger

Mix the first 7 ingredients together and pack into the cavity of the fish. Stitch up the opening.

Pour half the oil into an ovenproof baking dish large enough to hold the fish comfortably. Place the stuffed fish in the dish and pour the remaining oil over. Add the lemon juice and sprinkle the fish with the ground chilli and ginger.

Bake for 40 minutes in a pre-heated oven at 180°C/350°F/gas 4.

Stuffed Shad

A festive speciality from the ancient city of Fez, this dish is one of the masterpieces of Moroccan cuisine. The exotic stuffing of prunes filled with rice and nuts makes this an unusual party dish that is ideal for busy hostesses looking for something a bit different, as it can all be prepared well in advance. It needs nothing more than a fresh salad and a bowl of *harissa** to become a spectacular main course.

SERVES 6

- 3–4 cups cooked rice
- 3 tablespoons chopped almonds
- 1 teaspoon sugar
- ½ teaspoon ground cinnamon
- ½ teaspoon ground ginger
- 500 g/1 lb cooked prunes, or fresh or dried dates, or a mixture of prunes and dates
- 1 large shad or salmon weighing about 2 kg/4 lb, gutted and washed
- 3 tablespoons butter or *smen* (*ghee**)
- 1 teaspoon ground chilli
- ½ teaspoon salt
- ¼ teaspoon ground black pepper
- ¼ teaspoon ground ginger
- 1 small onion, finely sliced
- ½ teaspoon ground cinnamon
- thin lemon slices

Mix the cooked rice, almonds, sugar, cinnamon and ginger together in a bowl. Remove the stones from the prunes or dates and stuff with a little of the rice mixture. Fill the cavity of the fish with the stuffed fruit and stitch up the opening.

Use half the butter or *smen* to grease a large oval baking dish big enough to hold the fish comfortably. Mix together the ground chilli, salt, black pepper and ginger, and sprinkle half the mixture into the dish.

Place the fish in the dish and spread with the remaining butter or *smen*. Pour in 3 tablespoons of water and sprinkle the fish with the remaining chilli mixture. Scatter with the sliced onion.

Cover the dish with foil and cook for 45 minutes in a pre-heated oven at 180°C/350°F/gas 4. Remove the foil and continue cooking for 30 minutes at 200°C/400°F/gas 6 until the skin of the fish is golden. Remove from the oven and sprinkle with a little ground cinnamon.

Very carefully transfer the fish to a warm serving platter. Open up the cavity and spoon some of the filling out around the lower edge of the fish. Decorate with thin lemon slices and serve immediately.

VARIATIONS

Figs can also be used for the filling, and cooked *couscous* can replace the cooked rice.

Fish with Tomato Sauce
Poisson à la Tomate

The French-speaking countries of West Africa are fond of using typical French herbs such as thyme and bay leaves in their cooking. The *aja* sauce in this recipe is a popular fish accompaniment, combining a basically Provençal tomato sauce with African ingredients such as ground dried prawns, ginger and chillies.

SERVES 8

FOR THE AJA SAUCE

- 4 tablespoons oil
- 1 large onion, finely chopped
- 3 cloves garlic, finely chopped
- 6 tomatoes, peeled and chopped
- 1 teaspoon ground chilli
- 1 tablespoon ground dried prawns*
- 2 teaspoons finely chopped fresh ginger
- 1 *bouquet garni*
- ½ teaspoon salt or more to taste
- juice of 1 lemon

FOR THE FISH

- 1 large fish weighing about 2 kg/ 4 lb, gutted, scaled and washed
- 1 bunch thyme
- 2 cloves garlic, halved
- ½ small onion
- salt and freshly ground black pepper
- 2 tablespoons cornflour
- ½ teaspoon ground chilli
- 4 tablespoons oil

To make the *aja* sauce, heat the oil in a heavy frying-pan and gently fry the onion until it is just turning gold. Add the garlic and tomatoes and simmer for about 10 minutes until thick and pulpy. Add the remaining ingredients and simmer for a further 10 minutes.

To prepare the fish, stuff the thyme, garlic and onion into the fish cavity. Season the cavity with salt and pepper. Mix the cornflour with the ground chilli and dredge the fish, shaking off the excess. Put half the oil in a large ovenproof dish that will hold the fish comfortably. Put the fish in the dish and pour in the remaining oil. Cover with foil and bake in a pre-heated oven at 190°C/ 375°F/gas 5 for 30 minutes. Remove the foil and continue cooking for a further 15–20 minutes, until the fish is cooked through and the skin is golden. Baste occasionally with the oil in the dish.

Transfer the fish to a warm serving dish and serve the sauce separately. Rice and salad make good accompaniments. Alternatively serve with a vegetable and *pommes frites* or crusty French bread.

Indian Battered and Fried Fish
Tali Machchi

The batter for this dish is best made with a blend of ordinary flour and *besan** (ground chickpea flour) which gives a delicious crunchy texture.

SERVES 4

- 500 g/1 lb fish fillets
- 1 tablespoon lemon juice
- 3 tablespoons plain flour
- 3 tablespoons *besan**
- 1 teaspoon *garam masala**
- 1 teaspoon ground chilli
- ½ teaspoon ground turmeric
- ½ teaspoon salt
- 1 tablespoon oil
- 175 ml/6 fl oz water
- 1 egg white, beaten to form frothy peaks
- oil for deep-frying

Wash and dry the fish fillets, sprinkle them with lemon juice, and set aside.

Put the flour, *besan*, *garam masala*, chilli, turmeric and salt in a bowl and mix well. Add the oil and water and beat to make a smooth batter. Fold in the beaten egg white.

Dip the fish fillets in batter to give an even coating. Deep-fry in medium hot oil until golden. Drain on kitchen towels.

Serve with lemon wedges on a bed of lettuce as a fish course. Alternatively, garnish with paper-thin onion rings and finely sliced fresh green chillies, and serve with plain rice and a selection of chutneys and pickles. *Tali Machchi* is also good served with chips.

Chermoula

Found in slightly different forms all over the Meghrib, *Chermoula* is a delicious way of marinating and then frying either white fish fillets or a whole fish such as shad or sea bream. It is equally good eaten hot or cold. The fish can simply be marinated, drained, floured and fried in olive oil, or – as here – the marinade can be made into a sauce in which the fish steeps after frying, so that even more flavour penetrates the flesh.

I think *Chermoula* is best served cold (room temperature, not straight from the refrigerator) with a crispy salad, bowls of *harissa*, olives and lemon wedges, and warm flat bread (*pitta*).

SERVES 6

- 1 small onion, thinly sliced
- 2 cloves garlic, finely chopped
- 1 teaspoon *harissa** or 1 fresh red chilli, deseeded and finely chopped
- ½ teaspoon salt
- ¼ teaspoon ground black pepper
- ½ teaspoon paprika

Mix the first 8 ingredients together to make a marinade. Wash and dry the fish, place in a shallow dish and pour the marinade over. Cover with foil and leave in a cool place for 4 hours, turning the fish once.

Drain the fish, reserving the marinade, and dry on paper kitchen towels. Dredge the fish with flour. Heat the oil in a large, heavy frying-pan that will hold the fish comfortably, and fry the

½ teaspoon ground cumin
3 tablespoons lemon juice or vinegar
1 kg/2 lb white fish fillets or a 1.5 kg/3 lb whole fish, cleaned and scaled
flour
3 tablespoons olive oil
2 tablespoons water
5 cm/2 in cinnamon stick
1 teaspoon finely chopped parsley or coriander leaves
2 tablespoons raisins or sultanas

fish over a medium heat until it is golden on both sides and just cooked through. Remove the fish and add the marinade plus all the remaining ingredients to the juices left in the pan. Bring to the boil and simmer, uncovered, for 5 minutes, then return the fish to the pan and simmer for 3 minutes. Transfer the fish and the sauce to a serving dish and leave until cold. Remove the cinnamon stick before serving.

NOTE
For a sweeter dish, add 1 tablespoon of honey to the sauce ingredients but not to the marinade.

Fried Fish with Thai Ginger Sauce

This typical Thai fish dish has a hot sharp sauce, strongly flavoured with ginger. It is worth experimenting with the amounts of chillies, lemon juice (vinegar can be used instead) and sugar to achieve your preferred balance of tastes.

SERVES 4–6
4 tablespoons oil
1 whole white fish, cleaned and scaled
4 spring onions, chopped
3 cloves garlic, finely chopped
1 tablespoon finely shredded fresh ginger
3 fresh red chillies, deseeded and finely chopped
2 tablespoons lemon juice
2 tablespoons light soy sauce*
4 tablespoons water
2 teaspoons brown sugar
¼ teaspoon ground black pepper
1 teaspoon cornflour, mixed with a little water
1 tablespoon finely chopped coriander leaves
red chilli flowers to garnish

Heat the oil and fry the fish on both sides until it is golden and cooked through. Transfer the fish to a serving dish and keep warm.

Tip off all but 2 tablespoons of oil from the pan. Add the spring onions, garlic, ginger and chillies and stir-fry for 3 minutes. Add the lemon juice, soy sauce, water, sugar and pepper. Stir in the cornflour mixture and bring to the boil, continuing stirring to prevent lumps. Simmer for 1 minute until the sauce has thickened and become transparent. Pour over the fish. Sprinkle with the chopped coriander.

Serve garnished with red chilli flowers (p. 223).

Sweet and Sour Fish

In Singapore the ever-popular Chinese sweet and sour sauce has undergone an inevitable transformation – it is chilli-hot. There are many variations, ranging from a mixture that is basically tomato ketchup to one that is overwhelmingly sweet. There is no right or wrong sweet and sour blend, it is just a matter of preference. This is the way I make it, and I think it is best with fried fish, although batter-coated prawns and pork are also all-time favourites. Any whole fish or fish fillets will do, but in Singapore either pomfret (a flat fish) or grouper are considered the greatest delicacies and are simply deep-fried and served accompanied by the sauce and steamed rice.

SERVES 4

FOR THE SAUCE

- 4 fresh red chillies
- 5 cloves garlic, chopped
- 1 teaspoon finely chopped fresh ginger
- 2 tablespoons oil
- 1 small onion, halved and cut in thick chunks
- 250 ml/8 fl oz thick tomato juice
- 4 tablespoons light soy sauce*
- 2 tablespoons vinegar
- 1 tablespoon sugar
- ½ teaspoon salt
- 4 canned pineapple rings, cut into chunks, + 4 tablespoons juice
- 75 ml/3 fl oz water
- 2 teaspoons cornflour, mixed with a little water

FOR THE FISH

- 1 whole firm-fleshed fish weighing about 750 g/1½ lb, gutted, scaled and cleaned; or 500 g/1 lb white fish fillets
- egg and flour for coating
- oil for deep-frying

Deseed the chillies and finely chop 3 of them. Cut the fourth into shreds and set this one aside. Pound the chopped chillies to a paste with the garlic and ginger. Alternatively, chop the garlic and ginger very finely and mix them with the chopped chillies. Heat the oil in a heavy frying-pan or wok and gently fry the chilli mixture for 1 minute. Add the onion and stir-fry for 30 seconds. Add all the other ingredients (including the shredded chilli) except the cornflour. Bring to the boil and simmer, uncovered, for 3 minutes. Add the cornflour, stirring constantly until the sauce thickens. Set aside.

Dry the fish on paper towels, dip in beaten egg and dredge in flour, shaking off the excess. Deep-fry in medium hot oil. Drain and serve immediately on a warm platter with some hot sauce poured over and the rest in the bowl. Serve with steamed rice.

Fish in Taucheo Sauce

This is the chilli-hot Singaporean version of a well-known Chinese fish dish which is flavoured with salted soy beans – *taucheo*. They are available tinned from Chinese grocery shops and are usually in the form of a paste or sauce. If using whole beans, mash them lightly before use.

SERVES 4

- 3 fresh red chillies, deseeded and chopped
- 2 cloves garlic, chopped
- 1 teaspoon chopped fresh ginger
- 4 tablespoons oil
- 4 white fish steaks, weighing about 500 g/1 lb in total
- 1 medium onion, finely sliced
- 2 teaspoons *taucheo* paste*
- 1 teaspoon light soy sauce*
- 125 ml/4 fl oz water
- salt and lemon juice to taste

Use a pestle and mortar to pound the first 3 ingredients to a paste. Set aside.

Heat the oil in a large, heavy frying-pan until fairly hot. Quickly fry the fish for 1 minute on each side until browned. Remove from the pan and set aside. The fish should not be cooked through.

Turn down the heat and tip off all but 2 tablespoons of oil from the pan. Add the onion and fry until soft. Add the chilli mixture and stir-fry for 1 minute. Add the *taucheo* paste and stir-fry for 1 minute. Return the fish to the pan and add the soy sauce and water. Bring to the boil and simmer, uncovered, for about 5 minutes until the fish is cooked. Transfer to a warm serving dish.

The sauce should have reduced to about 2 tablespoons of thick gravy. If it has not, boil it vigorously for 1 minute to encourage evaporation. Taste, and add salt and lemon juice. Pour the sauce over the fish and serve immediately with rice as a main course. Alternatively, serve the fish with a salad as an unusual light lunch dish.

Grilled Fish

Fish Kebabs

These kebabs are made with marinated fish, cut into chunks, threaded on skewers and grilled. Serve them as a starter course just with lemon wedges, or as a light lunch with salad and *chapatis* or crusty bread. If 1 tablespoon of ground rice or *besan** is added to the marinade, the fish will have a slightly crunchy coating. Use any firm-fleshed thick white fish fillets that will hold their shape while cooking. If wooden skewers are used, soak them in water for 1 hour first.

SERVES 6

- 1 kg/2 lb white fish fillets, cut into 2.5 cm/1 in cubes
- 250 ml/8 fl oz yoghurt
- 1 teaspoon ground coriander
- 1 teaspoon ground cumin
- ½ teaspoon ground ginger
- ½ teaspoon ground chilli
- ¼ teaspoon ground cloves
- ½ teaspoon salt
- ¼ teaspoon ground black pepper
- 1 clove garlic, finely chopped
- 1 tablespoon lemon juice
- oil for basting

Put the fish in a bowl with all the other ingredients except the oil, and leave for up to 1 hour. Thread the pieces of fish on skewers and brush with oil. Grill for 5 minutes, baste again and turn. Grill for a further 5 minutes.

Serve with a chilli dip.

Javanese Grilled Fish
Ikan Panggang Djawa

A useful way to cook the cheaper and less delicately flavoured flat fish such as dab and flounder. Choose small fish which provide an individual portion.

SERVES 4

- 6 fresh red chillies, deseeded and chopped
- 3 cloves garlic, chopped
- 6 tablespoons dark soy sauce*
- 2 tablespoons brown sugar
- 3 tablespoons lemon juice
- 1 teaspoon grated lemon rind (zest only)
- 4 small flat fish, cleaned
- oil for basting

Put the first 6 ingredients into the container of an electric blender or food processor and blend to a purée. Make 2 slashes on each side of the fish, place in a shallow bowl and pour the chilli mixture over. Leave to marinate for 1 hour. Remove the fish (reserving the marinade) and brush with oil. Grill or barbecue (barbecuing gives the best results) for about 6 minutes either side.

Meanwhile add 2 tablespoons of water to the marinade and simmer for 5 minutes.

Serve the fish with the sauce in a bowl as a dip.

Otak Otak

These fragrant fish parcels are a Malaysian speciality and are traditionally wrapped in banana leaves and roasted over embers. Even if banana leaves are not available, they still make an unusual starter for a barbecue meal wrapped in more mundane kitchen foil. Prepare them in advance and roast them quickly to make an exotic appetizer while the main meats are cooking. Alternatively, they can be cooked on a table-top barbecue grill.

SERVES 6

- 1 large onion, chopped
- 4 cloves garlic, chopped
- 1 teaspoon chopped fresh ginger
- 8 fresh chillies, deseeded and chopped
- 1 tablespoon chopped nuts (candlenuts,* macadamias or almonds)
- 1 teaspoon ground coriander
- 1 stalk lemon grass* (bottom 5 cm/2 in only), chopped or ½ teaspoon grated lemon rind
- 150 ml/¼ pint coconut milk (p. 32)
- 2 tablespoons lemon juice
- 1 teaspoon salt or to taste
- 1 teaspoon sugar or to taste
- ¼ teaspoon ground white pepper
- 750 g/1½ lb white fish fillets

Put the first 8 ingredients into the container of an electric blender or food processor with enough thick coconut milk to allow the blades to operate properly. Blend to a purée. Transfer to a bowl and stir in the remaining coconut milk with the lemon juice, salt, sugar and pepper.

Remove any skin and bones from the fish. Chop the fish finely and stir into the mixture.

Cut 15 cm/6 in squares out of double thickness kitchen foil. Put 2 tablespoons of the mixture in the centre of each square and fold up to make a packet, making sure that the ends are well sealed. (This can be done in advance.) Barbecue over hot embers for 5 minutes each side. Eat – steaming hot – from the packet. *Otak Otak* can also be eaten cold with salad.

Grilled Mackerel Indian Style

This dish is nicest if mackerel fillets are used, rather than whole fish. If you don't enjoy filleting fish, ask your fishmonger to do it.

SERVES 4

- 4 medium mackerel, weighing about 200 g/7 oz each, filleted
- 2 tablespoons lemon juice
- 2 fresh green chillies, deseeded and finely chopped
- 3 tablespoons finely chopped coriander leaves
- 1 clove garlic, finely chopped
- ½ teaspoon ground turmeric
- ¼ teaspoon salt
- ¼ teaspoon ground black pepper
- oil for basting
- lemon wedges

Wash and dry the fish fillets. Mix together the lemon juice, chillies, coriander, garlic, turmeric, salt and pepper, and rub into both sides of the fish. Chill for 1 hour. Brush with oil and cook over hot coals or under a hot grill for about 4 minutes each side. Serve with lemon wedges.

Fish Parcels

A superbly fragrant way of cooking fish that makes life very easy for the cook.

SERVES 4

- 4 small whole fish (e.g. trout, mullet, bream or whiting), weighing about 250 g/8 oz each, cleaned and scaled
- 1 teaspoon salt
- 1 tablespoon oil
- 1 large onion, chopped
- 2 cloves garlic, chopped
- ½ teaspoon chopped fresh ginger
- 2 fresh green chillies, deseeded and chopped
- 4 tablespoons desiccated coconut
- 2 tablespoons chopped mint
- 2 tablespoons chopped parsley
- 1 teaspoon sugar
- 1 teaspoon lemon rind (zest only)
- juice of 1 lemon
- ⅛ teaspoon ground white pepper
- 4 bay leaves

Rub the fish with salt inside and out. Set aside. Heat the oil in a frying-pan and gently fry the onion, garlic and ginger until soft. Transfer to the container of an electric blender or food processor and add all the remaining ingredients except the bay leaves. Add the absolute minimum of water to allow the blades to operate properly, and blend to a paste. Put a little of the paste inside each fish. Lay the fish in a shallow dish, cover with the remaining paste, and leave to marinate for 30 minutes.

Lay each fish on a double thickness of kitchen foil. Divide the marinade between them and lay a bay leaf on top of each. Wrap up loosely and fold the ends over to fasten securely.

Barbecue or grill for 15 minutes each side. Serve in the packet.

Seafood

Goan Mussels

From the west coast of India, these mussels are rather like spiced *moules marinières*.

SERVES 6

- 1 kg/2 lb mussels
- 4 tablespoons oil
- 1 large onion, finely chopped
- 6 cloves garlic, finely chopped
- 1 tablespoon finely chopped fresh ginger
- 2 fresh green chillies, deseeded and finely chopped
- ½ teaspoon ground turmeric

Wash and scrub the mussels. Make sure the shells are free of all beards and gritty bits, and discard any shells that are open.

Heat the oil in a large heavy saucepan and gently fry the onion, garlic, ginger and chillies for 5 minutes. Add the turmeric, cumin, coriander and ground chilli and fry for 1 minute, stirring constantly to prevent burning. Add the salt and water, bring to boil, and add the mussels. Simmer, covered, for about 8 minutes and then discard any shells that are still closed. Stir in the

- 1 teaspoon ground cumin
- 1 teaspoon ground coriander
- ½ teaspoon ground chilli
- ½ teaspoon salt
- 250 ml/8 fl oz water
- 1 tablespoon finely chopped coriander or parsley leaves
- lemon juice to taste

chopped coriander and lemon juice to taste.

As part of an Indian-style meal, serve these mussels with rice. They also make an interesting starter course for a Western-style meal with crusty French bread or *chapatis*.

Singaporean Chilli Crab

One of the great Singaporean eating experiences – luscious sweet-fleshed crab in a hot-sweet chilli sauce. Authentically this dish is always made with live crabs, which are prepared immediately before cooking. If – like me – you are too squeamish to do this yourself, use ready-prepared crab legs that have been cracked for easier eating. The chilli sauce used in this recipe can be either commercially bottled Singaporean-style chilli sauce (available from oriental grocers) or one of the recipes that appear on p. 274.

There is only one way to eat chilli crabs, and that is with the fingers, so provide plenty of paper towels for mopping up sticky chins and hands.

SERVES 4

- 6 fresh red chillies, deseeded and chopped
- 4 cloves garlic, chopped
- 1 tablespoon chopped fresh ginger
- 4 tablespoons oil
- 2 medium crabs, cleaned and cut into portions, or 1 kg/2 lb crab legs
- 4 tablespoons tomato ketchup
- 2 tablespoons chilli sauce
- 2 tablespoons light soy sauce*
- 1 tablespoon sugar
- 4 tablespoons water

Using a pestle and mortar, pound the first 3 ingredients to a paste. Heat the oil in a large heavy frying-pan or wok and gently fry the paste for 3 minutes, stirring frequently to prevent burning. Add the crab and stir-fry until it changes colour. Add all the remaining ingredients, bring to the boil and simmer, uncovered, for 5 minutes. Keep turning the crab pieces so that they cook evenly. Serve immediately, with side bowls of rice.

Caribbean Crab Curry

This lovely light fresh curry incorporates traditional Indian spices but has a very un-Indian taste.

SERVES 3

- 2 tablespoons oil
- 1 medium onion, finely chopped
- 2 cloves garlic, finely chopped
- 1 teaspoon finely chopped fresh ginger
- 2 fresh red chillies, deseeded and finely chopped
- 1 teaspoon coriander seeds
- 1 teaspoon cumin seeds
- 1 teaspoon black mustard seeds*
- ½ teaspoon black peppercorns
- ½ teaspoon ground turmeric
- a 200 g/7 oz can tomatoes, including juice
- 1 bay leaf
- ½ teaspoon salt
- 1 tablespoon finely chopped parsley
- juice of ½ lemon
- 250 g/8 oz cooked crabmeat

Heat the oil in a large heavy frying-pan and gently fry the onion, garlic, ginger and chillies for 5 minutes. Add all the ground spices and cook for 1 minute, stirring constantly. Add the tomatoes and fill up the empty can with water. Pour the water into the pan and gently mash the tomatoes with a fork to break them up. Add the bay leaf and salt. Bring to the boil and simmer, uncovered, for about 10 minutes until the sauce has thickened. Check the seasoning and add more salt if necessary. Just before serving, stir in the parsley and lemon juice, add the crabmeat, turn off the heat, and leave for 1 minute for the crab to heat through.

Serve with boiled rice, a salad and Caribbean Peach Chutney (p. 257).

Chilli Cream Scallops

A special party dish – it can be made with frozen scallops but they should be thawed out before use.

SERVES 4

- 2 tablespoons butter
- 1 small onion, finely chopped
- 1 clove garlic, finely chopped
- 2 fresh green chillies, deseeded and finely chopped
- 2 teaspoons fish curry powder (p. 37)
- 125 ml/4 fl oz yoghurt

Heat the butter in a heavy frying-pan and gently fry the onion, garlic and chillies until soft but not coloured. Add the curry powder and cook for 1 minute. Do not allow to burn. Add the yoghurt a little at a time, stirring constantly to prevent curdling. Stir in the milk, ground ginger, salt and bay leaf. Add the scallops, bring to the boil and simmer very gently, uncovered, for about 5 minutes until the scallops are tender. Stir in the cream and parsley. Transfer to a warm serving

- 3 tablespoons milk
- ⅛ teaspoon ground ginger
- ½ teaspoon salt
- 1 bay leaf
- 500 g/1 lb scallops (weight without shells)
- 2 tablespoons thick cream
- 1 tablespoon finely chopped parsley
- 2 tablespoons toasted flaked almonds

dish and scatter the toasted almonds on top.

Serve with *Arroz Blanco*, p. 217, or *Arroz Verde*, p. 218 and a salad.

Malaysian Chilli-fried Prawns
Sambal Udang

A fiery-hot and pungent dish that combines fresh prawns with plenty of chillies and *blachan*. For anyone who has learnt to live with *blachan*, this is a superb way of serving prawns.

SERVES 4–6

- 1 kg/2 lb large raw prawns
- 2 large onions
- 4 cloves garlic, chopped
- 2 teaspoons chopped fresh ginger
- ½ teaspoon *blachan**
- 15 dried red chillies, deseeded, torn into pieces and soaked for 15 minutes
- 3 tablespoons oil
- ½ teaspoon sugar
- ½ teaspoon salt
- 1 teaspoon concentrated tamarind extract* diluted in 150 ml/¼ pint water

Peel the prawns, discarding the black spinal thread. Set aside. Chop one onion coarsely and thinly slice the other. Put the chopped onion, garlic, ginger, *blachan* and drained chillies into the container of an electric blender or food processor. Add 2 tablespoons of oil and blend to a paste. Set aside.

Heat the remaining 1 tablespoon of oil in a large heavy frying-pan. Add the sliced onion and gently fry until just turning gold. Add the chilli paste and fry for 3 minutes, stirring frequently to prevent burning. Add the prawns and fry for 1 minute, tossing and turning the prawns so that each is coated with paste. Add the remaining ingredients. Bring to the boil and simmer, uncovered, for 5 minutes until the prawns are cooked. There should be only a little thick, oily gravy. Serve with boiled rice.

NOTE

Quartered tomatoes could be added 2 minutes before the end of the cooking time. They not only look attractive but help to stretch the expensive prawns a little further.

Bahraini Prawns

The warm waters that surround the island of Bahrain, in the Persian Gulf, are aswim with the most delicious big juicy prawns. This favourite way of cooking them uses *baharat* – a fragrant spice mixture that gives Gulf dishes their distinctive taste.

SERVES 6

- 1 kg/2 lb large raw prawns
- 3 tablespoons oil or *ghee**
- 1 large onion, finely chopped
- 3 cloves garlic, finely chopped
- 5 cm/2 in cinnamon stick
- 1 teaspoon *baharat**
- 1 teaspoon ground chilli
- 1 teaspoon ground turmeric
- ½ teaspoon ground ginger
- 6 tomatoes, peeled and chopped
- 1 teaspoon finely chopped lemon rind (zest only)
- 1 teaspoon salt

Peel the prawns and remove the thin black spinal thread across the back. Heat 2 tablespoons of oil or *ghee* in a large heavy frying-pan and fry the prawns for a couple of minutes until they turn pink. Remove them with a slotted spoon and set aside. Add the remaining 1 tablespoon of oil or *ghee* to the juices in the pan and gently fry the onion, garlic and cinnamon stick until the onion is soft. Add all the remaining ingredients, plus a teacup of water. Bring to the boil and simmer, uncovered, for 5 minutes. Add the prawns and continue cooking for a further 5 minutes. Serve immediately with *Muhammar* (p. 217) or Rice and Dates (p. 219) and a salad with a lemon juice dressing.

Prawns with Coconut Milk

A quick and easy dish to make with solid coconut cream and concentrated tamarind extract.

SERVES 3–4

- 3 tablespoons oil
- 2 medium onions, finely sliced
- 4 cloves garlic, finely chopped
- ½ teaspoon finely chopped fresh ginger
- 1 teaspoon ground cumin
- 1 teaspoon ground turmeric
- 1 teaspoon ground chilli
- pinch fenugreek seeds*
- 300 ml/½ pint water
- pinch black pepper
- ½ teaspoon salt

Heat the oil in a heavy frying-pan and gently fry the onions, garlic and ginger until golden. Stir in the cumin, turmeric, chilli and fenugreek seeds and fry for 2 minutes, stirring constantly. Add the water, pepper, salt and coconut cream. Bring to the boil, stirring constantly to prevent curdling, and keep stirring until the coconut cream is completely dissolved. Add the tamarind and simmer, uncovered, for 15 minutes until the gravy has thickened.

Add the prawns and simmer for 3 minutes if raw or 1 minute if pre-cooked. Stir in the parsley before serving.

25 g/1 oz solid coconut cream (p. 31)
½ teaspoon concentrated tamarind extract*
250 g/8 oz shelled prawns, fresh or frozen (and thawed)
1 tablespoon finely chopped parsley

Madras Prawn Curry

Fiery hot in both colour and taste, this curry is easy to make and delicious. It is perfectly good made with frozen prawns, but if they are to be added while still frozen, make the sauce a bit thicker because the thawed juices will dilute it.

SERVES 3

2 tablespoons oil
1 medium onion, finely sliced
2 cloves garlic, finely chopped
2 teaspoons *garam masala**
1 teaspoon ground turmeric
1–1½ teaspoons ground chilli
½ teaspoon paprika
1 small can (about 200 g/7 oz) tomatoes, mashed with their juice
175 ml/6 fl oz water
½ teaspoon salt
250 g/8 oz shelled prawns, fresh or frozen
2 teaspoons lemon juice
1 tablespoon finely chopped coriander or parsley

Heat the oil in a large, heavy frying-pan and gently fry the onion and garlic until golden brown. Add the *garam masala*, turmeric, chilli and paprika, and fry for 30 seconds, stirring constantly. Add the tomatoes and simmer for about 3 minutes until pulpy. Add the water and salt and simmer for about 8 minutes until the sauce thickens. (This can all be done in advance if preferred.) Add the prawns and simmer for 1 minute only if ready cooked and thawed out. If still frozen (see note above) or raw, simmer for 3 minutes. Do not over-cook. Stir in the lemon juice and fresh herbs.

Serve immediately, with plain boiled rice, a vegetable (I like Cauliflower with Cumin, p. 185) and a salad or pickles.

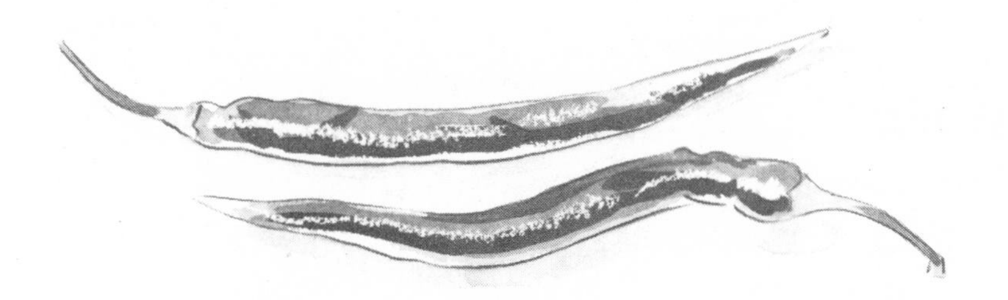

Tandoori Prawns

The bigger, fatter and juicier the prawns, the better!

SERVES 6–8

- 1 kg/2 lb large raw prawns
- 125 ml/4 fl oz yoghurt
- 3 tablespoons lemon juice
- 4 cloves garlic, finely chopped
- 1 teaspoon finely chopped fresh ginger
- 1 teaspoon ground chilli
- 1 teaspoon paprika
- 1 teaspoon ground turmeric
- 2 teaspoons *garam masala**
- 1 tablespoon chopped mint
- 1 tablespoon chopped coriander or parsley leaves

Shell the prawns but leave the tails intact. Remove the black spinal thread. Mix all the other ingredients together and use this to marinate the prawns for at least 30 minutes. Drain. Cook over hot coals or under a hot grill for 3 minutes each side. The prawns could also be threaded on to skewers (if using bamboo skewers, soak them in water for 1 hour).

Prawn Creole

SERVES 4

- 25 g/1 oz butter
- 1 large onion, finely chopped
- 3 stalks celery, chopped
- 4 tomatoes, skinned and chopped
- 300 ml/½ pint chicken stock, or water+stock cube
- 250 g/8 oz frozen peas
- 250 g/8 oz raw peeled prawns
- 1 tablespoon flour
- 2 teaspoons ground chilli
- 1 teaspoon sugar
- 1 tablespoon vinegar or lemon juice
- 2 teaspoons water
- ½ teaspoon salt

(flour, ground chilli, sugar, vinegar or lemon juice, water, salt:) Mix together as a smooth paste.

Heat the butter in a large, heavy frying-pan and gently fry the onion and celery until soft but not coloured. Add the tomatoes and stock, bring to the boil, cover, and simmer for 15 minutes. Add the peas and simmer for 5 minutes. Add the prawns and simmer for 2 minutes. Add the chilli paste and stir constantly until the sauce thickens. Add the salt and simmer for 2 minutes.

Serve immediately, with rice, a salad and crusty French bread.

Prawn Patia

This unusual and delicious prawn curry is a well-known Parsee dish associated with Bombay. It was here that the Parsees settled over 1,200 years ago after fleeing from their native Persia and the influence of their distinctive cooking is still evident today. Quite unlike most curries, the predominant flavours are hot, sweet and sour. The balance of these three aggressive tastes is very much a matter of personal preference. The quantities stated here are, therefore, only a guide and are open to experimentation.

SERVES 3–4

FOR THE SPICE PASTE

- 1 medium onion, chopped
- 2 cloves garlic, chopped
- 1 teaspoon chopped ginger
- 1 fresh green chilli, chopped
- handful of coriander or parsley leaves
- 2 teaspoons paprika
- 1 teaspoon ground coriander
- 1 teaspoon ground cumin
- ½ teaspoon ground chilli
- ½ teaspoon ground turmeric
- ¼ teaspoon ground fennel seeds
- ¼ teaspoon ground black peppercorns
- 1 tablespoon oil

FOR THE GRAVY

- 1 tablespoon oil
- a 125 g/4 oz pot yoghurt
- 1 teaspoon tomato purée
- 1 tablespoon brown sugar
- 1 teaspoon honey
- 1 teaspoon concentrated tamarind pulp or juice of 1 lemon
- 1 teaspoon vinegar
- salt to taste
- 250 g/8 oz cooked and peeled prawns

Put all the spice paste ingredients into the container of an electric blender or food processor and add the minimum water needed to allow the blades to operate properly. Blend to a paste.

Heat the oil in a large heavy frying-pan and fry the paste gently for 5 minutes, stirring constantly. Remove from the heat and stir in the yoghurt. Bring to the boil, stirring constantly. Fill the yoghurt pot with water and add to the mixture together with all remaining sauce ingredients. Simmer, uncovered, for 10 minutes until the sauce has thickened and the oil has separated into a vivid red rim. (This sauce can be made in advance.)

Add prawns and heat through. Do not allow them to over-cook.

VARIATION

Make a pork patia with 500 g/1 lb pork, cut into bite-sized pieces. Fry the pork in a little oil then add the prepared gravy and simmer for 10 minutes. The fennel seeds could be omitted and replaced with black mustard seeds and/or fenugreek seeds.

MEAT

Meat is subject to more taboos and dietary fads and fancies than any other foodstuff. The Chinese are the world's biggest pig-eaters. Muslims will not touch it; they prefer mutton or lamb, but only if it is killed in a certain way. Thus, in the Muslim north of India, they eat no pork . . . the pig is dirty. In the Hindu south, they eat no beef . . . the cow is sacred. Indian Buddhists and hundreds of thousands of vegetarian Tamils eat no meat at all.

In the cattle-rearing regions of South America, beef – naturally – reigns supreme. In Peru, they breed and eat llamas. Mexicans traditionally eat guinea-pigs. In the Caribbean, they like goats. Desert dwellers eat camels, and various people are reputed to eat cats and dogs.

In coastal communities the world over, all meat is scorned in favour of fish, and for the poor and hungry – many of whom live in the chilli-eating belt – there is precious little choice in what they eat, or when, or how much. With a staple diet of cereals and beans, meat in any form is a rare event.

Even so, international cooking offers such a rich and diverse repertoire of meat and chilli dishes that it is difficult to know where to begin. The original chilli stews from the Aztec kitchen, therefore, make a sensible starting point.

Mexican Moles and Tingas

Until the Spaniards introduced oil and lard into the Aztec cooking of Mexico, the frying process was unknown and stewing was the main method of cooking meat. Today's *moles* are based on the original Aztec stews and the word *mole* is derived from *molli* – a Nahuatl (the language of the Aztecs) word meaning a sauce made of chillies. Pre-Columbian *moles* were made by pounding chillies, tomatoes and herbs in a *molcejete* or heavy mortar, then simmering this chilli paste with fish or meat. Contemporary *moles* are still made from a chilli paste but this includes onions and garlic, and the paste is fried before any liquid is added, in much the same way that some Indian curries are prepared. In the modern Mexican kitchen, electric blenders and food processors have superseded the *molcejete* and do the job of producing a chilli paste in a fraction of the time.

Meat Stew
Mole de Olla para Carne de Res

This simple Mexican meat stew has many variations. It is basically meat – usually pre-cooked or partially pre-cooked – in a rich sauce made from dried chillies that have been soaked and puréed. In order to achieve the characteristic deep, rusty-red colour, at least one type of dried black chilli must be used in the sauce, i.e. *ancho*, *pasilla* or *mulato*.

SERVES 4–6

- 1 kg/2 lb lean stewing beef, pork or lamb cut into 2.5 cm/1 in cubes
- sprig of coriander leaves or a bouquet garni
- 2 *ancho* chillies
- 1 *pasilla* chilli
- 1 small onion, chopped
- 2 cloves garlic, chopped
- a 400 g/13 oz tin tomatoes
- 1 tablespoon lard or oil
- salt and pepper to taste

Put meat into a heavy saucepan with herbs and enough water to just cover. Simmer until tender. Strain and reserve stock. Discard herbs.

Prepare the chillies as explained on p. 25. Put into the container of an electric blender or food processor with the onion, garlic and tomatoes. Purée and add enough liquid – either reserved stock or chilli soaking water – to produce the consistency of thin cream.

Heat the lard or oil in a heavy saucepan and add the purée. Simmer for about 15 minutes until the purée has thickened and lost any raw onion taste. Season to taste. Add the meat and heat through.

Serve with rice or *tortillas*.

VARIATIONS

Vegetables may be added to the above basic recipe. Put them in the pan with the meat towards the end of the cooking time so that they are barely cooked. Simmer in the chilli sauce with the meat. Try any combination of vegetables – new potatoes, carrots, courgettes and green beans. Tinned sweetcorn, drained and added just before serving is also good.

Green Stewpot
Mole de Olla Verde

The green sauce in this dish is produced from fresh green chillies, canned green tomatoes and sweet green peppers.

SERVES 4–6

- 1 kg/2 lb lean pork, cut into 2.5 cm/1 in cubes
- 1 whole small onion, peeled and stuck with 2 cloves
- a 200 g/7 oz can Mexican green tomatoes* with juice
- 4 fresh green chillies, chopped, or 4 canned *serrano* chillies
- 1 medium sweet green pepper, chopped
- 2 tablespoons chopped parsley or coriander leaves
- 3 cloves garlic, chopped
- 1 medium onion, chopped
- 2 tablespoons oil or lard
- 1 teaspoon salt
- ½ teaspoon ground coriander
- 4 medium potatoes, peeled and quartered
- 125 g/4 oz frozen peas

Put the pork and the whole onion in a large heavy saucepan. Add enough water to cover, bring to the boil, and simmer for 30 minutes.

Meanwhile, drain the green tomatoes, reserving the juice. Put them in the container of an electric blender or food processor, adding half the juice (reserve the rest). Add the chillies, sweet pepper, parsley or coriander, garlic and onion, and blend to a purée.

Heat the oil or lard in a heavy frying-pan and fry the purée as described in the previous recipe. Add to the meat with the reserved green tomato juice, salt and ground coriander. Top up with water if necessary. Simmer for 30 minutes, then add the potatoes. Simmer for a further 15 minutes and add the peas. Simmer for 10 more minutes, by which time the meat and vegetables should all be tender.

Serve with rice or *tortillas*.

Adobo de Carnero

The Mexican *adobo* is prepared in a similar way to the *mole* but the sauce is much thicker. Lamb is used here, but pork or beef would also be suitable.

SERVES 6

- 1 kg/2 lb lean lamb, cut into large cubes
- 2 medium onions, one left whole, one chopped
- 2 cloves garlic, one left whole, one chopped
- 1 bay leaf
- ½ teaspoon salt

Put the lamb in a large heavy saucepan with the whole onion, the whole garlic clove, bay leaf, salt, thyme and oregano. Add just enough water to cover, and simmer for about 1½ hours until the meat is tender. Drain and reserve the stock.

Meanwhile, drain the chillies and tear them into pieces. Put them into the container of an electric blender or food processor with the remaining onion and garlic, tomato, vinegar and cumin. Add enough of the stock to allow the

- ½ teaspoon dried thyme
- ½ teaspoon dried oregano
- 6 dried red chillies, or 3 *ancho* and 3 *mulato* chillies, soaked
- 1 tomato, peeled and chopped
- 1 tablespoon vinegar
- ½ teaspoon ground cumin
- 2 tablespoons oil or lard

blades to operate properly, and blend to a purée.

Heat the oil or lard in a heavy frying-pan until moderately hot. Add the chilli purée (it will spit and splatter), turn down the heat, and fry for 5 minutes, stirring constantly. Add 250 ml/8 fl oz reserved stock so that the purée is thinned to the consistency of a thick cream. Add the lamb and simmer, covered, for 20 minutes.

Pork Tinga

Unlike the Mexican *mole* stews which have as their base a purée of chillies, onions and tomatoes, *tingas* are based on the Spanish *sofrito* – onions are fried and tomatoes are added and simmered until thick. *Chorizo* is often added for additional colour and flavour.

SERVES 6

- 2 tablespoons oil or lard
- 1 kg/2 lb boneless pork, cut into 2.5 cm/1 in cubes
- 200 g/7 oz *chorizo** sausage (bought or home-made, p. 135), sliced
- 1 medium onion, finely chopped
- 2 cloves garlic, finely chopped
- 4 tomatoes, peeled and chopped
- ½ teaspoon salt
- ¼ teaspoon ground black pepper
- ½ teaspoon dried marjoram
- 3 fresh red or green chillies, finely chopped
- 450 ml/¾ pint stock, or water+stock cube
- ½ teaspoon sugar

Heat the oil or lard in a heavy frying-pan and fry the pork until it is evenly browned, in two batches. Transfer the pork to a large heavy saucepan as it is cooked. Fry the *chorizo* and add to the pork. Add the onion and garlic to the oil or lard remaining in the frying-pan, and gently fry until soft but not coloured. Add the tomatoes and cook for about 5 minutes until thick and pulpy. Add all remaining ingredients and transfer to the saucepan containing the meat. Bring to the boil and simmer, covered, for about 1¼ hours or until the pork is tender and the sauce has thickened.

Alternatively the pork can be browned and transferred to a saucepan, covered with water and simmered until tender. Drain and reserve the stock and return the pork to the saucepan. Fry the *chorizo* and add to the pork. Make the *sofrito* as explained above, and add 250 ml/8 fl oz of the reserved stock. Add this to the pork and sausage and simmer for 20 minutes until the sauce has thickened.

Estofado

This Mexican meat stew has its origins in the Spanish conquest. When the Arabs came to North Africa, they brought with them fruits, nuts and spices from the Near and Middle East. The Moors of North Africa then introduced these delicacies into Spanish cooking, and when the Spaniards colonized Mexico they brought these ingredients with them, together with onions, garlic and sherry. Add the tomatoes and chillies that were native to Mexico and you have *Estofado*.

If dried *ancho* chillies are available, use 3. If not, follow the recipe below, using a mixture of sweet pepper and dried red chillies.

SERVES 6–8

- 4 dried red chillies, soaked in warm water for 15 minutes
- 1 medium sweet red pepper, deseeded and chopped
- 2 tablespoons oil or lard
- 1 large onion, finely chopped
- 2 cloves garlic, finely chopped
- 1.5 kg/3 lb boneless lamb, beef or pork cut into 2.5 cm/1 in cubes
- 4 tomatoes, peeled and chopped
- ¼ teaspoon ground cinnamon
- ¼ teaspoon cloves
- ¼ teaspoon ground black pepper
- ¼ teaspoon ground cumin
- 1 teaspoon salt
- 3 tablespoons seedless raisins or sultanas
- 250 ml/8 fl oz sherry
- 3 tablespoons flaked almonds

Drain the chillies and reserve their liquid. Tear the chillies into pieces and put them into the container of an electric blender or food processor with the sweet pepper and 4 tablespoons of the soaking liquid. Blend to a purée.

Heat 1 tablespoon of oil or lard in a large heavy saucepan and gently fry the onion and garlic until soft but not coloured. Remove with a slotted spoon and add the remaining 1 tablespoon oil or lard. Fry the meat in two batches, until evenly browned. Return the onion to the pan and add all the other ingredients except the almonds. Add the chilli purée and enough water to just cover the meat. Bring to the boil and simmer, covered, for 1½ hours or more, until the meat is tender and the gravy has thickened. Add the almonds before serving.

American Chili

The potent meat and ground chilli concoctions of the south-western United States are an all-American invention, but their culinary roots are firmly established with the Mexican *moles* and *tingas*. After all, it was only in 1853 that New Mexico – the American state that, with Texas, Arizona and California, has a common border with Mexico – became part of the United

States. Today, the chilies of New Mexico are generally acknowledged to be closest to true north Mexican cooking, with its strong emphasis on ground chilli and cumin seasoning. (Note that the one 'l' spelling of chili refers to the American dish made from meat and chillies. The two 'l' spelling denotes the vegetable or spice.)

The actual origins of chili, or *chili con carne*, are somewhat obscure, but certainly by the mid nineteenth century Texas prisons had acquired a reputation for the quality of their own particular brand of prison gruel. This was a one-pot stew of the cheapest possible ingredients – tough meat, which was chopped to make it more digestible then subjected to long simmering with chillies and herbs. Chain-gang chili eventually became such a gourmet dish that released prisoners were reported to do anything to get back inside again – back to a good bowl of chili!

There must be some truth, too, in the theory that Texan cowboys working on the great cattle ranches that were being developed in the south-west cooked up stews of beef – which was on hand – and of the chillies that grew wild over the vast grazing lands of the area.

By the turn of the century, San Antonio in Texas was the recognized chili centre of the day. Every evening, 'chili queens' appeared on all the main thoroughfares, serving passers-by from cauldrons. They remained there until the mid-1940s, when new American hygiene laws forced their closure.

From then on the south-western chili spread across the entire United States, until minced meat and tomato stews – labelled as chili or *chili con carne* – appeared on every roadside café and snack bar menu. They were, more often than not, insipid gastronomic shadows of the real thing, but they became accepted as typical American food, in the same culinary league as hotdogs and hamburgers.

While this adulteration was going on elsewhere, back in the south-west it was inevitable that the chili connoisseurs should take steps to preserve the integrity of their local gastronomy. The first official chili organization – the Chili Appreciation Society – was formed in the 1950s, but for the most part, cooking and eating chili was a fairly private affair, with like-minded enthusiasts meeting together to practise their art in an informal way. Then, in 1966, the first chili cookoff was held in Terlingua, Texas, as publicity for a recently published book on chili. The culinary contest was between two eminent chili-cooks and self-styled experts, and ended in a draw, but the event was such an unprecedented success that it triggered off a great chili-cult that took America by storm.

Infatuation with 'the pod' and 'the bowl of blessedness' still centred on

Texas and the south-west, but fanatics and *aficionados* throughout the country (and, ultimately, throughout the world) joined in the great chili craze. Other appreciation societies were formed, cookoffs became regular events in every state, chili books were published and newspaper articles debated the merits and demerits of various approaches to the gastronomic science of chili-making.

Chilimania continues unabated and offers enormous scope for the creative cook, for there are no rules. Every chili chef has his *own* rules, of course, but as nobody accepts any other than his own, the culinary field is wide open. The only point on which everyone agrees is that chili contains chilli . . . lots of it. However, American chili powder is not pure ground chilli but a mixture of ground hot chilli, ground sweet pepper, cumin, garlic and, perhaps, an extender and thickener such as *masa harina** (Mexican corn flour). American recipes can specify 4, 6, even 8 tablespoons of chili powder for 1 kg/2 lb meat, and you only have to use this amount of pure ground chilli once (as I did) to know that the most asbestos-mouthed chili-addict cannot eat chili *that* hot!

If using an American recipe, therefore, adjust the chilli powder quantities accordingly if you are not using American chili powder. For a mild mixture use 2 teaspoons of paprika, ½ teaspoon of ground chilli and ¼ teaspoon of ground cumin to replace 1 tablespoon of American chili powder. For a hotter mixture, use 1½ teaspoons of paprika, 1 teaspoon of ground chilli and ½ teaspoon of ground cumin to 1 tablespoon of chilli powder. All the recipes included here have already been converted, and 'ground chilli' means pure ground dried hot red chillies.

Apart from the essential chilli content, controversy reigns supreme. Beans, for example. Should beans be cooked in the chili? Should they be pre-cooked and added at the end? Should they be served on the side? Should they be red kidney beans, pinto beans or butter beans? Should beans be served at all?

What about other vegetables? In New Mexico, even tomatoes are shunned. The brilliant red sauces in New Mexican chilis are coloured by chillies alone. If tomatoes are included, are fresh or tinned tomatoes preferable? Or tomato purée? Or sweet peppers? Most people add onions, but there is the delicate question of garlic.

Then there is the all-important matter of meat. In New Mexico they chop it. In Texas they grind it coarsely. Further north they accept a fine-hamburger-type grind. Is pork acceptable? Or chicken? Or game?

What is the best oil? Perhaps butter, lard or dripping is better. Which herbs? How many spices? Should the sauce be thick or thin? Plentiful or sparse? Does simmering with a lid or without a lid improve the flavour?

The chili-buffs never tire of discussing the subtleties of chili-making, so – bearing in mind that no one chili can satisfy every chili palate – a selection of diverse chili recipes are included here. Experimentation is the name of the chili game and these are all tried and tested many times.

Serve chilis with rice, *tortillas*, crusty bread, crackers or even spaghetti. Salads, coleslaw and *Guacamole* (p. 50) make good accompaniments. Sour cream, grated cheese and finely chopped onion are great sprinkled over.

For drinks try chilled beer or rosé wine.

Chili con Carne Mark 1

For nearly ten years I made chili this way and was confident that it was *the* definitive chili. Then I met a few chili-buffs and my chilis were never the same again. This is, however, still a pretty mean chili. It is quite heavy on beans, so reduce the amount if you wish.

SERVES 4

- 6 tablespoons oil
- 2 large onions, coarsely chopped
- 500 g/1 lb lean stewing beef, cut into 1 cm/½ in cubes
- 4 cloves garlic, chopped
- 1 tablespoon ground cumin
- 1 tablespoon paprika
- 1½ teaspoons ground chilli
- a 200 g/7 oz can tomatoes, mashed with their juice
- 250 g/8 oz dried red kidney beans, soaked overnight
- ½ teaspoon dried oregano
- 1 tablespoon finely chopped parsley
- 2 fresh red or green chillies, deseeded and finely chopped
- salt and ground black pepper to taste

Heat 3 tablespoons of the oil in a large heavy saucepan and gently fry the onions until golden. Remove the onions and add the remaining 3 tablespoons of oil to the oil in pan. Turn up the heat and fry the meat (in two batches if necessary) until it is browned all over. Add the garlic, cumin, paprika and chilli. Fry for 1 minute and then return the onions to the pan. Add the tomatoes, drained kidney beans and enough water to cover by 2.5 cm/1 in. Add the oregano and parsley. Bring to the boil and simmer, covered, for 1 hour. Do *not* add salt at this stage.

Add the chillies, salt and pepper, and more water if there is any danger of sticking. Continue simmering until the meat and beans are tender and the sauce has reduced and thickened. Check frequently for sticking and add more water if necessary. If the sauce is too thin when the meat and beans are cooked, boil uncovered for a few minutes to encourage evaporation.

New Mexico Chili

This is the purists' chili, with no vegetables, not even tomatoes, and no beans, though pinto beans – definitely *not* red kidney beans – could be served on the side.

SERVES 4

- 1 kg/2 lb lean beef, coarsely ground
- 1 tablespoon ground chilli
- 1 tablespoon ground cumin
- 2 tablespoons paprika
- 2 cloves garlic, finely chopped
- 2 tablespoons lard, dripping or butter
- 1 large onion, finely chopped
- 1 teaspoon salt

Put the meat, chilli, cumin, paprika and garlic in a bowl and mix well.

Heat the fat in a large heavy saucepan and gently fry the onion until soft but not coloured. Add the meat mixture and fry until it changes colour, breaking up any lumps with a fork and stirring constantly. Add the salt and enough water to cover by 5 cm/2 in. Simmer, uncovered, for about 2 hours. Add extra water during cooking if necessary.

Serve with warm *tortillas* and pinto beans.

Mixed Bag Chili

This is pure invention, created in sheer exasperation one day when I was unable to find a selection of Mexican chillies for a *mole*. Instead, I used the different chillies that I had in the kitchen and so a new chili was born. It was so successful that it has been repeated many times. Beware: this is *hot*!

SERVES 4

- 2 fresh green chillies, chopped
- 2 fresh red chillies, chopped
- 2 pickled hot chillies, chopped
- 5 dried red chillies, soaked and torn into pieces
- 5 dried birdseye chillies, soaked and torn into pieces
- 1 medium onion, chopped
- 4 cloves garlic, chopped
- 4 fresh sage leaves or ¼ teaspoon dried sage
- 10 fresh basil leaves or ½ teaspoon dried basil
- ½ teaspoon dried oregano or marjoram
- 2 teaspoons paprika

Put all the ingredients except the last 3 into the container of an electric blender or food processor. Add just enough reserved tomato juice or water to allow the blades to operate properly, and liquidize to a purée.

Heat the lard or butter in a large heavy saucepan. Add the purée and cook for 5 minutes, stirring constantly. Add the pork, bay leaf and enough water to cover. If any tomato juice is left, add this too. Simmer, covered, for about 1 hour or until the meat is tender and the sauce has reduced and thickened.

Serve with boiled rice, Refried Beans (p. 198), *Guacamole* (p. 50), shredded lettuce and grated cheese.

2 teaspoons ground cumin
a 200 g/7 oz can tomatoes, drained and juice reserved
2 tablespoons chopped celery tops or ½ teaspoon celery salt
2 tablespoons chopped parsley or coriander leaves
1 teaspoon salt (slightly less if using celery salt)
¼ teaspoon ground black pepper
2 teaspoons lard or butter
500 g/1 lb boneless pork, cut into small cubes
1 bay leaf

Red Pork Chili

The sauce of this dish is brilliant red, which *can* be a warning that it is very hot. This recipe is, but tone it down if you like.

SERVES 4

1 medium onion, chopped
3 cloves garlic, chopped
1 large sweet red pepper (about 125 g/4 oz), deseeded and chopped
3 fresh red chillies (with seeds) chopped
1½ teaspoons ground chilli
1 teaspoon paprika
1 teaspoon ground coriander
1 teaspoon ground cumin
½ teaspoon dried marjoram
¼ teaspoon dried basil
1 tablespoon chopped parsley
250 ml/8 fl oz beer
4 tablespoons oil
500 g/1 lb boneless lean pork, cut into 2 cm/¾ in cubes
a 200 g/7 oz can tomatoes
375 ml/12 fl oz water
salt and black pepper to taste

Put the first 11 ingredients in the container of an electric blender. Add enough beer to make the blades work properly, blend to a purée and set aside.

Heat the oil in a large heavy saucepan. Fry the pork (in two batches, if necessary) for a few minutes until just turning golden. Add the purée and fry over a medium heat for 5 minutes, stirring to prevent burning. Add the remaining beer and the tomatoes, water, salt and pepper. Bring to the boil. Simmer, covered, for about 30 minutes, until the pork is tender and the sauce has thickened.

Serve with rice, Refried Beans (p. 198), *Guacamole* (p. 50), shredded lettuce and grated cheese.

Chili Antilles

Created around the fragrant Scotch Bonnet chillies that are so prized in the Caribbean, this chili combines heat with aromatic undertones. It has quite a distinctive taste.

SERVES 4

- 4 allspice berries*
- 8 cloves
- 12 black peppercorns
- 6 dried red chillies, stems removed, pods ripped into pieces
- 50 g/2 oz butter
- 1 medium onion, finely chopped
- 4 cloves garlic, finely chopped
- 500 g/1 lb boneless pork, cut into 2 cm/$\frac{3}{4}$ in cubes
- a 400 g/13 oz can tomatoes, mashed with their juice
- 2 tablespoons ground almonds
- $\frac{1}{4}$ teaspoon ground ginger
- $\frac{1}{4}$ teaspoon dried thyme
- $\frac{1}{4}$ teaspoon dried oregano
- 250 ml/8 fl oz water
- 1 chicken stock cube
- 1 Scotch Bonnet chilli, left whole
- 1 tablespoon finely chopped celery leaves
- 1 tablespoon finely chopped parsley
- salt to taste

Put the first 4 ingredients into an electric grinder and grind to a powder. Set aside.

Heat the butter in a large saucepan and fry the onions and garlic until golden. Add the pork and fry until it changes colour. Add all the remaining ingredients and bring to the boil. Simmer, covered, for about 1 hour, until the pork is tender and the sauce has thickened. Remove the whole chilli before serving.

Serve with Rice and Peas (p. 220) and a green salad garnished with sliced avocados.

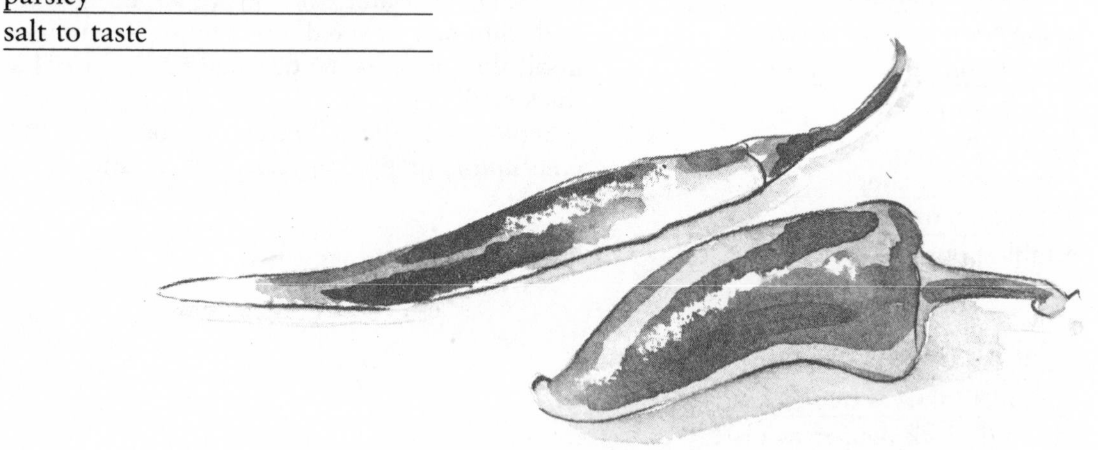

Chili Daube

We live in southern France, where beef stewed in red wine – known as a *daube* – is an everyday meal. The traditional *daube* ingredients – olive oil, tomato, garlic, salt pork, wine and the herbs that grow wild in Provence – provide the main flavourings for this robust, full-bodied chili.

SERVES 4

- 3 tablespoons olive oil
- 125 g/4 oz salt pork (or streaky bacon), cut into small dice
- 1 large onion, chopped
- 4 cloves garlic, finely chopped
- 500 g/1 lb lean stewing beef, cut into small dice
- 2 teaspoons ground cumin
- 2 teaspoons ground chilli
- 2 tablespoons tomato purée
- 1 large tomato, chopped
- 150 ml/¼ pint red wine
- 600 ml/1 pint water
- 1 teaspoon salt
- freshly ground black pepper to taste
- large sprig thyme or ¼ teaspoon dried thyme
- 8 basil leaves, chopped, or ¼ teaspoon dried basil
- 2 bay leaves
- 2 tablespoons chopped parsley

Put just a smear of the oil into a large heavy saucepan and fry the salt pork over a medium heat until it is beginning to crisp. Add the remaining oil and fry the onion and garlic until golden. Add the beef and fry until it changes colour, stirring constantly. Stir in the cumin, chilli, tomato purée and tomato and fry for a couple of minutes. Add all the remaining ingredients and bring to the boil. Cover and simmer for about 2 hours, until the meat is tender and the sauce is thick and rich. Add extra water during cooking if necessary.

Serve with boiled rice, a mixed green salad (no more tomatoes, please) with vinaigrette dressing and crusty French bread. A salad of grated carrot with a tiny amount of finely chopped onion, moistened with a little mayonnaise or vinaigrette, makes a good side dish.

For a rushed lunch one day, I served left-over Chili Daube with a left-over Pilaf with Pine Nuts (p. 220). The two went together so well that I now often serve them with *pitta* bread and a Greek-style salad with *feta* cheese ... which proves how extraordinarily flexible a chili can be!

NOTE

Like all daubes, this dish improves if cooked at least 24 hours in advance – 2 or 3 days even – and reheated. Add a small amount of water if the sauce is too thick.

Tajines

A *tajine* is a North African stew and also the vessel in which it is cooked – an earthenware casserole with a distinctive, tall, pointed lid like an inverted funnel, open at the top. Characteristically, *tajines* are a combination of meat – most commonly lamb, but beef, chicken and even fish are also used – and vegetables, simmered in plenty of liquid to produce a stew with a thin, soupy gravy. Generously seasoned with herbs, spices, dried fruits and nuts, they frequently contain chilli in some form – *harissa, hilba*, ground or fresh chillies.

Couscous or rice is the natural accompaniment to a *tajine*, and a fork and spoon are the most sensible cutlery for dealing with the copious gravy. As vegetables are always part of the stew, no other dishes are really necessary except, perhaps, bread and – of course – a small bowl of diluted *harissa* for extra piquancy.

Tajines can be cooked in any heavy-duty saucepan or casserole but the traditional pot does add an authentic touch, especially for entertaining. They are sold in shops specializing in North African food or, if you are on holiday in southern France, you can find them in ethnic Arab shops in all big towns and, sometimes, in department stores. Made in sturdy, glazed brown earthenware, they are available in a small individual size and in a selection of family sizes of various proportions. Although not really suitable for electric cookers, they can be placed directly on to low or medium heat gas rings. If in doubt, simply use the *tajine* as a serving dish.

The choice of *tajine* recipes is virtually limitless. In practice, almost anything that is cooked in a *tajine, is* a *tajine*, thus providing the chilli cook with great scope for experimentation.

Simple Meat and Potato Tajine

SERVES 6

- 3 tablespoons oil
- 1 kg/2 lb lamb or beef, cut into large cubes
- 1 large onion, finely sliced
- 1 teaspoon paprika
- 1 teaspoon *harissa** or ground chilli
- ½ teaspoon ground turmeric
- ½ teaspoon ground ginger

- ¼ teaspoon ground black pepper
- 3 tomatoes, chopped
- 1 teaspoon salt
- 500 g/1 lb potatoes, peeled and cut into 2.5 cm/1 in cubes

Heat the oil in a large, heavy saucepan and fry the lamb until browned on all sides. Add all the other ingredients except the potatoes, and enough water to cover by 4 cm/1½ in. Bring to the boil, cover the pan, and simmer for about 1 hour or until the meat is tender. Add the potatoes and simmer for a further 15 minutes until the potatoes are cooked but not disintegrating. The liquid should have reduced and thickened slightly – if necessary, simmer uncovered for 5 minutes to encourage evaporation.

Carrot Tajine

Another simple dish, this *tajine* comes from Libya. The chilli content is in the form of *hilba*, and the addition of tomato purée reflects the Italian influence on Libyan cooking. A further Italian touch – it can be served with spaghetti, as it is in Libya.

SERVES 6

- 2 tablespoons oil
- 50 g/2 oz butter
- 500 g/1 lb leg of lamb, cut into large cubes
- 3 chicken portions, each cut in half
- 1 large onion, thinly sliced
- 2 cloves garlic, finely chopped
- ½ teaspoon ground black pepper
- 5 cm/2 in cinnamon stick
- 2 teaspoons *hilba* (p. 42)
- 1 tablespoon tomato purée
- 1 teaspoon salt
- 500 g/1 lb carrots, scraped and left whole if young, cut into 5 cm/2 in lengths if old
- 2 tablespoons finely chopped parsley or coriander leaves
- 12 olives
- 1 tablespoon lemon juice

Heat half the oil and half the butter in a large heavy saucepan. Fry the lamb until nicely browned and remove from the pan with a slotted spoon. Add the remaining oil and butter and fry the chicken until crisp and golden. Remove the chicken, add the onions and garlic, and fry for 3 minutes. Return the lamb to the saucepan but set the chicken aside.

Add the ground black pepper, cinnamon, *hilba*, tomato purée, salt and enough water to cover by 4 cm/1½ in. Bring to the boil and simmer, covered, for 15 minutes. Add the chicken and simmer, covered, for 30 minutes. Add the carrots and simmer for about 20 minutes or until the lamb and chicken are cooked. The liquid should have reduced and thickened slightly – if necessary, simmer uncovered for 5 minutes.

Before serving, stir in the coriander or parsley, olives and lemon juice.

Tajine of Veal and Haricot Beans

Moroccan *tajine*, flavoured with saffron, ginger, cumin and coriander leaves.

SERVES 6–8

- 1.5 kg/3 lb stewing veal, cut into large cubes
- 2 tablespoons olive oil
- ½ teaspoon ground ginger
- 1 teaspoon ground cumin
- 1 teaspoon paprika
- good pinch saffron threads or ¼ teaspoon ground saffron*
- 2 fresh chillies, left whole
- 1 teaspoon salt
- ¼ teaspoon ground black pepper
- 1 kg/2 lb haricot beans, topped, tailed and cut in half
- 2 tablespoons lemon juice
- 3 tablespoons finely chopped coriander leaves

Put all the ingredients except the last 3 into a large heavy saucepan. Add enough water to cover by 2.5 cm/1 in, and bring to the boil. Simmer, covered, for 50 minutes. Add the beans, and top up with water if the liquid is not level with the top of the meat and beans. Bring back to the boil and simmer for 20 minutes. Stir in the lemon juice and coriander. This dish should have plenty of fairly thin gravy.

Meat Curries

Big G's Beef Curry

This is my husband's basic beef curry. It is a lethal concoction with an evil-looking dark red sauce.

SERVES 4

- 3 tablespoons oil
- 1 tablespoon butter
- 2 medium onions, chopped
- 3 cloves garlic, chopped
- 2 teaspoons ground coriander
- 2 teaspoons ground cumin
- 2 teaspoons *garam masala**
- 2 teaspoons ground turmeric
- 1 teaspoon ground chilli
- 2 dried chillies, with seeds

Heat the oil and butter in a large heavy frying-pan. Fry the onions and garlic over a moderate heat until well browned. Do not allow them to burn. Add the coriander, cumin, *garam masala*, turmeric, and the ground and dried chillies. Gently fry for 5 minutes, stirring constantly until the mixture becomes a thick paste. Add the beef and fry until it changes colour. Stir in the tomato purée and the dissolved stock cube. Take the pan off the heat and allow to cool for a few seconds. Add the yoghurt a little at a time, stirring well to prevent curdling. Add the remaining ingredients.

Transfer the mixture to a large pre-heated

- 350 g/11 oz lean stewing beef, cut into 2 cm/¾ in cubes
- 1 tablespoon tomato purée
- ½ beef stock cube, dissolved in 3 tablespoons water
- 125 g/4 oz yoghurt
- juice of ½ lemon
- ½ teaspoon salt
- 2 cloves
- 4 cardamom pods,* bruised
- generous grinding of black pepper
- 2 medium potatoes, cut into 8 chunks

ovenproof casserole. Add 450 ml/¾ pint of water, using some of it to rinse out the frying-pan. Cook for 2 hours at 180°C/350°F/gas 4. Check occasionally and add a little extra water if necessary. When ready, the sauce should be fairly thick and plentiful.

Serve with plain boiled rice, a salad and a selection of pickles and chutneys (preferably home-made).

NOTE

This curry is best if cooked the day before and reheated.

Burmese Beef Curry

This is a typical Burmese curry – hot and garlicky, fragrant with sesame oil and lemon grass. If fresh lemon grass is not available, add 1 teaspoon of grated lemon rind to the onion paste. The liquid in this curry should dry off completely. By the end of the cooking time the meat is frying in spiced oil.

SERVES 3–4

- 3 large onions, chopped
- 6 cloves garlic, chopped
- 2 teaspoons chopped fresh ginger
- 6 dried red chillies, soaked and chopped, or 2 teaspoons *sambal ulek**
- 4 tablespoons sesame oil*
- 500 g/1 lb lean stewing beef, cut into 5 cm/2 in cubes
- 1 teaspoon ground turmeric
- ¼ teaspoon ground black pepper
- 3 stalks lemon grass,* bruised
- ½ teaspoon salt

Put the first 4 ingredients into the container of an electric blender or food processor. Add a little of the sesame oil so that the blades will operate properly, and blend to a thick purée.

Heat the remaining oil in a heavy saucepan or frying-pan and gently fry the onion paste for 10–15 minutes, until the onion loses its raw smell. Stir constantly. Add the meat and stir until it changes colour. Stir in the remaining ingredients and add enough water to cover. Bring to the boil and simmer, covered, until the meat is tender. Add more water if necessary, but by the end of the cooking time all the liquid should have evaporated, leaving the meat frying in oil.

Serve with boiled rice, *Balachuang* (p. 263) and a cucumber salad.

VARIATION

For a pork curry, increase the garlic cloves to 10 and add 2 tablespoons of vinegar or fish sauce.* 1 teaspoon of *blachan* can also be added but is optional.

Malay Lamb Curry
Gulai Kambing

Hot, rich and fragrant, this is one of the most delicious curries I know.

SERVES 4–6

- 1 tablespoon coriander seeds
- 2 teaspoons cumin seeds
- 1 teaspoon fennel seeds*
- 6 black peppercorns
- 4 cloves
- 4 cardamom pods,* husks removed
- 2.5 cm/1 in cinnamon stick
- $\frac{1}{8}$ whole nutmeg
- 1 teaspoon ground turmeric
- 6 dried red chillies, soaked, drained and torn into pieces, or 2 teaspoons *sambal ulek**
- 12 shallots or 2 medium onions, chopped
- 4 cloves garlic, chopped
- 2 teaspoons chopped fresh ginger
- 4 tablespoons oil
- 500 g/1 lb lean boneless lamb or mutton
- 1 teaspoon salt
- 50 g/2 oz solid coconut cream (p. 32)
- 1 teaspoon concentrated tamarind extract*

Dry roast and grind the first 8 ingredients according to the instructions on p. 31. Mix with the turmeric and enough water to make a stiff paste, and set aside.

Put the chillies, shallots or onions, garlic and ginger into the container of an electric blender and add enough of the oil to make the blades operate properly. Blend to a purée.

Heat the remaining oil in a large heavy saucepan and gently fry the chilli purée for 5 minutes, stirring constantly to prevent sticking and burning. Add the spice paste and fry for 3 minutes, stirring constantly. Add the meat, tossing and turning it so that each piece is coated in spices. Fry until the meat changes colour. Add the salt and enough water to cover by 2.5 cm/1 in. Simmer, covered, for about 45 minutes until the meat is almost tender. (Mutton will take longer.) Take the pan off the heat and add the coconut cream, stirring constantly until the block has dissolved. Return to the heat and bring to the boil, stirring continuously. Add the tamarind and simmer, uncovered, for about 30 minutes until the meat is tender and the gravy has thickened.

Serve with boiled rice.

VARIATIONS

Add 3 medium potatoes, quartered, 20 minutes from the end of the cooking time, or add 3 tomatoes, quartered, 5 minutes before the end of the cooking time.

Thai Beef Curry

The base of many Thai dishes is a chilli paste strongly flavoured with dried shrimp paste (called *kapi* in Thailand and *blachan* in neighbouring Malaysia) and coriander leaves, including the stems and root. This dish features a red curry paste made with dried red chillies; a similar paste made with fresh green chillies is part of the Thai Fish Curry recipe that appears on p. 86.

SERVES 4–6

FOR THE CHILLI PASTE

6 dried red chillies with seeds, soaked in warm water for 10 minutes
1 teaspoon paprika
1 medium onion, chopped
1 teaspoon *blachan**
6 cloves garlic, chopped
3 tablespoons chopped coriander leaves and roots
1 teaspoon chopped lime or lemon rind
1 teaspoon *laos* powder*
1 teaspoon *serai* powder*
2 teaspoons ground coriander
1 teaspoon ground cumin
½ teaspoon ground black pepper
2 tablespoons oil

FOR THE CURRY

1 tablespoon oil
1 kg/2 lb lean stewing beef, cut into 1.5 cm/½ in cubes
6 cardamom pods*
1 teaspoon salt
500 ml/17 fl oz water
500 ml/17 fl oz thin coconut milk (p. 32)
250 ml/8 fl oz thick coconut milk (p. 32)
1 teaspoon chopped fresh basil leaves or ¼ teaspoon dried basil
2 fresh red chillies, deseeded and shredded
2 tablespoons fish sauce*

Drain the chillies and tear them into pieces. Put them into the container of an electric blender or food processor with all the other ingredients and blend to a paste.

Heat the oil in a heavy saucepan and fry the chilli paste gently for about 5 minutes, stirring constantly until the paste smells fragrant. Add the meat and stir-fry for 2 minutes. Add the cardamoms, salt, and 500 ml/17 fl oz water. Bring to the boil, cover, and simmer for 45 minutes. Remove the pan from the heat and allow to cool for a minute. Add the thin and the thick coconut milk, stirring constantly to prevent curdling. Return to the heat and bring to the boil, still stirring. Add all the remaining ingredients and simmer, uncovered, for about 45 minutes until the meat is tender and the gravy has reduced. Thai curries have plenty of gravy, so the liquid should not reduce too much.

Serve with boiled rice, salad and Nam Prik sauce (p. 264).

Kashmiri Lamb Curry

Although Indian curries do not normally contain dried fruit, those from Kashmir sometimes do. This is a fruit-growing area where apricots and sultanas are combined with delicate spicing to produce distinctive curried lamb dishes.

SERVES 3–4

- 500 g/1 lb lean boneless lamb, cut into 1.5 cm/½ in cubes
- 125 g/4 oz yoghurt
- 1 teaspoon meat curry powder (p. 37)
- 1 teaspoon *garam masala**
- ½ teaspoon ground chilli
- ½ teaspoon ground ginger
- ¼ teaspoon ground black pepper
- 3 tablespoons stoneless sultanas
- 6 dried apricots, chopped
- 2 tablespoons butter or *ghee**
- 1 large onion, finely chopped
- ½ teaspoon salt
- 3 tablespoons flaked almonds, lightly fried in butter

Put the first 7 ingredients in a bowl, mix well, and leave for 2 hours.

Soak the sultanas and dried apricots in a little warm water for 30 minutes.

Heat the butter or *ghee* in a large heavy saucepan and gently fry the onion until golden. Add the meat and yoghurt mixture. Bring to the boil, stirring constantly to prevent curdling. Drain the fruit and add to the meat. Add the salt. Simmer, covered, for about 1 hour, until the meat is tender. This is a fairly dry curry and it should not be necessary to add any extra liquid. If it does dry out before meat is cooked, add a few tablespoons of water. Garnish with almonds before serving.

This dish is good served with *chapatis* instead of rice.

Pork Vindaloo

This is a delicious dish, flavoured by a vindaloo paste made from spices and puréed fried onions.

SERVES 6

- 12 dried red chillies
- 1 tablespoon coriander seeds
- 2 teaspoons cumin seeds
- 1 teaspoon black mustard seeds*
- 1 teaspoon fenugreek seeds*
- 6 cardamom pods* (seeds only)
- 8 peppercorns
- 5 cm/2 in cinnamon stick
- small chunk nutmeg (about ⅛ whole nut)

Remove the stems from the dried red chillies (and the seeds, if preferred). Dry roast and grind the first 9 ingredients, following the instructions on p. 31. Mix these ground spices with the turmeric, vinegar, salt and brown sugar to make a paste.

Heat the butter and half the oil in a large heavy pan and fry the onion over a medium heat until brown and crisp. Do not allow it to burn. Remove from the pan with a slotted spoon (leaving the butter in the pan) and transfer to an electric blender or food processor. Add the garlic,

- ½ teaspoon turmeric
- 4 tablespoons vinegar
- 1 teaspoon salt
- 1 teaspoon brown sugar
- 25 g/2 oz butter
- 6 tablespoons oil
- 1 large onion, finely sliced
- 8 cloves garlic, chopped
- 1½ tablespoons chopped fresh ginger
- 750 g/1½ lb lean boneless pork, cut into 2 cm/¾ in cubes
- 300 ml/½ pint water
- ½ teaspoon salt

fresh ginger and 2 or 3 tablespoons of water. Blend to a purée.

Add the remaining oil to the butter juices in the pan and fry the pork (in two or three batches, if necessary) over a medium heat until nicely browned. Remove with a slotted spoon and put in a bowl.

Add the spice paste to the remaining oil in the pan and fry over a medium heat for 2 minutes, stirring constantly to prevent burning. If there is insufficient oil to fry the paste, add a little extra. Add the onion purée and fry for a further 2 minutes, stirring constantly. Add the meat and any juices that have accumulated. Add the remaining water and salt. Bring to the boil and simmer, covered, for about 1 hour or until the meat is tender and the liquid has reduced to a thick gravy.

The flavour of this vindaloo improves as it matures. Make it 1 or 2 days in advance and reheat it for best results.

Jamaican Curried Goat

Although commonly called curried goat, this Jamaican speciality is more generally made with kid meat. Lamb or rabbit can be substituted.

SERVES 4

- 3 tablespoons oil, lard or butter
- 1 kg/2 lb kid meat, cut into serving portions
- 1 large onion, finely sliced
- 2 cloves garlic, finely chopped
- 3 tablespoons Caribbean curry powder (p. 38)
- 3 fresh chillies, finely chopped
- 2 tomatoes, chopped
- ¼ teaspoon ground allspice*
- 1 bay leaf
- 1 stock cube
- salt and ground black pepper to taste

Heat half the oil, lard or butter in a heavy frying-pan or saucepan. Gently fry the kid until browned on all sides, in two batches if necessary. Remove the kid and add the onion and garlic to the juices left in the pan. Fry until soft and transparent. Add the remaining oil, lard or butter and fry the curry powder and chillies for 3 minutes, stirring constantly to prevent burning. Add the tomatoes and allspice.

Return the kid to the pan and add enough water to cover. Add the remaining ingredients and simmer, covered, for about 1½ hours or until the meat is tender. Add more water if necessary. When ready, there should be plenty of rich, thick gravy.

Serve with rice, mango chutney and salad.

Braised Meat Dishes

Pork in Red Sauce

Mexican or Indian? The answer is both. I adapted this recipe from two dishes – one Mexican and one from south-western India – when I realized how strikingly similar they were both in taste and in preparation. In the original versions large mild chilli peppers are used, but sweet peppers combined with dried chillies have been substituted here. Choose juicy, bright red, very ripe sweet peppers for their concentrated colour and flavour. They can be scorched and peeled (see instructions on p. 28) if you prefer, though I rarely bother.

SERVES 4

- 1 tablespoon coriander seeds
- 1 tablespoon cumin seeds
- 10 black peppercorns
- 4 cloves
- ½ teaspoon ground turmeric
- 2 tablespoons flaked almonds
- 1 tablespoon sesame seeds*
- 8 dried red chillies, soaked, with stems removed
- 2 large ripe sweet red peppers, deseeded and chopped
- 1 large onion, chopped
- 3 cloves garlic, chopped
- 1 teaspoon chopped fresh ginger
- 8 tablespoons oil
- 500 g/1 lb lean boneless pork, cut into 2 cm/¾ in cubes
- 400 ml/15 fl oz water
- 1½ teaspoons salt
- juice of ½ lemon
- 1 bay leaf

Grind the first 4 ingredients. Mix with the turmeric and set aside.

Put the almonds, sesame seeds, dried chillies, sweet peppers, onion, garlic and ginger into the container of an electric blender or food processor. Add enough of the oil to make the blades work properly, and blend to a paste. Mix with the ground spices.

Heat the remaining oil in a large heavy saucepan. When medium hot, add the spice paste and cook over a medium heat for 10 minutes, stirring constantly to prevent sticking and burning. As it cooks, the paste will reduce and the oil will separate. Add the pork and stir until the meat changes colour and each piece is coated with paste. This will take about 4 minutes. Add the remaining ingredients, mix well, and bring to the boil. Simmer, covered, for about 30 minutes, until the meat is tender and the sauce is thick. Add more water during cooking if the sauce reduces too quickly.

VARIATIONS

Try this dish with skinned chicken pieces or rabbit.

It also makes an interesting egg dish: follow this recipe without the pork and add halved hard-boiled eggs just before serving so that they heat through.

Tfina

Tfina is a North African stew that was originally a traditional Jewish dish, dating from the time when substantial numbers of Jews lived in the Maghreb. As the Jewish religion forbids any work – even food preparation – on the Sabbath, pots of meat and vegetables were assembled the day before and buried in the embers, of fire cooking slowly overnight, ready to be eaten for the Sabbath lunch. Only a few Jews remain in North Africa but *Tfina* (from the Arabic *dfi'ne*, meaning to bury) has been absorbed into local cooking.

This version is an exotic combination of meat, spices and dried fruit. It is ideal for entertaining, as all the work is done in advance. It also freezes well.

SERVES 6–8

- 25 g/1 oz butter
- 2 tablespoons oil
- 1.5 kg/3 lb lamb or stewing beef or both, cut into large cubes
- 1 litre/1¾ pints water
- 4 cloves garlic, finely chopped
- 4 fresh green chillies, deseeded and finely chopped
- 3 medium onions, finely sliced
- 1 sweet green pepper, deseeded and coarsely chopped
- 3 tomatoes, chopped
- ¼ teaspoon ground black pepper
- ¼ teaspoon ground allspice*
- ½ teaspoon ground turmeric
- ½ teaspoon ground coriander
- ½ teaspoon ground cumin
- 5 cm/2 in cinnamon stick
- 1 teaspoon salt
- 125 g/4 oz chickpeas, soaked for at least 8 hours and drained
- 50 g/2 oz prunes, soaked, stoned and chopped
- 50 g/2 oz dried apricots, soaked and chopped
- 50 g/2 oz sultanas or raisins
- 2 tablespoons finely chopped coriander or parsley leaves
- juice of 1 lemon

Heat the oil and butter in a large heavy frying-pan and fry the meat, a few pieces at a time, until nicely browned. As each batch is done, transfer it to a large ovenproof casserole. Use some of the water to rinse the meat juices out of the frying-pan, and add this, the rest of the water and all the remaining ingredients to the casserole. Stir well so that everything is evenly distributed. Cover and place in an oven pre-heated to 180°C/350°F/gas 4. Cook for about 2 hours, or longer if necessary, until the meat and chickpeas are tender. Check occasionally and add a little extra water if drying out. Serve with rice or *couscous* and a salad.

Indonesian Beef in Soy Sauce
Semur Daging

Hot, sweet and salty, this dish has a typical Indonesian flavour. The heat comes from chillies, the sweetness from palm sugar (or substitute dark brown sugar) and the saltiness from dark soy sauce. Add the fragrance of cinnamon, nutmeg, cardamom and cloves and this becomes a delectable dish.

SERVES 4–6

- 3 tablespoons oil
- 1 large onion, finely chopped
- 3 cloves garlic, finely chopped
- 1 teaspoon finely chopped fresh ginger
- 4 cloves
- 2.5 cm/1 in cinnamon stick
- 4 cardamom pods*
- 750 g/1½ lb lean stewing beef, cut into 2 cm/¾ in cubes
- ⅛ teaspoon ground nutmeg
- 3 tablespoons dark soy sauce*
- 1 tablespoon dark brown sugar or palm sugar*
- 2 tablespoons lemon juice
- ½ teaspoon salt

Heat the oil in a large heavy frying-pan or saucepan and gently fry the onion for 2 minutes. Add the garlic, ginger, cloves, cinnamon and cardamoms and continue frying until the onion is golden. Add the meat and fry until it changes colour. Add all the remaining ingredients and bring to the boil, then cover the pan and simmer until the meat is tender. Check frequently and add more water if the liquid dries up before the meat is tender. Remove the lid to reduce the liquid if too much remains when the meat is ready. The final sauce should be reduced and thick. Serve with boiled rice and a vegetable or salad.

South African Lamb Stew
Tomato Bredie

Of all South African *bredies*, Tomato Bredie is the most common. It is a simple stew of meat and vegetables, based on the original one-pot meal cooked on the back of a bullock cart by the early Dutch settlers. In those days it would probably have been springbok meat that was used; today lamb or mutton is more usual.

SERVES 4–6

- 1 kg/2 lb stewing lamb or mutton
- 2 tablespoons flour
- 2 tablespoons oil or butter
- 2 medium onions, finely sliced
- 6 cloves garlic, chopped

Cut the meat into large chunks and coat in the flour.

Heat 1 tablespoon of the oil or butter in a large heavy saucepan and gently fry the onions and garlic until golden. Remove the onions with a slotted spoon and add the remaining oil or butter

6 tomatoes, chopped
2 fresh chillies, finely chopped, or 1 teaspoon ground chilli
1 teaspoon salt
¼ teaspoon ground black pepper
1 teaspoon sugar

to the juices in the pan. Add the meat and fry until evenly browned. Add all the other ingredients and enough water to cover by 2.5 cm/1 in. Bring to the boil and simmer, covered, for about 1–2 hours or until the meat is tender and the gravy has thickened and reduced. Add a little extra water if necessary during cooking. Serve with boiled rice.

VARIATIONS

Prepare as above but omit the tomatoes and add one of the following:

Cabbage or cauliflower: shred a medium cabbage or cut a medium cauliflower into florets. Add to the meat 30 minutes before the end of the cooking time and grate a little nutmeg over the *bredie* before serving.

Potatoes and/or carrots: 4 medium potatoes, quartered, and/or 4 medium carrots, cut lengthwise. Add to the meat 1 hour before the end of the cooking time.

Green beans: 500 g/11 lb of green beans, cut into 5 cm/2 in lengths. Add to the meat 45 minutes before the end of the cooking time, together with 2 large potatoes, diced.

Pumpkin, marrow or courgettes: 500 g/1 lb of diced pumpkin or marrow, or sliced courgettes. Add to the meat 45 minutes before the end of the cooking time, together with a pinch each of ground cinnamon and nutmeg, 1 bay leaf and a small strip of orange rind.

Spinach: remove the stems from 500 g/1 lb of spinach and shred the leaves. Add 200 ml/7 fl oz of white wine to the meat and reduce the water accordingly. Add the shredded spinach and 1 large potato (sliced) 30 minutes before the end of the cooking time.

Quinces or tart cooking apples: 3 medium quinces or apples, peeled, cored and sliced. Add 1 hour before the end of the cooking time with 2 teaspoons of brown sugar, ½ teaspoon of ground turmeric and a pinch of ground cloves.

Pork Chops with Orange Juice

The Spaniards introduced oranges to Latin America, where they found a natural culinary partner in the chilli to produce hot, sweet-sour dishes similar to those of the Far East. Chillies and oranges combine particularly well with pork and also with fish (see Pescado a la Veracruzana, p. 88).

SERVES 6

- 1 tablespoon oil
- 6 pork loin chops, skin and excess fat removed
- 25 g/1 oz butter
- 3 cloves
- 1 large onion, finely sliced
- 2 cloves garlic, finely chopped
- 200 ml/7 fl oz freshly squeezed orange juice
- 200 ml/7 fl oz chicken stock, or water + ½ stock cube
- 2 teaspoons finely shredded orange peel
- 2 fresh red chillies, deseeded and finely chopped, or Tabasco sauce* to taste
- ½ teaspoon salt or to taste
- few grindings black pepper
- 1½ teaspoons cornflour, mixed with a little water

Heat the oil in a heavy frying-pan large enough to hold the chops in a single layer. Fry the chops over a moderate heat until lightly browned on both sides. Remove the chops and add the butter to the juices remaining in the pan. Add the cloves, onion and garlic and fry gently until the onion is soft but not coloured. Add all the remaining ingredients except the cornflour. Bring to the boil and return the chops to the pan. Simmer, covered, for about 15 minutes until the meat is tender. Transfer the chops to a warm serving dish, and thicken the sauce with the cornflour. Pour the sauce over the chops and serve immediately.

Kerrieboontjies

Curried meat and beans South African style is reminiscent of the American chili, except that it is usually made with lamb.

SERVES 4–6

- 3 tablespoons oil
- 1 large onion, finely chopped
- 1 kg/2 lb boneless lamb, cut into 2.5 cm/1 in cubes
- 2 teaspoons South African curry powder (p. 38)
- 3 cloves garlic, crushed

Heat the oil in a large heavy saucepan and fry the onion until golden. Add the meat and fry until it changes colour. Pound the curry powder, garlic, salt and pepper together and add the vinegar to make a paste. Add to the meat and stir so that the meat is coated with the paste.

Add enough water just to cover the meat, and bring to the boil. Add the chillies and simmer, covered, until the meat is tender and the gravy has

- ½ teaspoon salt
- ¼ teaspoon ground black pepper
- 2 teaspoons vinegar
- 2 fresh green chillies, finely chopped
- 250 g/8 oz kidney or pinto beans, pre-cooked
- 2 tablespoons lemon juice
- 2 tablespoons finely chopped parsley

thickened and reduced by about half. Add the cooked beans and simmer for 10 minutes to heat through.

Before serving, sprinkle with lemon juice and parsley.

Minced Meat

Mincing, grinding or pounding meat before seasoning it with herbs and spices has been a popular culinary technique since earliest times. It is a sensible way of dealing with tougher cuts as, once minced, the meat can be cooked to tender succulence without long simmering. Flavourings can also be mixed in with the meat, rather than having to be absorbed by marination.

Many minced dishes – particularly those for meatballs and kebabs – were originally Arab-inspired. In Arab cuisine, a favoured way of treating minced meat is to blend in the seasonings and then either to squeeze it between the fingers or to pound it until it becomes a sticky paste. By this stage it has lost its true fibrous meat consistency but retains its essential meaty flavour. Grilled or fried so that the outside is crisp and browned, the inside remains deliciously smooth, soft and moist.

An alternative way of creating shaped balls or brochettes from minced meat is to use beaten egg and flour or breadcrumbs to bind the individual morsels of meat together.

Yet another approach to minced meat is to fry it and/or simmer it so that each particle keeps its individual identity.

All these methods are covered in the following recipes for minced meat with chilli.

Other minced meat recipes are included in the section on *tortillas* (pp. 241–7).

North African Kebabs
Kefta

MAKES 16

- 500 g/1 lb finely minced lean lamb
- 75 g/3 oz finely chopped beef suet
- ½ teaspoon ground chilli
- 2 teaspoons paprika
- 1 teaspoon cumin
- ½ teaspoon ground cinnamon
- ¼ teaspoon ground black pepper
- ½ teaspoon salt
- 3 tablespoons finely chopped parsley or coriander leaves
- 1 tablespoon finely chopped mint

Mix all the ingredients together and knead the mixture for a few minutes by squeezing it in your hands to produce a sticky paste.

Working with wet hands, divide the mixture into 16 portions and wrap each one around a metal skewer, shaping it into a sausage about 10 cm/4 in long. Take care to seal each *kefta* around the skewer at each end, so that it does not open during cooking.

Grill over hot coals or under a hot grill for about 10 minutes, turning frequently. Do not over-cook.

Merguez

These North African sausages have had obvious associations with the Spanish *chorizo* sausage at some time in the past. Highly spiced and deep chilli-red, they are always made of lamb or beef – never of pork, as most North Africans are Muslims.

Merguez are now popular in France (they were introduced into France when French nationals who had lived in North Africa returned to their homeland following Algerian independence in the 60s), and are available in every French butcher's shop and supermarket.

Traditionally, *Merguez* are long (about 15 cm/6 in) and thin; because of their high fat content they shrink considerably during cooking. They exude a bright red oil which stains badly but is excellent mopped up with bread, rice, *couscous* or potatoes. *Merguez* can be fried, grilled, baked or combined with other ingredients. They also freeze well.

MAKES ABOUT 20

- 1 kg/2 lb finely minced lamb or beef
- 150 g/5 oz fine beef suet
- 3 tablespoons olive oil
- 4 cloves garlic, very finely chopped
- ½ teaspoon paprika

Put all the ingredients (except the casings) into a bowl and knead with the hands for 5 minutes until smooth. Fill the casings and hang in a cool, airy place for 12 hours before using.

3 teaspoons *harissa** or 2 teaspoons ground chilli
2 teaspoons salt
½ teaspoon ground black pepper
1 teaspoon *ras-el-hanout**
½ teaspoon ground coriander
½ teaspoon ground cumin
½ teaspoon ground fennel*
sausage casings

Prepare as for previous recipe.

Chorizo

This is the Mexican version – with plenty of chilli, naturally – of the original Spanish *chorizo*. Like the *Merguez* of the previous recipe, it can be stuffed into a casing to make sausages, or it can simply be kept in the fridge for up to a week and used to flavour and/or extend other meats. For the latter, fry the *chorizo* in a little oil until dry and crumbly, then add to other dishes or sprinkle over as a garnish. It is especially useful in *tortilla*-based dishes, served with Refried Beans and *Salsa Cruda* (p. 268) or *Salsa de Jitomate* (p. 269). See the index for other dishes using *chorizo*.

MAKES ABOUT 12
500 g/1 lb minced belly pork
125 g/4 oz minced lean pork
3 cloves garlic, very finely chopped
2 teaspoons ground chilli
2 teaspoons paprika
1 teaspoon ground cumin
½ teaspoon mixed spice
1 teaspoon dried marjoram
1 teaspoon salt
¼ teaspoon ground black pepper
3 tablespoons vinegar
sausage casings (optional)

Prepare as previous recipe.

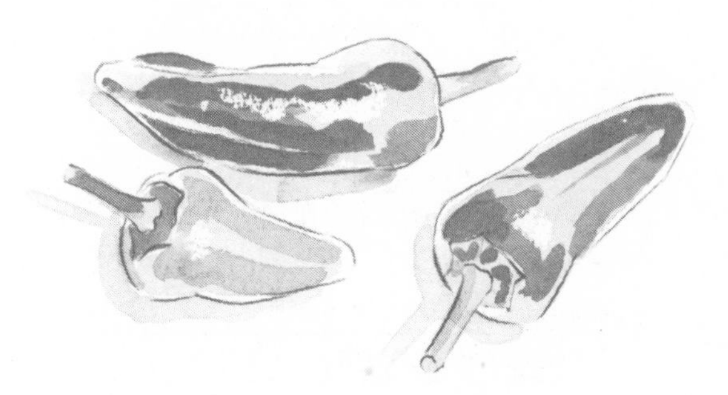

Dutch Frikkadels Sri Lankan Style

The Dutch took Ceylon from the Portuguese in the mid-seventeenth century and, of course, brought their food with them. The classic Dutch meatballs – *frikkadels* – are still popular in Sri Lanka today . . . with a few local additions.

MAKES ABOUT 36

- 500 g/1 lb finely minced beef
- 1 small onion, grated
- 2 cloves garlic, finely chopped
- ½ teaspoon finely chopped or grated fresh ginger
- 1 teaspoon *garam masala**
- ½ teaspoon ground fennel
- 2 fresh green chillies, deseeded and finely chopped
- 3 tablespoons fresh fine white breadcrumbs
- ½ teaspoon salt
- 1 egg, beaten
- 1 tablespoon lemon juice
- a little flour
- 2nd egg, beaten
- oil for deep-frying

Mix the first 11 ingredients together well, kneading a little with the hands. Shape into small balls 2.5 cm/1 in in diameter. Dip in flour and then in beaten egg. Deep-fry, a few at a time, in moderately hot oil for about 4 minutes – do not over-cook. The meatballs should be lightly crisped on the outside but moist and juicy inside. Drain on paper towels.

Serve with curries, or cold for picnics, or on cocktail sticks as nibbles with drinks.

Dutch Frikkadels Indonesian Style

The Dutch took their meatballs to Indonesia, too!

MAKES ABOUT 60

- 1 tablespoon dark soy sauce*
- 1 tablespoon lemon juice
- 2 teaspoons brown sugar
- ½ teaspoon *blachan**
- 2 teaspoons ground coriander
- 2 teaspoons ground cumin
- ½ teaspoon ground nutmeg
- 500 g/1 lb finely minced beef
- 2 small onions, grated
- 3 cloves garlic, finely chopped

Put the soy sauce, lemon juice, brown sugar and *blachan* in a small bowl. Mash and mix until the sugar and *blachan* are dissolved. Stir in the ground coriander, cumin and nutmeg.

Mix together the meat, onions, garlic, *sambal ulek* and salt. Add the potatoes and the soy sauce mixture. Blend really well with the hands and add enough beaten egg to bind. Shape into small balls and chill for 1 hour.

Proceed as for the previous recipe.

1 teaspoon *sambal ulek**
1 teaspoon salt
3 medium potatoes, boiled and mashed (do not add milk or butter)
1 egg, beaten
oil for deep-frying

Shami Kebab

These Indian patties are made from minced lamb and lentils boiled together with chillies and spices, and then ground to a paste and fried.

MAKES ABOUT 24

75 g/3 oz yellow split peas, soaked overnight
1 kg/2 lb minced lamb
1 small onion, chopped
4 cloves garlic, chopped
½ teaspoon chopped fresh ginger
3 fresh green chillies, chopped
1 teaspoon ground coriander
1 teaspoon *garam masala**
½ teaspoon salt
2 eggs
oil or *ghee** for frying

Drain the split peas and put them in a saucepan with the minced lamb. Add 450 ml/¾ pint of water and all the remaining ingredients except the eggs. Bring to the boil and simmer, covered, for about 45 minutes until the meat and split peas are tender and all the liquid has been absorbed. If the mixture dries out before the meat and split peas are cooked, add a little extra water.

Mince the mixture finely and then pound to a paste, using a pestle and mortar. Beat in the eggs, by hand or using a food processor. However, no extra liquid should be added and the mixture might prove to be too stiff for some machines.

Shape into patties about 5 cm/2 in in diameter and 2.5 cm/1 in thick. Fry in oil or *ghee* until golden on both sides. Serve with lettuce, thinly sliced onions and lemon wedges.

VARIATION

Shami Kebab can also be shaped around ½ teaspoon of filling made by mixing together 1 finely chopped hard-boiled egg, 1 tablespoon of seedless raisins or sultanas, 2 teaspoons of finely chopped mint and 2 fresh green chillies, finely chopped. If using this filling, omit the fresh chillies from the meat mixture and use 1 teaspoon of ground chilli.

Albondigas

Latin American meatballs – *albondigas* – were almost certainly introduced by the Spaniards, who in turn had taken the idea from the Moors (most Spanish words beginning with *al* have Arabic associations). *Albondigas* come in many forms, and are usually simmered in stock, wine or chilli and/or tomato sauce. They can be seasoned with herbs or spices and may have a secret centre – a mini-stuffing of a small piece of hard-boiled egg, an olive or a few chopped nuts. The meat can be beef, pork, veal or ham.

SERVES 4–6

- 250 g/8 oz finely minced beef
- 250 g/8 oz finely minced pork or veal
- 125 g/4 oz minced ham
- 1 small onion, grated or finely chopped
- 1 clove garlic, finely chopped
- 3 tablespoons fine fresh breadcrumbs
- ½ teaspoon ground cumin
- ½ teaspoon ground chilli
- ½ teaspoon dried oregano
- 1 egg, beaten
- ½ teaspoon salt
- ¼ teaspoon ground black pepper
- flour for coating
- oil for frying
- ½ quantity *Salsa de Jitomate* (p. 269)

Mix together the first 12 ingredients. If the mixture seems dry, moisten with a little milk. If too soft, add more breadcrumbs. Shape into balls 2.5 cm/1 in in diameter. Coat with flour. Chill for 30 minutes and fry, a few at a time, until lightly browned.

Transfer to a shallow ovenproof dish. Spoon the *salsa* over and bake for 30 minutes in an oven pre-heated to 180°C/350°F/gas 4. Alternatively, transfer the *albondigas* to a saucepan and simmer in the *salsa* for 20 minutes.

Bobotie

A classic South African minced meat dish with echoes of India and South-East Asia.

SERVES 4–6

- 50 g/2 oz butter
- 2 medium onions, finely sliced
- 1 tablespoon oil
- 1 tablespoon South African curry powder (p. 38), or standard mild curry powder with 1 teaspoon ground turmeric added
- 1 tablespoon vinegar
- 500 g/1 lb minced beef or lamb (or buck or venison)
- 1 thick slice bread, soaked in a little milk
- 2 tomatoes, chopped
- 3 bay leaves
- 2 tablespoons seedless raisins or sultanas
- 1 tablespoon flaked almonds
- 1 tablespoon mango chutney or peach or apricot jam
- 1 chicken stock cube
- 2 tablespoons lemon juice
- ½ teaspoon salt
- 125 ml/4 fl oz water
- 2 eggs
- 250 ml/8 fl oz milk
- 1 lemon, thinly sliced horizontally

Use a little of the butter to grease a shallow ovenproof baking dish. Heat the rest in a large heavy frying-pan and gently fry the onions until golden. Add the oil and curry powder and fry for 1 minute, stirring constantly. Add the vinegar and minced meat and cook for 5 minutes until the meat changes colour. Use a fork to break up any lumps in the meat. Squeeze the bread dry and stir into the meat. Add the tomatoes, 1 of the bay leaves, the raisins or sultanas, almonds, chutney or jam, stock cube, lemon juice and salt. Pour in the water. Bring to the boil and simmer, uncovered, for 15 minutes.

Transfer to the buttered dish. Beat the eggs with the milk and season. Pour over the minced meat and arrange the sliced lemon and remaining bay leaves on top. Bake for 30 minutes in a pre-heated oven set at 180°C/350°F/gas 4.

Serve with rice, sweet chutney and salad.

Picadillo

Picadillo is a fried minced meat dish, highly seasoned and incorporating as many chillies as desired. It is popular in Mexico and the Spanish-speaking Caribbean islands. There are many versions.

SERVES 8

- 4 tablespoons oil or oil and butter
- 1 large onion, finely chopped
- 2 cloves garlic, chopped
- 1 medium sweet green pepper, deseeded and chopped
- 4 fresh green chillies, deseeded and chopped
- 1 kg/2 lb minced beef or half beef/half pork
- 3 tomatoes, chopped
- 1 tablespoon tomato purée
- 150 ml/4 fl oz water
- 3 tablespoons seedless raisins
- 3 tablespoons flaked almonds
- 20 stuffed olives, chopped
- ½ teaspoon dried oregano
- 1 teaspoon salt
- ¼ teaspoon ground black pepper
- 1 stock cube, crumbled

Heat the oil in a large heavy frying-pan and gently fry the onion, garlic and sweet pepper until the onion is soft but not coloured. Add the chillies and meat and cook over a medium heat until the meat is browned, stirring constantly. Use a fork to break up any lumps in the meat. Add all the remaining ingredients and simmer for about 20 minutes. Serve with boiled rice.

VARIATION

A popular Cuban version of *Picadillo* is cooked as above with the addition of chopped capers. Serve with rice, Cuban Black Beans (p. 200) and deep-fried eggs. To cook the eggs, heat about 5 cm/2 in of oil in a heavy frying-pan, break the eggs into a dish and then slide them into the fat. Cook over a moderate heat for about 2 minutes, gently lifting the whites to enclose the yolks. Drain on paper towels and serve immediately.

Chiles en Nogada

This famous Mexican dish comes from Puebla but is popular nationwide, especially on 15 September – Mexico's Independence Day. The colours of *Chiles en Nogada* are those of the Mexican flag – red, green and white. This is also the time when fresh walnuts are in season and are easy to peel to make the cream sauce that coats the stuffed chillies.

Traditionally the mild green *poblano* chillies would be used for this dish. If these are not available, substitute large sweet green peppers.

SERVES 6

- 6 *poblano* chillies or sweet green peppers
- 500 g/1 lb *Picadillo* (p. 140)

Skin the chillies or peppers according to the instructions on p. 28 Carefully cut the top off each chilli or pepper and scoop out the seeds and ribs. Stuff with *Picadillo*.

- 125 g/4 oz cream cheese
- 150 ml/¼ pint single cream
- 75 g/3 oz walnuts, finely ground
- 50 g/2 oz blanched almonds, finely ground
- pinch salt
- pinch sugar
- pinch ground cinnamon
- 1 small sweet red pepper, blanched and cut into thin strips
- Sprigs of parsley or coriander leaves

Beat together the cream cheese and cream. Stir in the nuts, salt, sugar and cinnamon. Pour over the stuffed chillies or peppers and garnish with red pepper strips and sprigs of parsley or coriander leaves.

This dish is easiest to serve cold, perhaps on a bed of lettuce with hot rice served separately. To serve it warm, make the sauce in advance, heat the *Picadillo* and assemble while the chillies or peppers are still warm from skinning. Pour the cold sauce over the warm chillies.

VARIATION
Red pomegranate seeds are frequently used as a garnish to give the red, green and white colours.

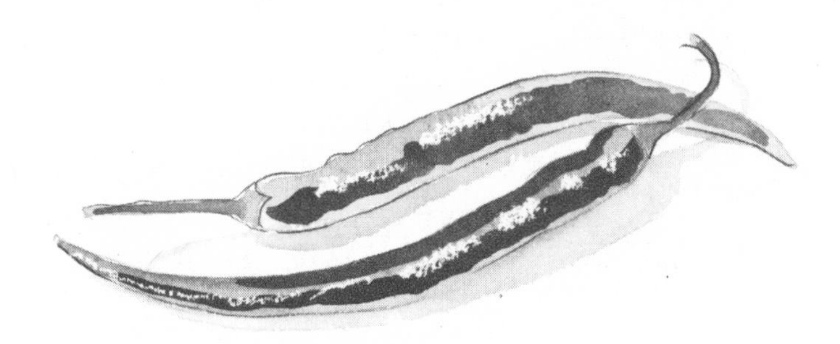

Marinated Meat

Satay

Anyone who has visited South-East Asia will know that *satay* are a way of life in Malaysia, Singapore and Indonesia. Small cubes of meat are soaked in a fragrant marinade, threaded on to bamboo skewers, grilled and then dunked into a chilli and peanut sauce. Two or three skewers of *satay* make an exciting appetizer or snack, a dozen make a meal in themselves.

The bamboo skewers can be bought in shops specializing in Chinese and South-East Asian food and should be soaked in water for at least 1 hour before use. If not available, ordinary metal skewers will do the job just as well, but as the meat is usually pulled off the skewers with the teeth, care must be taken if metal skewers are used – burned lips can be painful.

Satay are traditionally barbecued or cooked on a small table charcoal grill, which adds to the fun.

ENOUGH FOR ABOUT 36 SKEWERS

650 g/1¼ lb lean boneless beef, lamb or pork

FOR THE MARINADE

- 2 teaspoons coriander seeds
- 1 teaspoon cumin seeds
- ½ teaspoon fennel seeds*
- 1 teaspoon ground turmeric
- ¼ teaspoon ground cinnamon
- ¼ teaspoon ground black pepper
- 1 teaspoon salt
- 6 shallots or ½ small onion, chopped
- 2 cloves garlic, chopped
- ½ teaspoon chopped fresh ginger
- 2 tablespoons roasted peanuts (unsalted) or 1 tablespoon smooth peanut butter
- ½ teaspoon grated lemon rind
- 2 teaspoons brown sugar
- 1 tablespoon oil
- 1 tablespoon light soy sauce*

FOR THE SATAY SAUCE

- 6 dried red chillies, soaked, drained and torn into pieces, or 2 teaspoons *sambal ulek**
- 6 shallots or ½ medium onion, chopped
- 2 cloves garlic, chopped
- 1 tablespoon flaked almonds or 4 macadamia nuts
- ½ teaspoon grated lemon rind
- ½ teaspoon *blachan** (optional)
- 2 tablespoons oil
- 250 ml/8 fl oz coconut milk (p. 32)
- 4 tablespoons crunchy peanut butter

Cut the meat into 1 cm/½ in cubes. (If they are any larger the marinade will not be absorbed properly.)

Dry roast and grind the coriander, cumin and fennel seeds according to the instructions on p. 31. Mix with the turmeric, cinnamon; black pepper and salt.

Put the remaining marinade ingredients into the container of an electric blender or food processor and blend to a paste. Stir in the mixed spices and mix with the meat. Chill for at least 5 hours. Thread on to bamboo skewers (about 6 pieces per skewer) so that the meat takes up no more than two-thirds of the skewer. (This allows room for holding it.) Grill over hot coals or under a hot grill for about 5 minutes, turning at least once. Serve immediately.

While the meat is marinating, make the sauce which should be served at room temperature.

INSTRUCTIONS FOR SATAY SAUCE

Put the first five or six ingredients into the container of an electric blender or food processor. Add the minimum amount of water to allow the blades to operate and blend to a thick purée.

Heat the oil in a heavy frying-pan and gently fry the chilli purée for 5 minutes, stirring frequently. Add coconut milk and bring to the boil, stirring constantly. Add all remaining ingredients and simmer, uncovered, for a further 5 minutes. The sauce may be diluted with extra water if it seems too thick.

NOTE

This sauce freezes well.

1 teaspoon concentrated tamarind extract*
1 tablespoon brown sugar
½ teaspoon salt or more to taste

Sosaties

Sosaties are a South African barbecue speciality which no doubt began life as *satay*, brought by the Malay slaves whom the Dutch imported into South Africa during the seventeenth century. The name may be a derivation of 'sauce *satay*' and these marinated meat cubes, threaded on skewers and grilled, have unmistakable links with the South-East Asian *satay* in the previous recipes.

MAKES ABOUT 36

1.5 kg/3 lb lean boneless lamb, cut into 2 cm/¾ in cubes
1 clove garlic
1 teaspoon salt
¼ teaspoon ground black pepper
¼ teaspoon ground ginger
2 tablespoons oil
4 medium onions, finely chopped
1 teaspoon South African curry powder (p. 38)
1 teaspoon ground coriander
½ teaspoon ground cumin
1 fresh red chilli, finely chopped
2 teaspoons brown sugar
1 tablespoon apricot jam
3 tablespoons lemon juice
2 bay leaves

Put the meat in a bowl and rub with the garlic clove. Chop the garlic and scatter over. Mix together the salt, pepper and ginger and sprinkle over the meat. Set aside for 1 hour.

Heat the oil in a heavy frying-pan and fry the onions until golden. Stir in the curry powder, coriander and cumin and fry for 1 minute. Add 250 ml/8 fl oz of water and all the other ingredients. Bring to the boil and simmer for 1 minute. Remove from the heat and allow to cool completely. Pour over the meat and leave in the fridge for 12 hours, turning the meat occasionally.

Drain the meat and reserve the marinade. Thread the meat on to skewers and grill or barbecue, turning frequently, until evenly browned.

Put the marinade in a saucepan and bring to the boil. Simmer until reduced and thickened, or thicken with 1 tablespoon of flour mixed with a little water. Serve the sauce separately and accompany the *Sosaties* with fresh crusty bread and salad.

Indian Skewered Lamb
Seekh Kebab

This marinade is sufficient for 750 g/1½ lb lean boneless lamb, cut into 2.5 cm/1 in cubes. It could also include 2 tablespoons of yoghurt.

The kebabs are excellent served with chutney, salad and *chapatis*. Alternatively, serve them with rice and the curry sauce given below.

FOR THE MARINADE

- 1 small onion, finely sliced
- 4 cloves garlic, crushed
- 1 teaspoon chopped fresh ginger
- 1 teaspoon ground coriander
- 1 teaspoon *garam masala**
- 1 teaspoon ground chilli
- 1 teaspoon salt
- 3 tablespoons oil
- 2 tablespoons lemon juice

FOR THE CURRY SAUCE

- 3 tablespoons oil, butter or *ghee**
- 1 medium onion, finely chopped
- 2 cloves garlic, finely chopped
- 1 teaspoon finely chopped fresh ginger
- 2.5 cm/1 in cinnamon stick
- 4 cloves
- 4 cardamom pods*
- 1 tablespoon meat curry powder (p. 37)
- 125 g/4 oz yoghurt
- ½ teaspoon salt
- ¼ teaspoon ground black pepper
- 2 fresh green chillies, deseeded and sliced vertically
- 2 tablespoons finely chopped coriander or parsley leaves

Mix all the marinade ingredients together and add the cubed meat. Leave in a cool place for 4–12 hours, turning the meat occasionally. Drain and thread the meat on to skewers. Brush with the oil and grill or barbecue, turning frequently until evenly browned.

To make the sauce, heat the oil, butter or *ghee* in a heavy frying-pan and gently fry the onion, garlic and ginger until soft but not coloured. Add the cinnamon, cloves and cardamoms and fry for 1 minute. Add the curry powder and fry for a further 2 minutes, stirring constantly to prevent sticking. Remove the pan from the heat and add the yoghurt, a little at a time, stirring vigorously to prevent curdling. Return to the heat and bring to the boil, still stirring. Add the salt, pepper, chillies and 3 tablespoons of water. Simmer, uncovered, for 10 minutes. Stir in the chopped herbs before serving.

Ginger Beef

- 1 kg/2 lb lean steak
- 150 ml/¼ pint light soy sauce*
- 75 ml/3 fl oz sherry
- 1 clove garlic, mashed
- 1 teaspoon sugar
- ½ teaspoon ground chilli
- ¼ teaspoon ground ginger
- fresh ginger root

Cut the steak into 2.5 cm/1 in chunks and marinate in a sauce made with all the other ingredients except the fresh ginger. Thread the meat on to skewers with paper-thin slices of fresh ginger between the pieces, and barbecue or grill.

Venezuela Pork

Serve these pork skewers as an appetizer before barbecued steaks.

- 1.5 kg/3 lb lean pork
- 1 small onion, thinly sliced
- 2 cloves garlic, mashed
- 4 tablespoons white wine vinegar
- 4 tablespoons olive oil
- 3 tablespoons finely chopped parsley
- ½ teaspoon salt
- ¼ teaspoon ground black pepper
- 2 fresh chillies, chopped

Cut the pork into 2 cm/¾ in chunks and marinate in a vinegar and parsley sauce made with the remaining ingredients. Thread the meat on skewers, and barbecue or grill.

Japanese Steaks

Combine all the ingredients and use this marinade for thinly cut steaks (no more than 80 mm/¼ in) and marinate for 20 minutes. Enough for 350 g/11 oz meat.

- 3 tablespoons Japanese soy sauce*
- 3 tablespoons rice wine or dry sherry
- ¼ teaspoon ground chilli
- 1 teaspoon finely chopped fresh ginger
- 4 spring onions, halved
- 1 teaspoon sugar

Churrasco Steak

A *churrasco* is a barbecue party, Brazilian style. Traditionally the meat is threaded on to long skewers or 'swords', which are then stuck in the ground at an angle to the fire.

The recipe given below will serve as both a marinade and a condiment and is sufficient for 4 rump steaks. Use half to marinate the steaks for 4 hours and serve the rest as a sauce.

150 ml/¼ pint olive oil	Mix all the ingredients together.
5 tablespoons wine vinegar	
4 cloves garlic, finely chopped	
1 teaspoon ground chilli	
4 tablespoons finely chopped coriander or parsley leaves	
½ teaspoon dried thyme	
1 bay leaf	
½ teaspoon salt	
¼ teaspoon ground black pepper	

Texan Steaks

The Texans are masters of the art of barbecueing and enjoy spicy marinated steaks. Mix all the ingredients together and use this marinade again during cooking, to baste the meat. This amount is sufficient for about 2 kg/4 lb steaks.

- 250 ml/8 fl oz oil
- 1 small onion, finely sliced
- 2 cloves garlic, finely sliced
- ½ teaspoon Tabasco sauce*
- 1 fresh green chilli, halved (with or without seeds)
- ½ teaspoon paprika
- 1 teaspoon grated horseradish
- 2 tablespoons tomato ketchup
- 2 teaspoons Worcester sauce
- 2 tablespoons lemon juice
- 2 bay leaves
- 1 teaspoon salt
- few grindings black pepper

Singapore Spareribs

Sweet, spicy and hot, these spareribs are a winner to eat with the fingers.

- 4 cloves garlic
- ½ teaspoon *sambal ulek** or ground chilli
- ½ teaspoon chopped fresh ginger
- 1 tablespoon runny honey
- 1 tablespoon sesame oil*
- 3 tablespoons light soy sauce*
- 1 teaspoon dark soy sauce*
- ½ teaspoon five spice powder*
- ½ teaspoon salt
- 1.5 kg/3 lb meaty pork spareribs, cut into 7.5 cm/3 in lengths, ribs separated
- oil for shallow frying

Use a pestle and mortar to pound the first 3 ingredients to a paste. Add the honey, sesame oil, soy sauces, five spice powder and salt. Rub this mixture all over the spareribs. Heat the oil in a heavy frying-pan and fry the ribs, a few at a time, until crisp and browned. Return all the ribs to pan and add 125 ml/4 fl oz of water. Simmer, covered, for about 45 minutes until tender. Serve immediately, or allow to cool and grill or barbecue for a few minutes either side when needed.

Californian Spareribs

Hot and sweet, these spareribs are flavoured with herbs rather than the oriental spices of the previous recipe.

- 4 tablespoons oil
- 1 large onion, finely chopped
- 2 cloves garlic, finely chopped
- 3 tablespoons tomato purée
- 4 tablespoons vinegar
- 4 tablespoons runny honey
- ¼ teaspoon dry mustard
- 1 teaspoon Tabasco sauce*
- 1 tablespoon Worcester sauce
- ½ teaspoon salt
- ½ teaspoon dried basil
- ½ teaspoon dried thyme
- 2 kg/4 lb spareribs

Heat the oil in a heavy pan and fry the onion and garlic until golden. Add all the remaining ingredients except the spareribs and simmer for 5 minutes.

Line a large baking tray with kitchen foil to prevent drips burning. Use a pastry brush to brush the spareribs with the sauce, and place the spareribs in the baking tray. Bake in a moderately hot oven pre-heated to 200°C/400°F/gas 4, for about 1 hour, basting every 10 minutes with more of the sauce. Serve immediately with any remaining sauce.

POULTRY

Chicken

Many chicken dishes were originally conceived to cope with birds that have a long and busy life before reaching the cooking pot. Fresh and full of flavour they may be, but long braising is necessary to reduce their flesh to tender succulence. Commercially bred birds will reach that state in a far shorter time. A chicken portion, for example, will need about 40–45 minutes simmering in liquid to be perfectly cooked. Purists may say that such birds are bland and lacking in flavour, and that the sauces in which they cook must suffer as a consequence . . . perhaps, but the following recipes have been geared to producing satisfactory results with fresh, commercially reared oven-ready birds. If you are using a bird that has been raised more naturally, please adjust the cooking times accordingly, if necessary. Frozen birds should, of course, be completely thawed before use.

Chicken pieces for currying should not be too large, as it is an essential that the spices should penetrate into the chicken meat. A 1.5 kg/3 lb bird should be cut into 12–14 equal portions, which will allow for sufficient flavour absorption to take place within the average 40 minutes cooking time required for a cut-up oven-ready bird. During this time, the mixture of simmering liquid and spices will produce either a thick or a thin gravy, depending upon the recipe, or – in the case of a dry curry – will reduce to a spice coating.

Mild Chicken Curry

A typical North Indian curry that uses butter or *ghee* as the frying medium. Freshly ground spices, whole fragrant spices and yoghurt combine to produce just a little thick sauce, which can be scooped up with Indian bread.

SERVES 6

- 2 teaspoons coriander seeds
- 1 teaspoon cumin seeds
- ¼ teaspoon black peppercorns
- 1 teaspoon ground turmeric
- ½ teaspoon ground chilli
- 50 g/2 oz butter or *ghee**
- 1 medium onion, finely chopped

Dry roast and grind the first 3 ingredients according to the instructions on p. 31. Add the ground turmeric and chilli.

Heat the butter or *ghee* in a large heavy frying-pan or saucepan. Add the onions, garlic, ginger, cinnamon, cloves and cardamoms and fry gently until the onion is golden, stirring frequently. Stir in the ground spices and fry for 2 minutes. Add the chicken pieces and stir so that each piece is

- 3 cloves garlic, finely chopped
- ½ teaspoon finely chopped fresh ginger
- 2.5 cm/1 in cinnamon stick
- 4 cloves
- 3 cardamom pods,* bruised
- a 1.5 kg/3 lb chicken, cut into 12–14 pieces and skinned
- 125 ml/4 fl oz yoghurt
- ½ teaspoon salt
- 2 teaspoons lemon juice

coated with spices. Remove the pan from the heat and add the yoghurt, a little at a time, stirring vigorously after each addition to prevent curdling. Return to the heat and bring to the boil, still stirring continuously. Add the salt and 2 tablespoons of water. Simmer, covered, for about 40 minutes, until the chicken is tender and the sauce has thickened. Sprinkle with lemon juice just before serving.

Serve with *chapatis*, a vegetable or salad, and an assortment of pickles and chutneys.

Dry Chicken Curry
Bhuna Murgh

- 3 tablespoons oil, butter or *ghee**
- ½ teaspoon black mustard seeds*
- 1 medium onion, finely chopped
- 4 cloves garlic, finely chopped
- 1½ teaspoons finely chopped fresh ginger
- 2 bay leaves
- 2 teaspoons meat curry powder (p. 37)
- 1 teaspoon *garam masala**
- 1 tablespoon paprika
- ½ teaspoon ground chilli
- 4 cardamoms,* husks removed
- ½ teaspoon salt
- a 1.5 kg/3 lb chicken, cut into 12–14 pieces and skinned
- 2 tablespoons lemon juice

Heat the oil in a large heavy frying-pan or saucepan. Add the mustard seeds and fry until they jump and pop. Add the onion, garlic, ginger and bay leaves and gently fry until golden. Add the curry powder, *garam masala*, paprika, chilli and cardamoms. Fry for 2 minutes, stirring constantly to prevent sticking. Add the salt and the chicken and mix well so that the chicken pieces are coated in spices. Add the lemon juice and 2 tablespoons of water. Simmer, tightly covered, for 40 minutes until the meat is tender. Add a little water if necessary to prevent sticking, but the finished dish should be dry.

Serve with *chapatis* and a wet vegetable dish.

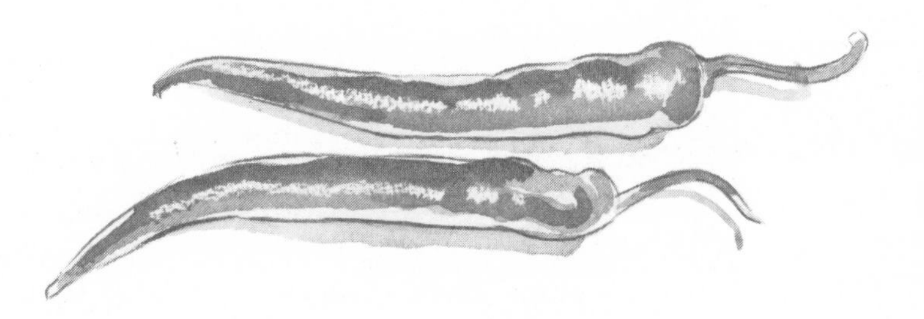

Malay Chicken Curry
Gulai Ayam

Malay curries have a strong affinity with those of southern India, so *Gulai Ayam* has much in common with the previous recipe. However, the addition of nuts (authentically these would be candlenuts,* but almonds make a perfectly acceptable alternative) as a thickening and enriching agent for the sauce is typically Malay. So is the use of fennel and the strong emphasis on fragrant spices – cinnamon, nutmeg and cloves.

This deliciously aromatic curry *must* be made with freshly roasted and ground spices. It has lots of thick, rich gravy and can be made hotter or quite mild. This is one of my favourite curry tastes, and one that is rarely found outside South-East Asia.

SERVES 6

- 2 tablespoons coriander seeds
- 1 tablespoon cumin seeds
- 2 teaspoons fennel seeds*
- 6 black peppercorns
- 6 cloves
- 5 cm/2 in cinnamon stick
- ⅛ whole nutmeg
- 1 teaspoon ground turmeric
- 3 medium onions, chopped
- 4 cloves garlic, chopped
- 1 tablespoon fresh ginger, chopped
- 8 dried fresh chillies, soaked and chopped, or 3 teaspoons *sambal ulek**
- 1 teaspoon paprika
- 2 tablespoons flaked almonds
- 1 teaspoon powdered lemon grass* or finely chopped lemon rind
- 5 tablespoons oil
- a 1.5 kg/3 lb chicken, cut into 12–14 pieces
- 1 litre/34 fl oz water
- 125 g/4 oz creamed coconut (p. 32)
- 1 teaspoon salt or to taste

Dry roast and grind the first 7 ingredients as explained on p. 31. Add the ground turmeric and set aside.

Put the onions, garlic, ginger, chillies, paprika, almonds and powdered lemon grass into the container of an electric blender or food processor. Add 3 tablespoons of the oil and blend to a paste. If necessary, add 1 tablespoon of water to make the blades work properly.

Follow the instructions in the previous recipe for frying chicken and spice paste.

Return the chicken pieces to the pan with any juices that have accumulated. Add the water and creamed coconut and heat gently until the coconut has melted. Bring to the boil, stirring constantly to prevent curdling. Add the salt and simmer *uncovered* for 40 minutes or until the chicken is tender.

VARIATIONS

To make an economical and substantial meal, add quartered potatoes for the final 15 minutes cooking. Do not allow them to disintegrate. If necessary, remove them when they are cooked and return them to the pan just before serving. Small, tender okra are also suitable for adding for the last 10 minutes, or quartered tomatoes for the final couple of minutes.

This sauce is so flavoursome that I often make it without the chicken (or just with wing tips, which are discarded after cooking) but with

assorted vegetables to make a meatless curry. Try it with any combination of the following, adding vegetables that require long cooking first: potatoes, carrots, shallots, green beans, okra, aubergines, shredded cabbage, tomatoes.

South Indian Chicken Curry with Coconut Milk Gravy

A classic chicken curry in the South Indian style – hot with dried red chillies that are ground to a paste together with the other wet spices. The simmering liquid is coconut milk, but more thick coconut milk is added just before serving to give extra richness to the gravy. If fresh curry leaves and lemon grass are not available, use bay leaves and lemon rind. If using lemon rind, put it in the blender as part of the paste. This curry will have lots of orange-red sauce.

SERVES 6

- 1 large onion, chopped
- 4 cloves garlic, chopped
- 1 tablespoon chopped fresh ginger
- 10 dried red chillies, soaked and chopped
- 4 tablespoons oil
- 1 tablespoon coriander seeds
- 2 teaspoons cumin seeds
- ½ teaspoon fenugreek seeds*
- ¼ teaspoon black peppercorns
- 1 teaspoon ground turmeric
- a 1.5 kg/3 lb chicken, cut into 12–14 pieces
- 600 ml/1 pint coconut milk (p. 32)
- ½ teaspoon salt or to taste
- 6 curry leaves* or 2 bay leaves
- 1 stalk lemon grass,* bruised, or ½ teaspoon shredded lemon rind
- 125 ml/4 fl oz thick coconut milk (p. 32)
- juice of ½ lemon
- 2 tablespoons finely chopped parsley or coriander leaves

Put the onion, garlic, ginger and dried chillies into the container of an electric blender or food processor. Add enough of the oil to make the blades work properly and blend to a paste. Set aside.

Dry roast and grind the coriander, cumin, fenugreek and peppercorns as explained on p. 31. Add the turmeric and set aside.

Heat 2 tablespoons of the oil in a large heavy saucepan and fry the chicken pieces a few at a time until the skin is golden. Remove the chicken. Add the remaining oil (if any), and fry the spice paste over a medium heat for about 4 minutes until all the liquid has evaporated. Stir constantly. Add the ground spices and fry for about 3 minutes until the spices smell fragrant.

Return the chicken pieces to the pan and turn in the spice paste so that each piece is coated. Add the coconut milk, stirring constantly to prevent curdling. Add the salt, curry or bay leaves and lemon grass. Simmer, *uncovered*, for about 40 minutes, until the chicken is tender. Check frequently for sticking as the gravy thickens. Add the thick coconut milk, stirring constantly. Simmer for 2 minutes. Stir in the lemon juice and parsley immediately before serving.

Serve with rice, a vegetable, *chapatis*, and a selection of pickles or chutneys.

Sri Lankan Chicken Curry

In the Sri Lankan manner, whole spices are roasted to a deep brown before grinding, giving an unmistakable colour, aroma and taste to the dish. Another local practice is to use tinned evaporated milk which has been soured with lemon or lime juice, instead of coconut milk. The result is a hot, rich, full-bodied curry. Use paprika in place of some of the red chillies, if preferred.

SERVES 6

- a 1.5 kg/3 lb chicken, cut into 12–14 pieces
- 2 teaspoons ground turmeric
- 1 teaspoon salt
- 2 teaspoons coriander seeds
- 1 teaspoon cumin seeds
- 1 teaspoon fennel seeds*
- ½ teaspoon fenugreek seeds*
- 24 dried red chillies, stems removed (and seeds if preferred)
- ½ teaspoon turmeric
- 2 tablespoons oil
- 1 teaspoon black mustard seeds*
- 2 medium onions, finely sliced
- 4 cloves garlic, finely chopped
- 1 teaspoon finely chopped fresh ginger
- 1 tablespoon water
- 1 teaspoon salt
- 250 ml/8 fl oz evaporated milk
- 2 teaspoons lemon or lime juice
- 3 cardamom pods,* bruised
- 1 stalk lemon grass* or 1 teaspoon finely chopped lemon rind
- 125 ml/4 fl oz water

Rub the turmeric and salt into the chicken pieces and set aside.

Dry roast and grind the coriander, cumin, fennel, fenugreek and dried red chillies as explained on p. 31, but extend the roasting time so that the seeds are chocolate brown and the chillies become crisp. This will take at least 5 minutes. Do not allow them to burn, however, as this will give a bitter taste. Grind the chilli seeds as well as the pods for a really fiery curry! Mix in ½ teaspoon of ground turmeric and set aside.

Heat the oil in a large heavy pan. Add the mustard seeds and fry over a medium heat until the seeds jump. Turn the heat to low and fry the onions, garlic and ginger until soft and golden. Add the ground spices and fry for 2 minutes. Add a little extra oil if necessary. Add the chicken pieces and mix well so that all the pieces are coated. Add the water and salt. Cover and simmer for 20 minutes.

Stir in the evaporated milk and the lemon or lime juice and bring to the boil, stirring constantly. Add the cardamoms, lemon grass and water, and simmer *uncovered* for a further 20 minutes until the chicken is tender and the sauce has reduced and thickened.

Burmese Chicken Curry

Soy sauce and sesame oil – typical Burmese ingredients – are combined with Indian curry powder for this interesting curry. Authentically the chicken would be cut into smaller pieces than is normal for an Indian curry – about 20–24, rather than 12–14. This can become a bit bony for some tastes, so please yourself. Alternatively, use boned chicken breasts cut into 2.5 cm/1 in cubes and reduce the simmering time to 15 minutes. Reduce the amount of water, too.

SERVES 6

- 2 teaspoons meat curry powder (p. 37)
- 1 teaspoon turmeric
- 1 teaspoon ground chilli or *sambal ulek**
- 1 tablespoon light soy sauce*
- a 1.5 kg/3 lb chicken, cut into small pieces
- 3 tablespoons sesame oil*
- 1 medium onion, grated or very finely chopped
- 4 cloves garlic, very finely chopped
- 7.5 cm/3 in cinnamon stick
- 3 bay leaves
- a little salt if necessary

Mix the first 4 ingredients together to make a paste. Mix with the chicken pieces and set aside for 30 minutes.

Heat the oil in a large heavy frying-pan or saucepan and gently fry the onions and garlic until golden. Add the chicken, scraping all the juices into the pan. Fry gently for 5 minutes, stirring constantly to prevent sticking. Add the cinnamon, bay leaves and enough water to cover barely. Simmer, covered, for about 30 minutes, until the chicken is tender and the gravy has reduced. Check the seasoning and add a little salt if needed.

Serve with boiled rice, a salad and Balachaung (p. 263).

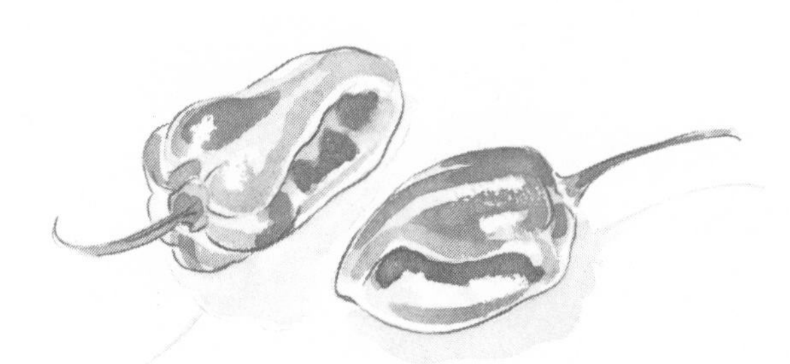

Jamaica Chicken

Scotch Bonnet chillies are much favoured in Jamaica for their special flavour. They are, however, extremely hot as well as having a beautiful fragrance. Many cooks, therefore, add them whole, discarding the pod before serving. I also add chopped cayenne-type chillies for extra body, and plenty of herbs for a really delicious dish.

SERVES 4

- 4 chicken quarters, each cut in half
- 3 cloves garlic, chopped
- 1 generous bunch thyme or ½ teaspoon dried thyme
- 1 teaspoon chopped basil leaves or ¼ teaspoon dried basil
- 1 bay leaf
- juice of 1 lemon
- 10 allspice berries,* coarsely crushed
- 2 fresh red or green chillies, deseeded and finely shredded
- 2 large tomatoes, chopped
- salt and ground black pepper to taste
- 3 tablespoons oil
- 1 large onion, finely sliced
- 1 glass dry white wine
- 1 Scotch Bonnet chilli, left whole, or ½ teaspoon West Indian hot pepper sauce*

Put the first 9 ingredients in a shallow bowl. Season with salt and pepper and leave for 1 hour to marinate. Remove the chicken pieces, scrape off any marinade ingredients that cling, and dry the chicken on kitchen paper. Reserve the marinade.

Heat the oil in a large heavy frying-pan. Add the onion and fry until soft. Remove from the pan and add the chicken pieces. Fry until golden. Return the onion to the pan with the reserved marinade, white wine and Scotch Bonnet or hot pepper sauce. Add enough water just to cover the chicken. Bring to the boil and simmer, covered, for about 45 minutes, until the chicken is tender and the sauce has thickened. If necessary, reduce the sauce by removing the cover for the last few minutes of the cooking time.

Serve with Rice and Peas (p. 220) and a salad of lettuce, spring onions, cucumber and avocado slices, dressed in vinaigrette.

Canari Chicken

This dish comes from the Ivory Coast and takes its name from a round earthenware pot called a *canari*, which is used both for storing drinking water and as a cooking vessel. The chicken and seasonings are put in the *canari* and the lid is then sealed so that the chicken simmers completely in its own juices. Traditionally the *canari* is set to cook very gently in the embers of a fire and its rounded bottom allows the pot to be tipped and tilted at intervals, preventing sticking and encouraging the chicken to cook evenly. The modern cook, however, must be content with using a heavy casserole on a gas or electric ring. It is also a good idea to use an asbestos mat for slow, even cooking. The casserole should be sealed around the lid with a stiff flour and water paste. Fill any ventilation holes in the lid with paste as well.

SERVES 6

- a 1.5 kg/3 lb chicken, cut into 12 even-sized pieces
- 2 large onions, finely sliced
- 6 tomatoes, peeled and chopped
- 4 cloves garlic, finely chopped
- 2 tablespoons finely chopped fresh ginger
- 4 fresh chillies, deseeded and finely chopped
- 1 bay leaf
- ½ teaspoon salt
- ½ teaspoon ground black pepper

Put all the ingredients in a heavy casserole suitable for use on top of the cooker. The ingredients should fit comfortably, with at least 5 cm/2 in clear at the top. Seal with flour and water paste. Set on low heat. After 5 minutes, gently tilt and shake the casserole to prevent sticking. This shaking should be repeated every 5 minutes during cooking. To time the cooking, listen carefully after about 10 minutes, for a hissing sound inside the casserole. When you hear this, cook the chicken for a further 40 minutes.

Serve directly from the pot, with rice and a salad.

NOTE

Canari Chicken can be cooked in the oven but it is a nuisance having to remove the casserole every 5 minutes. Oven-top cooking is far less trouble.

African Chicken Stews

All over Black Africa, one-pot stews are the most favoured method of cooking, and as chicken is generally regarded as a special-occasion dish, it is chicken stews that are given particular attention. Invariably highly spiced, often containing an assortment of vegetables and sometimes seasoned with dried fish or prawns, they are suited to cooking over a fire or a kerosene burner and can be stretched out – with the addition of a few extra vegetables – to feed large family groups and unexpected guests.

Most distinctive of all the African chicken stews are those cooked in a sauce thickened with ground peanuts (or groundnuts, as they are called locally). The peanuts are first roasted and then ground to a paste with, if necessary, a little peanut oil. For most Western cooks, however, commercially prepared smooth peanut butter (unsweetened) is quicker and easier to use. As a rough guide, allow 175 g/6 oz of peanut butter for 250 g/8 oz of roasted peanuts. Before adding the peanut butter or ground peanut paste to the cooking pot, mix it with a little of the hot simmering liquid. In this way it is thinned down and blends in more easily.

Chickennat

In this Ugandan peanut stew hard-boiled eggs are used as a garnish.

SERVES 6

- 4 tablespoons oil
- a 1.5 kg/3 lb chicken, cut into 12 pieces
- 3 medium onions, finely chopped
- ½ teaspoon ground cumin
- 2 teaspoons ground chilli
- 600 ml/1 pint chicken stock, or water, or water+stock cube
- 1 teaspoon salt
- ½ teaspoon ground black pepper
- 500 g/1 lb roasted peanuts, ground to a paste, or 375 g/12 oz smooth peanut butter
- 1 egg yolk
- 6 hard-boiled eggs, shelled

Heat 2 tablespoons of the oil in a large heavy saucepan and gently fry the chicken, a few pieces at a time, until golden. Set aside. Add the remaining oil to the pan and gently fry the onions until golden. Stir in the cumin and ground chilli. Add the chicken stock, salt and pepper. Return the chicken to the pan and bring to the boil. Simmer, covered, for 15 minutes.

Spoon some of the hot liquid into a bowl and mix with the peanut paste. Add to the pan and stir in well. Simmer, covered, for a further 25 minutes. Take the pan off the heat and beat a little of the sauce with the egg yolk. Add to the pan, stirring well. Add the hard-boiled eggs and return to a very low heat for a few minutes so that the eggs heat through. The sauce must not boil again or the egg yolk will curdle.

Serve with rice, salad, mango chutney and sliced bananas.

Mafé

A substantial chicken and vegetable stew that is found in many parts of West Africa, especially Mali and Senegal. It can also be made with mutton or beef and is sometimes seasoned with dried fish. This version includes dried prawn powder, which can be made by grinding dried prawns (obtainable in Chinese and West Indian food shops) in an electric coffee grinder.

SERVES 6–8

- 4 tablespoons oil
- a 1.5 kg/3 lb chicken, cut into serving pieces
- 1 large onion, coarsely chopped
- 2 cloves garlic, finely chopped
- 4 tomatoes, peeled and chopped, or a 200 g/7 oz tin tomatoes
- 2 tablespoons tomato purée
- 1 tablespoon dried prawn powder*
- 1 teaspoon salt
- ½ teaspoon dried thyme
- 1 bay leaf
- 250 g/8 oz roasted peanuts, ground to a paste, or 175 g/6 oz peanut butter
- 2 teaspoons ground chilli
- 4 carrots, peeled and cut into large chunks
- 3 turnips, peeled and cut into large chunks
- ½ small cabbage, shredded
- 3 potatoes or sweet potatoes, peeled and cut into large chunks
- 10 whole okras (optional)
- 3 fresh chillies, deseeded and finely chopped
- 1 medium onion, grated
- ½ teaspoon ground black pepper

Heat 2 tablespoons of the oil in a large heavy saucepan and gently fry the chicken, a few pieces at a time, until golden. Remove from the pan and add the remaining oil. Gently fry the onion and garlic until golden. Add the tomatoes, tomato purée and prawn powder and stir well. Return the chicken to the pan and add enough water to cover by 2.5 cm/1 in. Add the salt, thyme and bay leaf, bring to the boil, and simmer for 15 minutes.

Mix a little of the hot liquid with the peanut paste and add to the pan with the ground chilli, carrots and turnips. Bring to the boil and simmer for 5 minutes. Add the cabbage, potatoes and okras. The liquid should just come level with the vegetables – top up with water if necessary. Bring back to the boil and simmer for 15 minutes. Add the last 3 ingredients and simmer for about 10 minutes more until the meat and vegetables are tender.

Serve with rice.

Wat

An Ethiopian stew, fiery hot with *berber* – a chilli and spice mixture (p. 40).

SERVES 6

- 50 g/2 oz butter
- 2 large onions, finely chopped
- 6 cloves garlic, finely chopped
- 2 tablespoons *berber* (p. 40)
- 3 tomatoes, chopped
- 3 tablespoons tomato purée
- a 1.5 kg/3 lb chicken, cut into serving pieces and skinned
- 1 teaspoon salt
- ½ teaspoon ground black pepper
- 6 hard-boiled eggs, shelled
- 2 tablespoons finely chopped parsley or coriander or mint

Heat the butter in a large heavy saucepan and gently fry the onions and garlic until golden. Stir in the *berber* and fry for 1 minute, stirring constantly to prevent burning. Add the tomatoes and purée and simmer for a couple of minutes. Add the chicken, turning each piece so that it is coated in the spice paste. Add the salt and pepper and enough water just to cover the chicken. Bring to the boil, cover, and simmer for about 40 minutes until the chicken is tender and the sauce is rich and thick. Add the eggs and simmer a few minutes to heat through. Stir in the fresh herbs before serving.

Serve with rice, flat bread, a green salad (no more tomatoes) and pickles.

Assorted Chicken Dishes

Chicken Assam Pedas

In the Malay language *assam* means sour and *pedas* means hot. There are many hot-sour dishes in Malay, Indonesian and Indian cuisine but most are for fish and shellfish. This chicken version is the only one that I have come across. It is very hot, with a thin, bright red sauce.

SERVES 4–6

- 5 chicken quarters, cut in half
- 1 teaspoon salt
- ½ teaspoon turmeric
- pinch ground black pepper
- 4 tablespoons oil
- 15 dried red chillies, ripped up and soaked in warm water for 10 minutes
- 1 medium onion, chopped
- 3 cloves garlic, chopped
- 1 teaspoon *laos* powder* (optional)

Score the chicken and sprinkle with the salt, turmeric and pepper. Leave for 10 minutes.

Heat the oil in a large saucepan and fry the chicken gently until it is golden on all sides. Put on the lid, turn the heat to very low and cook for 30 minutes, checking regularly for sticking.

While the chicken is cooking, put the chillies into the container of an electric blender with about 1 tablespoon of their soaking liquid. Blend for 30 seconds, adding a little more soaking liquid if necessary to make the blades work properly. Add the onion, garlic, ginger, *laos* powder, lemon rind and flaked almonds and blend to a paste.

- 5 cm/2 in ginger, chopped
- 1 teaspoon finely shredded lemon rind
- 1 teaspoon flaked almonds
- ½ teaspoon sugar
- 1 small aubergine, halved and sliced
- 1 litre/1½ pints water
- 2 medium tomatoes, quartered
- ½ teaspoon salt

When the chicken is cooked, remove from the pan and add the onion paste and sugar to the remaining oil. Fry very gently for about 20 minutes, until the oil separates. Stir frequently to prevent sticking. Add the aubergine and fry for 5 minutes. Add the water, tomatoes and salt. Return the chicken to pan. Bring to the boil, then simmer for 5 minutes. Taste for salt and add more if necessary. If the sauce is too hot, add 1 tablespoon of tomato ketchup. It probably won't make much difference but our cook used to say it takes some of the heat away!

Serve with boiled rice and fried vegetables such as *Baba-Bindi* (okra and beans, p. 188).

Pepperpot

A classic Trinidadian stew that has very ancient origins, although some of the spices are a more modern addition. Cassareep is an essential ingredient. It is made by boiling the juice of grated cassava root, and mixing it with brown sugar. Bottled cassareep is available in specialist West Indian shops. A tasty pepperpot can be made without cassareep but it will, of course, lack some of the authentic flavour.

SERVES 6–8

- a 1.5 kg/3 lb chicken, cut into serving portions
- 1 pig's trotter or calf's foot, halved
- 1 kg/2 lb boneless pork, cut into large cubes
- 250 g/8 oz salt beef or pork (optional)
- 4 tablespoons cassareep
- 2 medium onions, thickly sliced
- 4 fresh chillies, deseeded and finely chopped
- 2 tablespoons brown sugar
- 6 cloves
- 5 cm/2 in cinnamon stick
- ¼ teaspoon dried thyme
- salt to taste
- 2 teaspoons vinegar

Put all the ingredients except the vinegar into a large heavy saucepan. If salt beef or pork is being used, do not add salt yet. Add enough water barely to cover and bring to the boil. Simmer, covered, for about 1 hour until the meat is tender. The liquid should become fairly thick from the gelatinous juices of the trotter or calf's foot. Taste for salt and add extra if necessary. Stir in the vinegar just before serving.

Serve with boiled rice or potatoes.

Aji de Gallina

A classic Peruvian dish that combines boiled potatoes, chicken and a chilli sauce thickened with ground walnuts and bread.

SERVES 4–6

- a 1.5 kg/3 lb chicken
- 4 tablespoons fresh white breadcrumbs
- 250 ml/8 fl oz milk
- 2 oz walnuts
- 2 canned tomatoes+2 tablespoons juice
- 2 teaspoons *aji** or 1½ teaspoons ground chilli
- ¼ teaspoon turmeric
- 3 tablespoons olive oil
- 1 medium onion, finely chopped
- 3 cloves garlic, finely chopped
- salt and freshly ground black pepper to taste
- 750 g/1½ lb potatoes, peeled and freshly boiled
- 2 hard-boiled eggs, peeled and cut into segments
- black olives
- 2 fresh red chillies, deseeded and cut into long thin shreds

Poach the chicken in lightly salted water until just tender. When cool, skin the chicken and take the meat from the bones. Cut or shred into bite-size pieces and keep warm.

Put the breadcrumbs, milk, walnuts, tomatoes, *aji* or ground chilli and turmeric into the container of an electric blender or food processor and blend to a purée.

Heat the oil in a heavy saucepan and gently fry the onion and garlic until soft but not coloured. Gradually add the purée from the blender and bring to the boil, stirring constantly until the sauce thickens. Simmer for 5 minutes. Add the chicken and heat through. Season to taste.

To assemble, slice the hot potatoes and spread in a shallow serving dish. Pour the chicken and sauce over. Garnish with hard-boiled eggs, black olives and shredded chillies.

VARIATION

2 tablespoons of parmesan cheese or 3 tablespoons of grated Cheddar cheese can be added to the sauce just before the chicken is added. Heat through until it melts.

Chicken Stew
Dak Jim

The liberal use of garlic, chilli, sesame oil and soy sauce makes this classic Korean dish full of flavour. A salad of cucumber with toasted sesame seeds is the perfect side dish to accompany it, and plain boiled rice, of course.

SERVES 4

- 3 tablespoons oil
- 4 chicken portions, each cut into 2 or 3 pieces
- 3 spring onions, finely sliced

Heat the oil in a heavy frying-pan and fry the chicken pieces – a few at a time – until golden brown. As they are done, transfer to a large saucepan. Add 1 teaspoon of the oil from the frying-pan and all the other ingredients. Simmer,

- 5 cloves garlic, finely chopped
- 1 small onion, finely chopped
- 1 carrot, peeled and diced
- 2 tablespoons sesame oil*
- 5 tablespoons thin soy sauce*
- 125 ml/4 fl oz water
- ¼ teaspoon crushed black peppercorns
- ½ teaspoon ground chilli
- 1 fresh green chilli, deseeded and finely chopped
- ½ teaspoon sugar
- salt to taste (remember soy sauce is salty)

covered, for about 40 minutes until the chicken is tender.

Chicken with Olives

This is my version of a classic Algerian dish – *djej bil zaitun*. The hot, thin, red sauce makes it quite a light dish, suitable for a summer lunch with a difference.

SERVES 4

- 3 or 4 chicken portions, each cut into 3 pieces
- 2 tablespoons oil
- 25 g/1 oz butter
- 1 small onion, thinly sliced
- 4 cloves garlic, finely chopped
- 3 tablespoons paprika
- 1 teaspoon ground chilli
- 1 teaspoon ground ginger
- 1 teaspoon ground cumin
- ¼ teaspoon ground black pepper
- 2.5 cm/1 in cinnamon stick
- ½ teaspoon salt
- 450 ml/¾ pint water
- 12 green olives, stoned and coarsely chopped
- 1 tablespoon finely chopped parsley
- 2 tablespoons lemon juice

Pat the chicken portions dry on paper towels. Heat the oil and butter in a large heavy frying-pan or saucepan and fry the chicken pieces, a few at a time if necessary, until crisp and golden. Return all the pieces to the pan and scatter the onions and garlic over them. Sprinkle with the paprika, chilli, ginger, cumin and black pepper, mix in well, and continue frying gently for 1 minute. Add the cinnamon stick, salt and water. Bring to the boil and simmer, covered, for about 40 minutes until the chicken is tender. Add the remaining ingredients and simmer for a further 5 minutes. The sauce should have thickened slightly but still be rather thin. Check for salt. If the olives are not very salty, a little extra may be needed.

Serve with plain white rice, Green Pepper Salad (p. 208) and crusty French bread.

Texan Ranch Style Chicken Barbecue

The spice mixture in this recipe is both a marinade and a basting sauce. It is best made 24 hours in advance to allow the flavours to blend. Ideally, the chicken should be turned and basted every 3 or 4 minutes while barbecueing – the Texans take their barbecueing seriously! The final chicken is beautiful – but it's not much fun for the cook! Every 7 or 8 minutes is probably a reasonable compromise.

SERVES 6

- 3 tablespoons oil
- 3 tablespoons vinegar
- 1 teaspoon Worcester sauce
- 2 teaspoons tomato ketchup
- ¼ teaspoon mustard powder
- ½ small onion, minced or very finely chopped
- 2 cloves garlic, minced or very finely chopped
- 1 teaspoon salt
- ½ teaspoon Tabasco or hot pepper sauce*
- 6 chicken quarters, each cut in half
- 2 tablespoons melted butter

Make up a marinade with the first 9 ingredients. Put the chicken pieces in a bowl, pour the marinade over and leave for 1 hour. Drain, reserving the liquid. Dry the chicken on kitchen paper and brush with melted butter. Barbecue over hot coals, turning the chicken pieces frequently and basting with the reserved marinade at every turn. Cooking time is about 35 minutes.

Serve with crusty French bread, a crisp salad and a selection of chilli dips and chutneys (pp. 52, 264–6, 274).

Lebanese Drumsticks

Similar drumstick treatments are found all over the Middle East – sometimes using *sumac* powder (made from the dried berries of the sumac bush) to give the required tartness. Either way, the chicken is delightfully fresh and tangy. The drumsticks can be eaten hot or cold with *pitta* bread, salad and black olives; or as part of the *mezzeh* table.

MAKES 12

- 1 large onion, thinly sliced
- 3 cloves garlic, finely chopped
- 4 tablespoons olive oil
- 4 tablespoons lemon juice
- 1 teaspoon sugar
- 1 teaspoon salt

Mix the first 8 ingredients together and marinate the drumsticks in this mixture for 4 hours or longer. Cook over hot coals or under a medium-hot grill for 20–25 minutes until tender and evenly browned. Baste with the marinade during cooking.

- ½ teaspoon ground chilli
- 1 fresh green chilli, deseeded and shredded
- 12 chicken drumsticks, skinned if preferred

Piri-piri Chicken

In Mozambique, *piri-piri* is the name for chilli peppers and also for any dish cooked with chilli or steeped in a chilli marinade. This version makes an excellent barbecue dish.

SERVES 6

- 6 tablespoons oil
- 250 ml/8 fl oz coconut milk (p. 000)
- 1 teaspoon finely chopped parsley
- 2 teaspoons ground chilli
- 3 cloves garlic, finely chopped
- ¼ teaspoon ground black pepper
- ½ teaspoon salt
- 6 chicken portions

FOR THE SAUCE

- 25 g/1 oz butter
- 1 small onion, finely chopped
- 2 cloves garlic, finely chopped
- 1 teaspoon paprika
- ½ teaspoon ground chilli
- 2 fresh red chillies, deseeded and finely chopped
- 250 ml/8 fl oz coconut milk (p. 32)
- 1 tablespoon finely chopped parsley
- salt and black pepper to taste

Make a marinade with the first 7 ingredients and marinate the chicken pieces in it for at least 2 hours at room temperature or overnight in the refrigerator. Grill or barbecue the chicken for about 15 minutes either side, using the marinade for basting.

To make the sauce, heat the butter in a saucepan and gently fry the onion and garlic until golden. Stir in the paprika, ground chilli and fresh chillies. Fry for 1 minute. Add the coconut milk and bring to the boil, stirring constantly to prevent curdling. Stir in the parsley, season, and simmer uncovered for 5 minutes until the sauce has thickened.

Serve the chicken on a bed of rice, with the sauce in a separate bowl.

VARIATION

This recipe can also be made with boneless chicken breast. Cut into bite-size cubes before marinating and thread on skewers for cooking. The cooking time will, of course, be much shorter.

Sichuan Chicken with Dried Chillies

Dried red chillies are fried until dark brown, giving this dish an unmistakable flavour and aroma. Eat the fried chillies, or not, as you wish.

SERVES 4–6

- 10 long dried red chillies
- 2 teaspoons light soy sauce*
- 1 teaspoon sugar
- ½ teaspoon vinegar
- 2 teaspoons rice wine or dry sherry
- 2 teaspoons cornflour
- 3 tablespoons water
- 6 tablespoons oil
- 500 g/1 lb raw boneless chicken breasts, cut into 1.5 cm/½ in cubes
- ½ teaspoon five spice powder*
- 2 cloves garlic, finely chopped
- 1 teaspoon finely shredded fresh ginger
- 2 spring onions, cut into 2.5 cm/1 in lengths and then into quarters lengthwise
- few drops sesame oil*

Wash the chillies, remove the stalks and shake out the seeds. Roughly break the chillies into 2.5 cm/1 in lengths and set aside to dry completely.

In a small bowl, mix together the soy sauce, sugar, vinegar, rice wine or sherry, cornflour and water and set aside.

Heat the oil in a large heavy frying-pan or wok until fairly hot. Add the chicken and stir-fry for 2 minutes. Remove the chicken from the pan and pour off half the oil. Turn up the heat, add the chillies and stir-fry for 1–2 minutes until their colour changes to a dark reddish-brown. Do not burn. Remove the chillies and take the pan off the heat to cool down a little. Add the five spice powder, garlic and ginger, and gently fry for 1 minute, stirring constantly. Add the cornflour mixture and stir constantly until the sauce thickens. Put the chicken (and any juices that have accumulated) and chillies back in the pan together with the spring onions. Reheat over moderate heat, stirring all the time.

Transfer to a warm dish, sprinkle with sesame oil, and serve immediately with boiled rice.

Other Poultry

Drunken Duck
Pato Borracho

Found all over Latin America, this dish is so called because of the alcohol in the sauce.

SERVES 4

- 1 tablespoon butter
- a 2 kg/4 lb duck
- 2 medium onions, finely chopped
- 2 cloves garlic, finely chopped
- 300 ml/½ pint dry white wine

Heat the butter in a heavy frying-pan. Prick the duck all over with a fork (to release some of the fat under the skin) and fry until crisp and golden on all sides. Transfer the duck to an ovenproof roasting dish. Pour off all but 2 tablespoons of the fat from the pan and gently fry the onions and garlic until soft. Remove with a slotted spoon and

- 150 ml/¼ pint duck stock (made from the giblets), or water
- 2 tablespoons dry sherry
- 2 *jalapeños* or fresh green chillies, deseeded and finely chopped
- ⅛ teaspoon ground cinnamon
- ⅛ teaspoon ground cloves
- ¼ teaspoon ground cumin
- ¼ teaspoon ground coriander
- ¼ teaspoon ground black pepper
- ½ teaspoon salt
- 1 teaspoon tomato purée
- bay leaf

arrange around the duck. Add all the other ingredients, cover with foil, and cook for about 1½ hours or until the duck is tender in a pre-set oven at 180°C/350°F/gas 4.

Remove the duck from the oven and cut into serving pieces. Arrange them on a warm dish. Pour the sauce into a small saucepan, skimming off excess fat if necessary. Boil vigorously for a few minutes to reduce. Check the seasoning and pour the sauce over the duck.

Serve with rice and a salad of lettuce and fresh orange segments.

Duck Vindaloo

Hot, garlicky and tart, this Goan duck dish from the west coast of India is definitely not for the chilli-shy.

SERVES 4

- 125 ml/4 fl oz vinegar
- 6 cloves garlic, chopped
- 1 tablespoon chopped fresh ginger
- 12 dried red chillies, torn into pieces and soaked
- a 2 kg/4 lb duck, cut into serving portions
- 2 tablespoons oil
- 1 large onion, thinly sliced
- 2 teaspoons *garam masala**
- 2 teaspoons ground coriander
- 1 teaspoon turmeric
- ½ teaspoon ground black pepper
- 1 teaspoon sugar
- 1 teaspoon salt
- 1 bay leaf

Put the vinegar, garlic and ginger into the container of an electric blender or food processor with the drained chillies. Blend to a purée. Pour over the duck pieces in a bowl and leave to marinate for at least 3 hours. Remove the duck pieces and dry on kitchen paper towels. Reserve the marinade.

Heat the oil in a large heavy frying-pan. Add the duck and gently fry until golden on all sides. Remove with a slotted spoon and add the onion to the juices left in the pan. Fry the onion until golden. Add the *garam masala*, ground coriander, turmeric and black pepper and fry for 1 minute. Return the duck to the pan with the reserved marinade and all the other ingredients. Add just enough water barely to cover the duck. Bring to the boil and simmer, covered, for about 1 hour or until the duck is tender. If it is rather tough it may need longer cooking, in which case it may also be necessary to add a little extra water. Serve with rice and Cabbage with Coconut (p. 184).

Turkey with Chilli and Chocolate Sauce
Mole Poblano de Guajolote

One of the most famous Mexican festive dishes, the distinctive sauce really has to be made with the three dark Mexican dried chillies – *ancho, pasilla* and *mulato*. If these are not all available, use all *ancho* chillies. If none of these dried chillies are available, it is best to use a mixture of dried red cayenne-type chillies and sweet red peppers, although the taste will, of course, not be authentic. A small amount of unsweetened chocolate is added to the sauce at the end of cooking.

SERVES 10

- a 4 kg/8 lb turkey, cut into serving pieces
- bay leaf
- salt
- 4 *ancho* chillies
- 4 *pasilla* chillies
- 4 *mulato* chillies
- 2 fresh red chillies, deseeded and chopped
- 2 medium onions, chopped
- 4 cloves garlic, chopped
- 1 slice toast (or toasted *tortilla*), crumbled
- 2 large tomatoes, peeled and chopped
- 2 tablespoons ground almonds
- 3 tablespoons raisins
- 3 tablespoons toasted sesame seeds* + 1 tablespoon extra for garnish
- ½ teaspoon ground cumin
- ½ teaspoon ground coriander
- ¼ teaspoon ground black pepper
- ¼ teaspoon ground aniseed
- ½ teaspoon ground cinnamon
- ½ teaspoon ground cloves
- 2 tablespoons oil or lard
- 25 g/1 oz dark unsweetened chocolate

Put the turkey pieces in a large saucepan with just enough water to cover. Add the bay leaf and ½ teaspoon of salt. Bring to the boil and simmer, covered, for about 1 hour or until the turkey is tender. Drain and reserve stock.

Meanwhile remove the stems from the *ancho, pasilla* and *mulato* chillies. Shake out the seeds (reserve some if a hotter sauce is required) and tear out any tough veins. Rip the chillies into pieces, put in a bowl and cover with boiling water. Leave for 30 minutes. Drain and put into the container of an electric blender or food processor with the fresh chillies, onions, garlic, toast, tomatoes, almonds, raisins, sesame seeds, cumin, coriander, black pepper, aniseed, cinnamon and cloves. Blend to a purée, adding a little reserved stock if necessary for the blades to operate properly. The blending may have to be done in two or more batches.

Heat the oil or lard in a large heavy pan. Add the chilli purée and fry gently for 5 minutes. Add 450 ml/¾ pint of the reserved stock and bring to the boil. Add the turkey and stir in the chocolate until it melts. Simmer very gently, uncovered, for about 20 minutes until the sauce has thickened. Check frequently for sticking. Sprinkle with toasted sesame seeds before serving.

Serve with warm *tortillas, Frijoles* (p. 198) and *Arroz Blanco* (p. 217).

Chilli Stuffing for Turkey

For a spicy Christmas dinner, try this chilli stuffing.

ENOUGH FOR A 4–5 KG/8–10 LB TURKEY

- 3 tablespoons butter
- 1 large onion, coarsely chopped
- 2 cloves garlic, finely chopped
- 5 fresh green chillies, deseeded and finely chopped
- 250 g/8 oz minced pork or veal
- 250 g/8 oz fresh white breadcrumbs
- 150 ml/¼ pint dry white wine or chicken stock
- 3 tablespoons finely chopped parsley
- 50 g/2 oz toasted flaked almonds
- 50 g/2 oz coarsely chopped walnuts or pine nuts
- ⅛ teaspoon ground cloves
- ¼ teaspoon ground black pepper
- ½ teaspoon dried thyme
- salt to taste

Heat the butter in a heavy saucepan and fry the onion, garlic and chillies until the onion is soft. Add the pork and fry for 5 minutes. Transfer to a bowl and add all the remaining ingredients. Leave to stand for 10 minutes, and if the mixture seems too dry add a little extra wine or stock. Stuff the turkey and cook in the normal way.

EGGS

There is a special affinity between eggs, chilli and olive oil in the lands that border the Mediterranean. Locally grown herbs and vegetables are also incorporated, resulting in a distinctive repertoire of dishes that are quite different from the egg dishes of northern Europe. Beaten eggs, highly seasoned with fresh herbs and often spiced, are combined with cooked vegetables, meat and fish to produce thick omelette 'cakes' that are more akin to pastryless quiches than the soft, moist, folded omelette. Fried in olive oil, they have a rich, golden crust that cannot be achieved by frying with lighter oils. This crust is quite delicious, especially eaten cold.

For this type of omelette the size of frying-pan is important, as the egg mixture should form an omelette about 2.5 cm/1 in thick. The pan should also be heavy-bottomed to allow for slow cooking without burning, and either well-seasoned so that it does not stick, or non-stick.

Eggs Scrambled in Green Sauce
Huevos Revueltos en Salsa Verde

Until the Spanish arrived in Mexico, eggs were little used in local cooking. Today, however, there are dozens of egg dishes – most of them clearly in the Mediterranean tradition.

SERVES 4

- 2 fresh green chillies, deseeded and chopped
- 1 small sweet green pepper, deseeded and chopped
- a 250 g/8 oz can Mexican green tomatoes,* drained and liquid reserved
- 1 small onion, chopped
- 2 cloves garlic, chopped
- 2 tablespoons chopped coriander or parsley leaves
- 2 tablespoons oil or lard
- salt and pepper to taste
- 8 eggs, beaten

Put the first 6 ingredients into the container of an electric blender or food processor. Add enough of the reserved tomato liquid to allow the blades to operate properly, and blend to a purée.

Heat the oil or lard in a large heavy frying-pan and gently fry the purée for 5 minutes, stirring constantly. Season with salt and pepper. Pour in the eggs and cook over a low heat for about 5 minutes, stirring gently all the time until the eggs are cooked to the desired consistency. Turn on to a warm dish and serve immediately, with warm *tortillas*.

Tunisian Scrambled Eggs with Dersa Sauce

Dersa sauce is a standard spiced, hot sauce found all over North Africa. Scrambled with eggs, and served with black olives, it is a culinary world away from the bland scrambles with which we are more familiar.

SERVES 4

- 3 tablespoons olive oil
- 1 small onion, finely chopped
- 3 cloves garlic, finely chopped
- 2 teaspoons *harissa** mixed with 4 tablespoons water
- 1 tablespoon tomato purée
- ½ teaspoon ground cumin
- ½ teaspoon ground coriander
- ½ teaspoon paprika
- ½ teaspoon ground caraway
- ¼ teaspoon ground black pepper
- 1 teaspoon salt
- 8 eggs, beaten
- 1 tablespoon finely chopped parsley or coriander leaves

Heat the oil in a large heavy frying-pan and gently fry the onion and garlic until golden. Stir in the *harissa*, tomato purée, cumin, coriander, paprika, caraway, pepper and salt and simmer for 5 minutes. Pour in the eggs and cook over a low heat for about 5 minutes, stirring gently all the time until the eggs are creamy and set to the desired consistency. Stir in the chopped parsley or coriander leaves and tip on to a warm serving dish.

Serve immediately, with a bowl of olives and French bread or *pitta* bread.

Mexican Scrambled Eggs with Chorizo
Huevos Revueltos con Chorizo

The tomatoes in this dish can either be coarsely chopped so that they cook to a purée, or quartered so that they retain their shape. For the latter, choose tomatoes that are ripe but very firm.

SERVES 3–4

- 1 tablespoon butter or oil
- 1 small onion, finely chopped
- 175 g/6 oz *chorizo** sausage, skinned and finely chopped or crumbled
- 2 medium tomatoes, chopped or quartered
- 2 fresh green chillies, deseeded and finely chopped
- salt and black pepper
- 6 eggs, beaten

Heat the butter or oil in a heavy frying-pan and gently fry the onion until soft but not coloured. Add the *chorizo* and fry gently for 5 minutes. Add the tomatoes and chillies and fry for 3 minutes. Season with salt and pepper, then pour in the beaten eggs. Stir slowly until the eggs reach the desired creamy consistency.

Serve immediately, with warm *tortillas*, toast or crusty French bread.

Vietnamese Crab Omelette

No doubt due to the French influence in Indo-China, this omelette is usually served as a soft French-style folded omelette. Serve it with extra fish or light soy sauce in a sprinkler or a Chinese soy sauce pot, which is like a tiny coffee pot with a curved spout. Soy sauce is, by the way, a superb accompaniment to any omelette or scrambled egg.

SERVES 2–3

- 2 teaspoons oil
- 2 spring onions, finely sliced
- ½ teaspoon finely chopped fresh ginger
- 1 fresh red chilli, deseeded and finely chopped
- 125 g/4 oz cooked crabmeat (fresh, frozen or canned), picked over to remove all bony bits
- 1 teaspoon fish sauce* or light soy sauce*
- 4 eggs, lightly beaten
- salt to taste (remember that fish or soy sauce is salty)

Heat 1 teaspoon of the oil in an omelette pan and gently fry the spring onions, ginger and chilli for 1 minute. Stir in the crabmeat and the fish or soy sauce and cook for 1 minute longer. Tip into a bowl and wipe out the pan with a paper towel.

Heat the remaining 1 teaspoon of oil in the pan. Pour in the beaten eggs and cook in the normal way for an omelette, tilting the pan and drawing the egg mixture to the middle. When almost set, spoon the crab mixture on to one half, fold the other half over it with a spatula and carefully tip out on to a warmed plate.

VARIATIONS

Substitute cooked prawns (chopped, if large) or shredded cooked chicken for the crabmeat.

Malaysian Beansprout Omelette

SERVES 2, OR CAN BE PART OF A MULTI-DISH MALAYSIAN MEAL

- 2 tablespoons oil
- 3 spring onions, finely sliced
- 2 cloves garlic, finely chopped
- ½ teaspoon finely chopped fresh ginger
- 1 fresh red chilli, deseeded and finely chopped
- 250 g/8 oz beansprouts, washed and picked over 1 hour in advance, to allow them to dry completely
- 4 eggs, lightly beaten and seasoned with salt and pepper

Heat the oil in a heavy frying-pan and gently fry the spring onions, garlic, ginger and chilli for 1 minute. Add the beansprouts and stir-fry for 2 minutes. Pour in the eggs and gently stir for 5 seconds. Cook until well set and the underside has browned. Turn the omelette over, as Malaysian cooks do. Cut it into quarters then turn each quarter over separately with a spatula. Cook until browned.

In Malaysia, this would be served at room temperature.

Parsee Scrambled Eggs
Ekuri

Like conventional scrambled eggs, this is considered to be an ideal dish for invalids. My Indian cook used to make it for me whenever I was under the weather, but it is also a good lunch dish served with salad and warm *chapatis* or French bread . . . or try it as a starter course with hot buttered toast fingers. Kids like it that way, too!

SERVES 4

- 6 eggs
- salt to taste
- 3 tablespoons milk
- 1 tablespoon finely chopped parsley or coriander leaves plus extra for garnish
- 2 teaspoons butter, *ghee** or oil
- 1 small onion, finely chopped
- 1 teaspoon finely chopped fresh ginger
- 1 fresh green chilli, deseeded and finely chopped
- ½ teaspoon ground cumin
- ¼ teaspoon ground turmeric

Beat the eggs with the salt and milk. Stir in the 1 tablespoon of parsley or coriander and set aside.

Heat the butter, oil or *ghee* in a heavy frying-pan and gently fry the onion, ginger and chilli until soft. Stir in the cumin and turmeric. Pour in the egg mixture and cook over a very low heat, gently stirring, until soft and creamy. Turn on to a warmed serving dish and sprinkle with the extra chopped herbs. Garnish with tomato wedges and cucumber slices.

VARIATION

This mixture also makes an excellent flat cake-like omelette (see North African *Markude*, p. 179) to be eaten cold with salad. Omit the milk in this case and add a few cooked prawns or some diced cooked chicken.

Mexican Eggs Ranch Style
Huevos Rancheros

This classic Mexican dish makes a meal out of 2 eggs.

SERVES 4

- 2–4 *tortillas*, depending on size, per person
- oil for deep-frying
- Refried Beans (p. 198)
- 8 eggs
- *Salsa de Jitomate* (p. 269), heated
- shredded lettuce
- 2 avocados, peeled and sliced
- canned *serrano* chillies

Deep-fry the *tortillas* until golden. Arrange on 4 plates and spread with the beans. Fry the eggs and place 2 on each plate of *tortillas*. Spoon the *salsa* over the eggs. Scatter shredded lettuce around the edge of each plate and lay the avocado slices on top. Serve immediately with a bowl of *serrano* chillies.

Baked Chorizo Eggs

If these are going to be cooked in individual dishes – and I think that is the best way – you need shallow ovenproof dishes that are about 15 cm/6 in in diameter. The Spanish type made in brown earthenware or the French Le Creuset ones are ideal.

SERVES 4

- 50 g/2 oz butter
- 4 large tomatoes, skinned and coarsely chopped
- 125 g/4 oz *chorizo** sausage, skinned and crumbled or chopped
- ½ teaspoon ground chilli
- 1 teaspoon chopped fresh basil leaves or ¼ teaspoon dried basil
- 1 tablespoon finely chopped parsley
- salt and black pepper to taste
- 8 eggs
- 50 g/2 oz grated cheese, preferably Gruyère

Use a little of the butter to grease 4 shallow dishes (see above), and put the remainder in a frying-pan with the tomatoes, *chorizo* and ground chilli. Simmer for about 10 minutes until thick and pulpy, stirring frequently to prevent sticking. Stir in the basil and parsley, and season to taste.

Divide the tomato mixture between the 4 dishes and spread evenly. Break the eggs, one at a time, on to a saucer and carefully slide 2 into each dish. Sprinkle with the cheese and bake in a preheated oven, 180°C/350°F/gas 4, for about 15 minutes or until the whites are set. Serve immediately with hot toast – butter it if you like, but there is plenty of butter in the tomatoes.

Eggs in Coconut Milk

A typical way of cooking eggs in southern India and Sri Lanka, this dish is pale and creamy, making it an ideal contrast to other chilli dishes that are richer and darker in colour.

SERVES 3–6

- 2 tablespoons butter, *ghee** or oil
- 2 large onions, finely sliced
- 3 cloves garlic, finely chopped
- 2 teaspoons finely chopped fresh ginger
- 3 fresh green chillies, deseeded and shredded
- 500 ml/17 fl oz chicken stock, or water+stock cube
- 1 teaspoon ground turmeric
- 1 bay leaf

Heat the butter, *ghee* or oil in a large heavy frying-pan and gently fry the onions, garlic and ginger until soft but not coloured. Add the chillies, chicken stock, turmeric, bay leaf and salt. Take off the heat, add the creamed coconut, and stir until it is dissolved. Return the pan to the heat and bring to the boil, stirring constantly to prevent curdling. Simmer, uncovered, for about 10 minutes until the sauce has thickened. Add the eggs and peas or prawns. Heat through. Stir in the lemon juice just before serving.

Serve with rice Pilau, a colourful vegetable and pickles.

- 1 teaspoon salt
- 25 g/1 oz solid creamed coconut (p. 31)
- 6 hard-boiled eggs, shelled and halved
- 2 tablespoons cooked peas or 75 g/3 oz cooked prawns (optional)
- 1 tablespoon lemon juice

Chakchouka

Chakchouka is, perhaps, one of the best known and best loved of North African dishes. It appears in many, many forms but is basically a mixture of stewed vegetables (similar to *provençal* ratatouille) with eggs. The eggs can either be poached whole in the vegetable stew – as here – or the yolks can be gently broken so that they set firmer.

SERVES 6

- 4 tablespoons oil
- 1 medium onion, finely chopped
- 3 cloves garlic, finely chopped
- 2 courgettes, topped, tailed and cut into thin rounds
- 4 tomatoes, chopped
- 2 large sweet peppers (red or green), deseeded and chopped
- 2 fresh chilli peppers (red or green), deseeded and chopped
- 1 teaspoon salt
- ½ teaspoon ground black pepper
- 2 tablespoons finely chopped parsley
- 6 eggs

Heat the oil in a large heavy frying-pan and gently fry the onion and garlic until golden. Add the courgettes, tomatoes, sweet and chilli peppers, salt, pepper and half the parsley. Mix well and simmer over medium heat for about 15 minutes with the lid on the pan. Check frequently for sticking and add a little water if necessary. When cooked, the mixture should be thick and pulpy.

Make 6 slight hollows in the vegetable mixture. Break the eggs, one at a time, on to a saucer and carefully slide one into each hollow. Cook over a low heat for about 4 minutes with the lid on, until the eggs are set. Sprinkle with the remaining parsley and serve immediately.

Egg Curry

SERVES 6

- 3 tablespoons oil
- 1 large onion, finely sliced
- 4 cloves garlic, finely chopped
- 3 teaspoons finely chopped fresh ginger
- 1 tablespoon ground coriander
- 2 teaspoons ground cumin
- ½ teaspoon ground turmeric
- 1½ teaspoons ground chilli
- 4 tomatoes, chopped
- ½ teaspoon salt
- 6 hard-boiled eggs, peeled and halved
- ½ teaspoon *garam masala**

Heat the oil in a heavy frying-pan and fry the onion, garlic and ginger gently until golden. Add the coriander, cumin, turmeric and chilli and fry for 1 minute, stirring constantly. Add the tomatoes and salt and cook for 5 minutes. Add enough water just to cover, and simmer uncovered for about 10 minutes until the mixture is thick. Add the eggs and heat through. This will only take a few minutes. Do not overcook, as the eggs will turn leathery and become an unappetizing brown. Sprinkle with the *garam masala*.

Serve with boiled rice for a light lunch, or as part of a multi-dish Indian meal.

Eggs in Chilli Sauce
Sambal Telur

These chilli-fried eggs are found in both Malaysia and Indonesia. They combine two of the most powerful ingredients used in local cooking – chilli and *blachan* – in quantities that will deter many. They are an acquired taste and are eaten as a side dish – half an egg will be sufficient for most people. The recipe here is the Malaysia version. For Indonesian *Sambal Telur*, substitute coconut milk (p. 32) for the tamarind water and add ½ teaspoon each of *laos* powder* and *serai* powder.*

- 3 tablespoons oil
- 1 medium onion, chopped
- 3 cloves garlic, chopped
- 1 teaspoon *blachan**
- 3 teaspoons *sambal ulek** or 1 teaspoon chilli and 5 fresh red chillies
- 125 ml/4 fl oz tamarind water*
- 1 teaspoon salt
- 1 teaspoon brown sugar
- 6 hard-boiled eggs, shelled

Put the first 5 ingredients into the container of an electric blender or food processor and reduce to a paste. Add a little extra oil if necessary to allow the blades to operate properly.

Heat a heavy frying-pan, large enough to hold the 6 eggs comfortably, and add the paste. There is no need to add extra oil. Cook gently for 5 minutes, stirring constantly. During this time the oil will separate out and the paste will fry in its own oil. Add the tamarind water, salt and sugar, bring to the boil, and simmer for 1 minute. Put in the eggs and turn them so that they are thoroughly coated in the paste. Simmer for a couple of minutes longer, until the oil has once again separated out and the eggs are frying.

Serve at room temperature, with the eggs either whole or halved, as an accompaniment to rice and meat, fish or vegetable dishes.

Mashed Potato Markude

In North Africa thick, cake-like omelettes are called *markude*. They can contain a wide variety of vegetables, meat and even fish. Often eaten cold, they are served with lemon wedges, salad and pickles.

SERVES 6

- 2 large potatoes, boiled and mashed
- 4 cloves garlic, finely chopped
- 3 tablespoons finely chopped parsley
- 1 teaspoon ground coriander
- ½ teaspoon caraway seeds
- ½ teaspoon ground black pepper
- ½ teaspoon ground chilli
- ½ teaspoon paprika
- 1 teaspoon salt
- 8 eggs, beaten
- 3 tablespoons olive oil

Mix all the ingredients except the olive oil together in a bowl.

Heat the oil in a fairly large heavy frying-pan (about 25 cm/10 in). Pour in the egg mixture and cook over a low heat for 10–15 minutes, until well set. Turn upside down on to a plate and slide the omelette back into the pan. Cook the underside for a couple of minutes, then slide on to a serving plate.

I have had this *markude* served with French mustard but English-style piccalilli is even better.

VARIATIONS

Make a chicken markude with 500 g/1 lb of chopped cooked chicken; 2 hard-boiled eggs, chopped; 2 tablespoons of fresh breadcrumbs; 1 teaspoon of *harissa** mixed with 1 teaspoon water; 1 teaspoon of salt; ½ teaspoon of ground black pepper; 8 eggs, beaten.

Make a fish markude with 300 g/10 oz flaked cooked fish or drained canned tuna; 2 tablespoons breadcrumbs soaked in 2 tablespoons lemon juice; 3 tablespoons finely chopped parsley; 1 fresh green chilli, deseeded and finely chopped; salt and pepper; 8 eggs, beaten.

Make a meat markude with 200 g/7 oz lean cooked meat, chopped; 1 small onion, sliced and lightly fried; 3 cloves garlic, chopped; ½ teaspoon ground chilli; 3 tablespoons finely chopped parsley; 1 teaspoon *ras-el-hanout**; 2 hard-boiled eggs, chopped; 8 eggs, beaten.

VEGETABLES, PULSES AND SALADS

Millions of the world's most regular chilli-eaters are either totally vegetarian from religious conviction, or largely vegetarian through necessity. The result is a vast repertoire of superb vegetable dishes that offer not only a balanced and healthy diet but unusual and exciting tastes.

Vegetables

Aubergines in Coconut Milk

SERVES 6
1 large aubergine (about 250 g/8 oz)
150 ml/¼ pint oil
½ teaspoon salt
½ teaspoon ground turmeric
½ teaspoon black mustard seeds*
1 small onion, thinly sliced
2 cloves garlic
½ teaspoon cumin seeds
½ teaspoon fennel seeds*
1 teaspoon ground coriander
½ teaspoon ground chilli
⅛ teaspoon ground black pepper
250 ml/8 fl oz water
25 g/1 oz solid creamed coconut (p. 32)
1 teaspoon finely chopped parsley or coriander leaves

Cut the aubergine into 1 cm/½ in horizontal slices and then into halves or quarters, depending on size. Fry a few pieces at a time in hot oil until golden on both sides. Aubergines absorb oil when frying, so keep the oil fairly hot and top up as needed, using the minimum amount. When browned, transfer to a bowl and sprinkle with the salt and turmeric.

Heat 2 tablespoons of oil in a heavy frying-pan or saucepan. Add the mustard seeds and fry until they jump and pop. Add the onion, garlic, cumin and fennel seeds and fry gently until the onion is golden. Add the ground coriander and chilli and fry for 30 seconds. Add the black pepper, water and coconut cream and bring to the boil over a gentle heat, stirring constantly to prevent curdling and to encourage the coconut cream to dissolve. Simmer for 2 minutes, then add the aubergines and any juices that have accumulated. Simmer for a few minutes longer until the aubergines are cooked.

Stir in the chopped parsley or coriander and serve immediately.

Aubergines with Yoghurt

When fried, aubergines have a lovely nutty flavour that combines well with chilli and mint.

SERVES 6–8

- 1 kg/2 lb aubergines, washed and cut into 1 cm/½ in slices
- 1 tablespoon salt
- 300 ml/½ pint olive oil
- 3 cloves garlic, finely chopped
- 2 fresh green chillies, deseeded and finely chopped
- 1 tablespoon finely chopped mint leaves
- 400 ml/14 fl oz yoghurt

Lay the aubergine slices out on a tray and sprinkle with salt. Leave for 15 minutes and dry on kitchen paper.

Heat about 4 tablespoons of oil in a heavy frying-pan and add enough aubergine slices to fit comfortably in a single layer. Fry over a moderate heat until golden on both sides. Drain, and continue adding oil and frying until all the slices are cooked. Drain on kitchen paper. Allow to cool.

When ready to serve, mix the remaining ingredients together and pour over the fried aubergines. Serve immediately, as an accompaniment to kebabs, grills and roasts.

Chinese Sweet and Sour Cabbage

Generations of English cooks have abused the poor old cabbage by overcooking it, filling their kitchens with nasty lingering boiled cabbage smells and generally giving it a thoroughly bad reputation. This is a shame, because cabbage can be a very good vegetable indeed, especially combined with chilli.

SERVES 6

- 1 fresh red chilli, deseeded and finely shredded
- 2 tablespoons tomato ketchup
- 2 tablespoons light soy sauce*
- 2 tablespoons Chinese rice wine or dry sherry
- 3 tablespoons vinegar
- 4 tablespoons orange juice
- 2 tablespoons sugar
- 5 tablespoons water
- 1 tablespoon cornflour
- 4 tablespoons oil
- 1 large Chinese cabbage, outer leaves removed, cored and shredded
- 1 teaspoon salt

Make the sweet and sour sauce by mixing the first 9 ingredients together in a small saucepan. Bring to the boil, stirring constantly, until the sauce thickens and becomes translucent. Keep warm.

Heat the oil in a large heavy wok, frying-pan or saucepan. Add the cabbage and salt and stir-fry for 2 minutes over a medium heat. Reduce the heat to low and cook, covered, for about 4 minutes, stirring frequently.

Transfer to a warm serving dish and pour the sauce over.

Cabbage with Coconut

One of my favourite vegetable dishes, this is a typical south Indian way of cooking cabbage. Desiccated coconut gives very satisfactory results, but freshly grated coconut makes it even better.

SERVES 6

- 2 tablespoons oil
- 1 teaspoon black mustard seeds*
- 1 small onion, finely sliced
- 1 teaspoon finely chopped fresh ginger
- 2 fresh green chillies, deseeded and finely chopped
- 2 teaspoons black gram (*urid dahl*)*
- ½ firm white or green cabbage, core removed, shredded
- 1 teaspoon salt
- 4 tablespoons water
- 3 tablespoons desiccated coconut

Heat the oil and mustard seeds in a large heavy frying-pan until the mustard seeds start to jump and pop. Add the onion, ginger and chillies and fry gently until the onion begins to brown. Add the black gram and cabbage and stir-fry for 2 minutes. Add the salt and water, bring to the boil, and simmer, covered, for 3 minutes. Stir in the desiccated coconut and simmer, covered, for a further 5 minutes. Serve immediately or at room temperature. Do not re-heat.

NOTE

If using fresh coconut, stir in at the end of the cooking time.

Brazilian Cabbage with White Wine

SERVES 4

- ½ large firm white or green cabbage, core removed, shredded
- salt
- 2 tablespoons olive oil
- 1 medium onion, finely sliced
- 1 clove garlic, finely chopped
- 1 sweet green pepper, deseeded and thinly sliced
- 2 fresh green chillies, deseeded and finely chopped
- 4 tomatoes, chopped
- 2 tablespoons finely chopped parsley or coriander leaves
- salt and black pepper to taste
- 4 tablespoons white wine

Plunge the cabbage into a large pan of boiling salted water and boil for 3 minutes. Transfer to a colander, rinse in cold water and drain.

Heat the olive oil in a heavy saucepan and fry the onion, garlic, pepper and chillies until the onion is soft but not coloured. Add the tomatoes and cook for 3 minutes. Add all the remaining ingredients and the cabbage. Simmer for 3 minutes. Serve.

Tunisian Carrots
Mzoura

SERVES 4–6

- 500 g/1 lb carrots, peeled and sliced horizontally
- salt
- 2 tablespoons olive oil
- 2 cloves garlic, finely chopped
- 2 tablespoons vinegar
- 1 teaspoon *harissa*,* diluted with 3 tablespoons water
- ½ teaspoon cumin
- few grindings black pepper
- 1 tablespoon finely chopped parsley

Boil the carrots in salted water for 10 minutes so that they are tender but still crisp. Drain.

Heat the oil in a heavy frying-pan and gently fry the garlic for 1 minute. Stir in the vinegar, diluted *harissa*, cumin, black pepper and salt to taste. Bring to the boil. Add the carrots and simmer for a few minutes, stirring constantly, until the sauce has reduced and the carrots are coated. Stir in the chopped parsley and serve hot or cold.

Cauliflower with Cumin Seeds

SERVES 4–6

- 2 tablespoons oil
- ½ teaspoon black mustard seeds*
- 1 medium onion, finely sliced
- 1 teaspoon finely chopped fresh ginger
- 1 teaspoon cumin seeds
- 1–2 fresh green chillies, deseeded and finely chopped
- ½ teaspoon ground turmeric
- 1 small or ½ large cauliflower, cut into small florets
- 3 tablespoons water
- salt to taste

Heat the oil in a large heavy frying-pan and fry the mustard seeds until they pop and jump. Add the onion, ginger, cumin seeds and chillies and fry gently for 3 minutes, stirring constantly. Stir in the turmeric and add the cauliflower, water and salt. Bring to the boil and simmer, covered, until the cauliflower is just tender. Do not overcook. If the water dries up before the cauliflower is cooked, add a little more. The final dish should be almost dry.

Serve immediately with curries or grilled or roast meat.

Red and White Cauliflower

A good dish to add a little piquancy to roast or grilled meat, this dish has the advantage of being prepared in advance. Make a basic white sauce with 10 g/ ½ oz butter and a tablespoon of flour for the roux.

SERVES 6

- 1 medium cauliflower, divided into florets
- 250 ml/8 fl oz white sauce
- 1 quantity *Salsa de Jitomate* p. 269
- 4 tablespoons grated Gruyère or Cheddar cheese

Plunge the cauliflower florets into a large pan of boiling salted water and boil for 5 minutes, until barely tender. Drain and arrange in a shallow baking dish, the domed florets uppermost. Pour the white sauce over and then spoon the thick chilli *salsa* on top. Sprinkle with the grated cheese and bake for 15 minutes in a moderate oven, preheated to 190°C/375°F/gas 5. Serve immediately.

Fried Broccoli with Chilli and Oyster Sauce

SERVES 4–6

- 500 g/1 lb broccoli or calabrese
- 1 tablespoon oil
- ½ teaspoon finely shredded fresh ginger
- 1 clove garlic, finely chopped
- 1 fresh red chilli, deseeded and finely chopped
- 2 teaspoons oyster sauce*
- 2 teaspoons light soy sauce*
- pinch salt
- pinch sugar
- pinch ground black pepper
- 1 tablespoon water

Remove the outer leaves from the broccoli. Cut into florets with a 2.5 cm/1 in head and the same length of stem. Cut the remaining stems into slightly longer pieces. Keep the florets and stems separate.

Heat the oil in a large wok over a fairly high heat. Toss in the ginger, garlic, chilli and broccoli stems. Stir-fry for 30 seconds then reduce the heat, cover, and cook for 1 minute, stirring once during this time. Add the florets and stir-fry for 30 seconds. Add all the remaining ingredients, bring to the boil and simmer, covered, for 2 or 3 minutes until the broccoli is cooked but still crisp. Serve immediately as part of a Chinese or Western-style meal.

Courgettes Mexican Style

SERVES 4

- 2 tablespoons oil
- 1 tablespoon olive oil
- 1 medium onion, finely chopped
- 2 cloves garlic, finely chopped
- 4 tomatoes, chopped

Heat the oils in a heavy saucepan and gently fry the onion and garlic until soft but not coloured. Add all the remaining ingredients and simmer, covered, for about 30 minutes or until the courgettes are tender. Stir frequently, and check the seasoning before serving.

- 2 fresh green chillies, chopped
- 1 small sweet green pepper, deseeded and coarsely chopped
- 500 g/1 lb small courgettes, topped, tailed and cut in 1 cm/½ in slices
- 1 teaspoon finely chopped parsley or coriander
- salt and freshly ground black pepper to taste

The following recipe is suitable for either the flat green bean, which should be cut into horizontal slices, or the slim French bean, which should be cut into pieces about 4 cm/1½ in long. Other than topping and tailing, no preparation will probably be necessary, but some tropical green beans can be a little tough and may need stringing and slightly longer cooking.

Fried Green Beans

This is just about the nicest way to cook green beans that are young and tender. I always add a touch of ground turmeric – such a small amount does not affect the taste but heightens the green colour of the beans.

SERVES 3–4

- 2 tablespoons oil
- 1 small onion, finely sliced
- 1 clove garlic, finely chopped
- ½ teaspoon finely shredded fresh ginger
- 2 fresh green chillies, deseeded and finely chopped
- pinch ground turmeric
- 300 g/10 oz green beans, sliced
- salt and freshly ground black pepper to taste

Heat the oil in a large heavy frying-pan and gently fry the onion, garlic, ginger and chillies until the onion is soft but not coloured. Stir in the turmeric. Add the beans and mix well. Season with salt and pepper, cover, and cook for 5–10 minutes until the beans are just tender. Do not over-cook. Serve immediately.

Beans cooked this way can be served with Asian or Western dishes.

VARIATIONS

Add a handful of prawns (the colour contrast of green and pink is attractive) – if raw, allow 4 minutes cooking time; if cooked and frozen, allow 3 minutes cooking time; if cooked and thawed, allow 1 minute cooking time.

To accompany Latin American dishes, omit the ginger and add 1 small sweet green pepper, deseeded and cut in strips, with the beans.

Caribbean Okra and Tomato Stew

SERVES 8

- 3 tablespoons olive oil
- 500 g/1 lb small whole okra, stems removed
- 1 medium onion, finely chopped
- 2 cloves garlic, finely chopped
- 2 fresh red chillies, deseeded and finely chopped
- 1 fresh green chilli, left whole
- a 250 g/8 oz can tomatoes+3 tablespoons juice
- 1 medium sweet red or green pepper, deseeded and coarsely chopped
- 1 teaspoon salt
- ¼ teaspoon ground black pepper
- ¼ teaspoon ground allspice*
- pinch of sugar

Heat the oil in a large heavy frying-pan and fry the okra over a medium heat for 3–5 minutes until it is starting to brown. Stir constantly to prevent burning. Remove the okra from the pan and fry the onion and garlic until soft but not coloured. Add all the remaining ingredients including the okra. Bring to the boil and simmer, covered, for 10 minutes. Remove the whole green chilli before serving.

Fried Okra, Nonya Style
Baba Bindi

Nonya cooking is a mixture of Chinese and Malaysian and is found in Malaysia, Singapore and Indonesia.

SERVES 3–4

- 1 tablespoon dried prawns*
- 1 clove garlic, halved
- ½ teaspoon chopped fresh ginger
- 4 fresh red chillies, coarsely chopped
- 1 small onion, chopped
- 2 tablespoons oil
- 200 g/7 oz okra, topped, tailed and sliced diagonally
- 125 g/4 oz green beans, topped, tailed and sliced
- salt to taste

Put the dried prawns, garlic, ginger and chillies to soak in a little warm water for 10 minutes. Drain, reserving the liquid. Put the onions and the dried prawns mixture into the container of an electric blender or food processor and add enough of the soaking liquid to allow the blades to work properly. Blend to a paste.

Heat the oil in a large frying-pan and fry the paste for 3 minutes over a moderate heat, stirring constantly. Add the okra and stir-fry for 3 minutes. Add the beans and stir-fry for 1 minute. Add 1 tablespoon of water and turn the heat to low. Simmer, uncovered, for about 8 minutes. Stir occasionally and check for sticking. Season with salt and serve immediately or at room temperature.

Papas a la Huancaina

In Peru, these boiled potatoes with a cheese and chilli sauce would normally be served as a separate vegetable course but they could be offered as an accompaniment to grilled and roast meats or – with the addition of garnishes – as a complete light meal.

SERVES 4–6

- 500 g/1 lb potatoes
- 1 large onion, very finely sliced in rings
- 2 fresh red chillies, deseeded and finely shredded
- juice of 1 lemon
- ½ teaspoon sugar
- 250 g/8 oz Cheshire or Wensleydale cheese, grated
- 200 ml/7 fl oz single cream
- ½ teaspoon ground turmeric or a few drops yellow food colouring
- ½ teaspoon ground chilli
- 4 tablespoons olive oil

Boil the potatoes in salted water, either peeling them first or boiling them in their skins and peeling them when cooked. If not of a uniform size, cut them into equal chunks. Keep warm.

While the potatoes are cooking, put the onion and chillies in a bowl with the lemon juice and sugar. Set aside.

Mix the cheese, cream, turmeric or food colouring and ground chilli together. Heat the oil in a heavy saucepan and cook the cheese mixture over a low heat for about 5 minutes or until the cheese has melted and the sauce has thickened. Stir constantly.

To serve, put the cooked potatoes in a warm serving dish, pour the sauce over, and garnish with the drained onion rings and chilli shreds.

For a complete meal, serve on individual platters on a bed of lettuce with prawns, hard-boiled egg and olives.

Potatoes in Green Sauce
Patatas en Salsa Verde

SERVES 4–6

- 4 tablespoons olive oil
- 1 kg/2 lb potatoes, peeled and cut into 1.5 cm/½ in slices
- 1 medium onion, finely chopped
- 3 cloves garlic, finely chopped
- 2 fresh green chillies, deseeded and finely chopped
- 2 tablespoons finely chopped parsley
- 200 ml/7 fl oz water
- salt and freshly ground black pepper to taste

Heat the oil in a large heavy frying-pan and fry the potatoes over a medium heat for about 8 minutes until they are lightly browned but not cooked through. Add all the other ingredients, cover the pan, and simmer gently for about 10–15 minutes until the potatoes are soft and most of the liquid has been absorbed. Check occasionally for sticking and add a little more water if necessary, but do not stir as this will break up the potatoes. Gently shake the pan from time to time.

Serve from the pan or carefully transfer to a platter, using a fish slice.

Potatoes with Fenugreek

I love the combination of fenugreek, chilli and lots of garlic in this dish. Serve the potatoes fairly wet, as the sauce thickens as it cools.

SERVES 4

- 25 g/1 oz butter
- 2 tablespoons oil or 50 g/2 oz *ghee**
- 500 g/1 lb potatoes, peeled and cut into 1.5 cm/½ in cubes
- 2 teaspoons ground coriander
- 1 teaspoon ground turmeric
- ½ teaspoon ground chilli
- 1 teaspoon fenugreek seeds*
- 6 cloves garlic, finely chopped
- ½ teaspoon salt
- ¼ teaspoon ground black pepper
- 1 teaspoon chopped chives or green spring onion tops
- 1 tablespoon finely chopped parsley, coriander or mint

Heat the butter and oil or *ghee* in a large heavy frying-pan. Add the cubed potatoes and fry over a moderate heat for about 5 minutes until golden, stirring frequently. Remove the potatoes from the pan. Stir the ground coriander, turmeric, chilli, fenugreek and garlic into the oil remaining in the pan. Fry gently for 2 minutes, stirring constantly to prevent burning. Return the potatoes to the pan and mix well so that they are coated in the spice mixture. Add all the remaining ingredients, and pour in enough water to cover. Bring to the boil and simmer, covered, for about 5 minutes until the potatoes are tender and the sauce has become thick.

VARIATION

Omit the fenugreek and garlic and add 1 teaspoon of *garam masala*,* 1 bay leaf and 125 g/4 oz yoghurt (reduce the water accordingly).

Fried Potatoes with Dersa Sauce

North African style chips that are perfect with spicy *Merguez* sausages (p. 134), or indeed any sausages.

SERVES 4

- 500 g/1 lb potatoes, peeled and cut into thick chips
- oil for deep-frying
- 1 tablespoon olive oil
- 1 small onion, finely sliced
- 3 cloves garlic, finely chopped
- 1 teaspoon *harissa**
- 1 teaspoon caraway seeds
- 1 teaspoon salt
- ¼ teaspoon freshly ground black pepper

Quickly fry the potatoes in fairly hot oil until nicely golden and cooked through. Drain and set aside.

Heat the olive oil in a large heavy frying-pan and gently fry the onion and garlic until soft but not coloured. Stir in the *harissa* and caraway seeds and fry for 1 minute. Add 3 tablespoons of water, bring to the boil and simmer, uncovered, for 2 minutes. Add the potatoes and stir well so they are coated. Cook for a minute longer to evaporate all the liquid. Sprinkle with salt and black pepper and serve immediately.

Potato Croquettes with Pea Filling
Alu Chap

These fried mashed potatoes have a surprise filling of spiced peas. You can also make them with a spinach filling.

SERVES 6

- 1 kg/2 lb peeled potatoes
- 25 g/1 oz butter
- 1 medium onion, finely chopped
- 1 teaspoon finely chopped fresh ginger
- 1 fresh green chilli, deseeded and finely chopped
- ½ teaspoon ground turmeric
- ½ teaspoon ground cumin
- 1 tablespoon finely chopped parsley or coriander
- 200 g/7 oz frozen peas
- salt and ground black pepper to taste
- oil for deep-frying

Boil the potatoes in salted water until soft. Drain well and mash. Add salt and pepper, if you like, but no extra liquid or butter.

Heat the butter in a heavy frying-pan and gently fry the onion and ginger until golden. Add the chilli, turmeric and cumin and fry for 1 minute, stirring constantly. Add the chopped herbs and the peas (still frozen). Cover and simmer until the peas are tender. If necessary, add 1 tablespoon of water but allow this to evaporate at the end of cooking, by removing the lid for a minute. Season with salt and pepper.

Divide the mashed potato and pea mixture into 8 portions each. Shape each potato portion into a ball. Push a finger into the centre to make a cavity. Fill with the pea mixture and reshape the ball so that the peas are sealed in. Flatten the ball slightly and chill for 30 minutes.

Deep-fry in fairly hot oil, a few at a time, until golden. Drain on paper towels and serve as a curry accompaniment or with grilled or roast meat.

NOTE

If preferred, dip the croquettes into beaten egg and breadcrumbs before frying.

Red Chilli Potato Hash

The traditional American hash brown goes chilli red.

SERVES 4

- 3 tablespoons oil
- 4 rashers streaky bacon, diced
- 2 large potatoes, cut into 2 cm/1 in cubes
- 1 small onion, finely chopped
- 2 cloves garlic, finely chopped
- ½ teaspoon paprika
- ½ teaspoon ground chilli
- ½ teaspoon ground cumin
- 2 teaspoons finely chopped parsley or coriander leaves
- ⅛ teaspoon dried marjoram
- salt to taste

Heat 1 tablespoon of the oil in a large frying-pan and gently fry the bacon until crisp. Remove with a slotted spoon and set aside. Put the remaining oil in the pan and gently fry the potatoes until tender and lightly browned. Remove the potatoes and add the onion and garlic to pan. Fry gently until soft. Add the paprika, ground chilli and cumin and fry for 30 seconds. Return the potatoes to the pan and fry for 3 minutes, stirring constantly. Stir in the fresh herbs, marjoram and crispy bacon. Add salt to taste. Fry for 2 minutes longer and serve immediately.

Spinach with Sweet Peppers

A West African dish that combines spinach with peanut butter. Okra could be used instead of sweet peppers. For convenience, use frozen spinach.

SERVES 4

- 2 tablespoons oil
- 1 medium onion, finely sliced
- ½ teaspoon finely chopped fresh ginger
- 2 tomatoes, chopped, or 2 canned tomatoes with 1 tablespoon juice
- 1 medium sweet green pepper, deseeded and coarsely chopped
- 250 g/8 oz frozen chopped spinach
- 3 tablespoons smooth peanut butter diluted with 3 tablespoons water
- ½ teaspoon ground chilli
- salt and black pepper to taste

Heat the oil in a large heavy frying-pan and gently fry the onion and ginger until golden. Add the tomatoes and sweet green pepper. Simmer for 5 minutes, stirring frequently. Add the spinach (there is no need to thaw) and all the remaining ingredients. Simmer for 5–10 minutes until the spinach is cooked. Check for sticking and add a little extra water if necessary.

Indian Spinach
Saag

SERVES 3–4

- 50 g/2 oz butter or *ghee**
- 1 medium onion, finely sliced
- 2 teaspoons grated fresh ginger
- 2 fresh green chillies, deseeded and finely chopped
- ½ teaspoon ground turmeric
- 250 g/8 oz frozen chopped spinach
- 2 tablespoons water
- ½ teaspoon sugar
- ½ teaspoon salt
- ½ teaspoon *garam masala**
- 1 tablespoon lemon juice

Heat the butter or *ghee* in a heavy frying-pan and gently fry the onion, ginger and chillies until the onion is soft but not coloured. Stir in the turmeric, spinach, water, sugar and salt, and simmer for 5–10 minutes until the spinach is heated through and all the water has been absorbed. Stir in the *garam masala* and transfer to a warm serving dish. Sprinkle with lemon juice.

Serve with curries or grills.

Ethiopian Mixed Vegetables

This is a delicious way of dressing young boiled vegetables in a spiced butter sauce. Use a selection of vegetables, or serve small new potatoes in their skins like this.

SERVES 8

- 500 g/1 lb new potatoes in their skins or old potatoes peeled and cut in 2.5 cm/1 in cubes
- 4 carrots, peeled and sliced horizontally
- ½ cauliflower, cut into florets
- 75 g/3 oz butter
- 3 fresh green chillies, deseeded and finely chopped
- 1 large onion, finely sliced
- 1 clove garlic, finely chopped
- 1 teaspoon fresh ginger, finely shredded
- ¼ teaspoon ground turmeric
- pinch each ground nutmeg, cinnamon and cloves
- seeds from 2 cardamom pods*

Boil the potatoes, carrots and cauliflower – together or separately – in salted water until just tender. Drain.

Heat the butter in a large heavy saucepan and sweat the chillies, onion, garlic and ginger for about 5 minutes until the onion is soft but not coloured. Stir in the spices, add the cooked vegetables and mix well. Cover the pan and cook over a very low heat for a few minutes so that the vegetables heat through and are coated in the spiced butter sauce. Transfer to a warm dish and serve immediately.

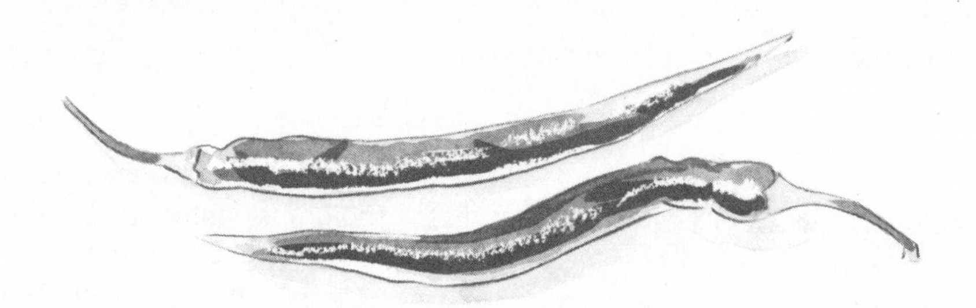

Stir-fried Mixed Vegetables

You really need a large wok in order to stir-fry this volume of vegetables successfully. Toss in a few cooked prawns and it becomes a flavoursome first course or the perfect light lunch dish.

SERVES 4

- 4 tablespoons oil
- 1 large onion, finely sliced
- 3 cloves garlic, finely chopped
- 1 teaspoon finely shredded fresh ginger
- 1 fresh red or green chilli, deseeded and finely chopped
- 1 sweet red or green (or half and half) pepper, deseeded and cut into thin strips
- ½ cucumber, unpeeled and cut into matchsticks
- 2 sticks celery, chopped
- 200 g/7 oz beansprouts, washed, picked over and well drained
- 3 spring onions (white and some green), sliced
- 1 small can bamboo shoots, drained (optional)
- 4 canned water chestnuts, drained and sliced (optional)
- 2 tablespoons light soy sauce*
- 2 tablespoons chicken stock
- ½ teaspoon salt
- ½ teaspoon sugar

Heat the oil over a fairly high heat in a large wok. Toss in the onion, garlic, ginger and chilli and stir-fry for 30 seconds. Toss in all the vegetables and stir-fry for 1 minute, mixing well so that all the vegetables come into contact with the oil but do not burn. Add the soy sauce, chicken stock, salt and sugar and continue stir-frying for 1 minute longer. Transfer to a warm dish and serve immediately as part of a multi-dish Chinese meal.

Malaysian Hot-sweet-sour Vegetables
Achar

Probably my favourite vegetable dish!

SERVES 3–4

- 5 dried red chillies, stems and seeds removed, soaked, or 2 teaspoons *sambal ulek**
- ½ medium onion, chopped
- 1 teaspoon chopped fresh ginger
- 1 teaspoon ground turmeric
- 1 tablespoon dried prawns,* soaked for 30 minutes and drained
- 2 macadamia nuts or 1 tablespoon flaked almonds
- 4 tablespoons oil
- 2 teaspoons sugar
- 1 tablespoon fresh ginger, finely shredded
- 6 cloves garlic, sliced
- 6 pickling onions, peeled and quartered
- ½ teaspoon salt
- 2 tablespoons vinegar
- 3 carrots, peeled and cut into matchsticks
- ½ large cucumber, unpeeled and cut into matchsticks
- 3 fresh red chillies, deseeded and quartered lengthwise

Drain the dried red chillies, break into pieces and put into the container of an electric blender or food processor with the next 5 ingredients and enough of the chilli soaking liquid to make the blades work properly. Blend to a paste.

Heat the oil in a large heavy frying-pan. Add the spice paste and fry for about 5 minutes until the oil separates, stirring frequently. Add the sugar, ginger, garlic and onions and fry for 2 minutes, stirring constantly. Stir in the salt and vinegar. Add the carrots and fry for 3 minutes, stirring frequently. Add the cucumber and chillies and cook for 3 minutes, stirring frequently.

Transfer to a serving dish and serve at room temperature.

The taste should be hot, sweet and sour. The vegetables should still be slightly crisp and coated in a thick, sticky sauce.

Sayor Loday

A delicious South-East Asian mixed vegetable dish with a chilli-hot coconut-milk gravy. Choose a selection of vegetables from the following: shredded white cabbage, green beans cut into 5 cm/2 in lengths, small whole okra, potato chunks, carrot chunks, aubergine chunks and quartered tomatoes (which should only be added at the last moment so that they remain intact).

Sayor Loday makes a superb buffet dish for a spicy food party, so the amounts given here will feed around 15 people, with other dishes.

- 6 shallots, chopped
- 2 cloves garlic, chopped
- 2 teaspoons *blachan**
- 3 candlenuts,* or 4 cashew nuts, or 1 tablespoon flaked almonds
- 2 teaspoons *sambal ulek** or 6 dried chillies, soaked and drained
- 1 teaspooon ground turmeric
- 1.5 litres/2½ pints coconut milk (p. 32)
- 3 tablespoons dried prawns,* ground to a powder
- 2 kg/4 lb assorted prepared vegetables (see above)
- 1 tablespoon salt
- 1 tablespoon sugar
- 3 tablespoons oil
- 1 medium onion, finely sliced
- 2 cloves garlic, finely chopped
- 1 tablespoon ground chilli
- 250 ml/8 fl oz thick coconut milk (p. 32)

Put the first 6 ingredients into the container of an electric blender or food processor. Add a few tablespoons of coconut milk and blend to a paste. Put the remaining coconut milk into a large heavy saucepan and stir in the chilli paste from the blender. Bring to the boil, stirring constantly to prevent curdling. Add the prawn powder, vegetables, salt and sugar. Continue stirring until the coconut milk comes back to the boil. Simmer, uncovered, for about 30 minutes until all the vegetables are tender.

Meanwhile, heat the oil in a heavy frying-pan and gently fry the onion and garlic until golden. Add the ground chilli and fry for 1 minute, stirring constantly. Pour in the thick coconut milk and bring to the boil, stirring constantly. Remove from the heat as soon as it comes to the boil.

When the vegetables are ready, remove the pan from the heat and stir in the fried chilli mixture. Continue stirring for about 2 minutes and serve.

NOTE
Fresh beansprouts can also be added for the last few minutes cooking time, but they will go soft if this is a buffet dish which is going to stand for any length of time.

A South Indian dish of mixed vegetables with yoghurt
Avial

SERVES 4–6

- 750 g/1½ lb mixed vegetables (all cut to approximately the same size – potato, green beans, cabbage, carrots, okra, aubergines, tomatoes
- 5 fresh green chillies, deseeded and halved lengthwise
- pinch of turmeric
- salt to taste
- 6 tablespoons desiccated coconut
- 300 ml/½ pint yoghurt

Put the vegetables and chillies in a large heavy saucepan with the minimum amount of water needed to boil them without sticking. Add the turmeric and salt. Cover and cook over a moderate heat until the vegetables are tender. Check frequently for burning. If any water remains when the vegetables are ready, simmer uncovered for a few minutes to encourage evaporation.

Take the pan off the heat and allow to cool slightly. Mix the coconut and yoghurt together and stir into the vegetables, a little at a time. Return to the heat and bring back to the boil, stirring constantly. Check the seasoning and serve immediately.

Pulses

Pulses are the seeds of leguminous plants – peas and beans – whose fruits are borne in pods. Strictly speaking, the term can apply to both fresh and dried seeds but, in practice, it is the dried seeds that are generally known as pulses. In some countries the words pea and bean are interchangeable, but lentils are always dried seeds that have been de-husked and split. Because pulses are rich in protein, supply valuable vitamins and are a useful source of fibre, they provide essential nutritional elements to simple peasant diets the world over – diets that consist of little other than pulses, a staple cereal and only occasional fish, meat or poultry.

Most pulses need soaking prior to cooking in order to restore the moisture lost during the drying process and thus cut down on cooking time. For whole seeds an 8-hour soak is normally adequate, though really hard seeds such as chickpeas or large broad beans benefit from longer. Yellow or green split peas need 1 hour but smaller lentils (including most of the Indian lentils) can be used after a brief 10-minute soak, or without any soaking at all. A good washing and picking over to remove stones and grit are, however, advisable. During soaking, pulses will swell to approximately double their original size. If time is short and extended soaking is really not possible, try the following method: soak for 15 minutes, bring to the boil and leave to stand in the hot water for 1 hour.

Some recipes state that pulses may need their skins removing either after soaking or after cooking, but that does not apply to any of the recipes included here.

Actual cooking time varies with the different types of pulses. Pulses also harden with age and will, therefore, demand longer cooking. Allow up to 4 hours for chickpeas and broad beans, up to 2 hours for other whole seeds, and up to 1 hour for split peas and lentils.

Slow simmering is preferable to vigorous boiling and if additional water is needed during cooking, try to use hot or boiling water as fluctuations in temperature can cause the pulses to toughen. Never add salt during the early cooking stages – especially with whole seeds – as this, too, can cause the pulses to toughen.

The dishes included in this section are all simple pulse recipes that are seasoned with chillies. Other recipes including pulses appear in the chapters on *hors d'oeuvre*, fish, meat, poultry and rice. Recipes combining pulses with other vegetables also appear earlier in this chapter.

Mexican Beans
Frijoles

With chillies, maize and tomatoes, beans have been a mainstay of the Mexican diet for thousands of years. They are still as essential today as they ever were and are invariably served with every meal. If you enjoy Mexican food, you will need plenty of beans, so – as they take so long to prepare – cook in bulk and freeze them.

SERVES 6

- 500 g/1 lb red, black or pinto beans, soaked overnight
- 4 cloves garlic, whole
- 1 bay leaf
- 3 fresh green chillies, whole
- 2 teaspoons salt
- 1 teaspoon sugar
- 2 tablespoons lard or oil
- 1 medium onion, finely chopped
- ½ teaspoon ground black pepper

Drain the beans and put them in a large heavy saucepan with 2 of the garlic cloves, the bay leaf and 1 chilli. Add enough water to cover by 2.5 cm/1 in and boil, covered, for about 2 hours or until very soft and tender. Check frequently and add more water (preferably hot) if the beans are drying out. Towards the end of the cooking time, stop adding extra water so that finally there are 2 or 3 teacups of liquid remaining. Remove the bay leaf and the whole chilli. Stir in the salt and sugar.

Finely chop the remaining 2 cloves garlic and 2 chillies. Heat the lard or oil in a heavy frying-pan and gently fry the onion, garlic and chillies until golden. Add 3 tablespoons of beans and 3 tablespoons of the cooking liquid. Heat through, mashing to a thick purée at the same time. Stir this purée into the pot of beans. Add black pepper and more salt if necessary. Simmer for 1 or 2 minutes and serve.

Refried Beans
Frijoles Refritos

Of all the ways of presenting *frijoles* in Mexico, this is probably the most usual – beans cooked according to the previous recipe are then mashed and fried to form a thick paste. Subsequent re-fryings are considered to improve the flavour even more. *Frijoles Refritos* are quite dry and become drier as they cool. They are widely used as a spread on *tortillas*, but as an accompaniment to main dishes they can be stodgy. It is, therefore, no accident that many Mexican meat and fish dishes are of a wet stew consistency. It is also no accident that fiery hot chilli sauces are served with *Frijoles Refritos* – they are perfect partners.

There are no hard and fast rules on the ratio of the frying medium – lard or oil – to beans. It is a matter of personal taste – more lard or oil will give a richer blend, more beans will result in a drier mix.

As a start, heat 3 tablespoons of lard or oil in a large heavy frying-pan. Add about 3 teacups of cooked beans and cook over a gentle heat, mashing with a fork or potato masher. Add more beans and keep mashing until a smooth purée is produced. For a creamier mixture, add more oil or lard or a little water. For a drier mix, keep cooking and stirring.

To refry refried beans, repeat this method but add a little water to the beans before frying, in order to soften them.

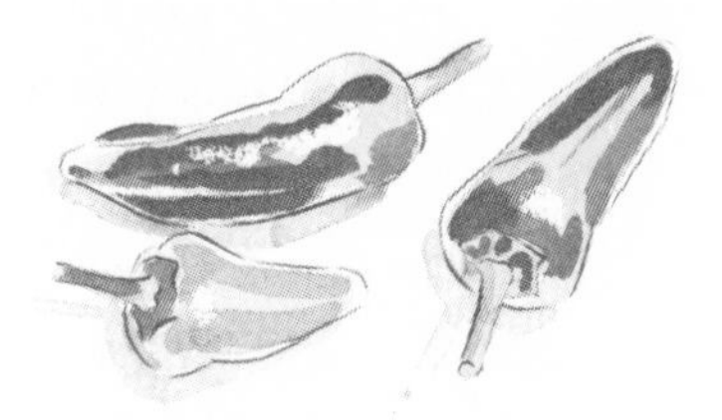

Cowpoke Beans

SERVES 6

- 500 g/1 lb dried pinto beans, soaked overnight
- 2 fresh or dried red chillies
- 1 ham or fresh pork hock
- 1 bay leaf
- 50 g/2 oz lard or butter
- 1 large onion, finely chopped
- 3 cloves garlic, finely chopped
- 2 tomatoes, chopped
- 1 teaspoon ground chilli
- 1 teaspoon paprika
- 1 teaspoon ground cumin
- ½ teaspoon dried oregano
- ½ teaspoon dried basil
- 2 tablespoons finely chopped parsley or coriander
- salt and ground black pepper to taste
- 125 ml/4 fl oz beer

Drain the beans and put in a large heavy saucepan with the chillies, ham hock and bay leaf. Pour in water to cover and simmer for about 2 hours until tender. Drain. Discard hock, chillies and bay leaf.

Rinse out the saucepan. Heat the lard and fry the onions and garlic gently until golden. Add all the remaining ingredients. Bring to the boil, add the beans and simmer for 30 minutes.

Cuban Black Beans

SERVES 4–6

- 250 g/8 oz black beans, soaked for at least 8 hours
- 4 tablespoons oil
- 1 medium onion, finely sliced
- 2 cloves garlic, finely chopped
- 1 fresh chilli, deseeded and finely chopped
- 1 small sweet pepper, deseeded and finely chopped
- ¼ teaspoon ground cumin
- 2 teaspoons finely chopped parsley or coriander
- 1 bay leaf
- salt and freshly ground black pepper to taste
- 1 teaspoon sugar
- 1 teaspoon cornflour, mixed with 1 tablespoon vinegar

Drain the beans and boil in 600 ml/1 pint of water without salt for 1–2 hours until tender. Drain and reserve the liquid.

Heat the oil in a large heavy saucepan and gently fry the onion and garlic until soft but not coloured. Add the chilli, sweet pepper and cumin. Cook for 1 minute, then add the drained beans and 200 ml/7 fl oz of their cooking liquid. Add the chopped herbs, bay leaf, salt and pepper. Bring to the boil and simmer, covered, for 15 minutes. Add the sugar and cornflour, stirring constantly until the sauce has thickened. Simmer for 1 minute longer and serve hot.

Red Bean Pepper Pot

SERVES 4

- 250 g/8 oz red kidney beans, soaked overnight
- 2 tablespoons oil
- 2 medium onions, finely sliced
- 4 cloves garlic, finely chopped
- 1 tablespoon paprika
- 1 large sweet red pepper, deseeded and chopped
- 6 fresh red chillies, deseeded and chopped
- a 750 g/1½ lb can tomatoes
- ½ teaspoon salt
- ¼ teaspoon ground black pepper
- ¼ teaspoon ground allspice
- 2 bay leaves

Drain the kidney beans and boil in plenty of *unsalted* water for 1 hour. Drain.

Heat the oil in a heavy frying-pan and gently fry the onions and garlic until golden. Stir in the paprika.

Combine all the ingredients in a large oven-proof casserole and bake for 1½ hours in an oven pre-heated to 170°C/325°F/gas 3. Taste before serving and add more salt if necessary.

Dahl

Stewed lentils are an essential part of the Indian diet, especially for India's many vegetarians. This is a very basic and simple recipe, which can be sloppy or thick, depending on preference and the other dishes being served. I like it best fairly runny, particularly as it tends to thicken as it cools. Though slightly irregular, I also like to eat *dahl* as a side dish from a small bowl, rather than on the same plate as the rest of the meal.

Dahl can be made with any lentils. Most Indian lentils do not need extended soaking, neither do the small red European lentils. Other types may require longer soaking.

SERVES 4

- 175 g/6 oz lentils
- 2 tablespoons oil or *ghee**
- 1 teaspoon black mustard seeds*
- 1 medium onion, sliced
- 2 cloves garlic, chopped
- 1 teaspoon finely chopped fresh ginger
- 1 teaspoon *garam masala**
- ½ teaspoon ground turmeric
- 600 ml/1 pint water
- 1 teaspoon salt
- 2 fresh green chillies, deseeded and sliced vertically

Rinse the lentils in a colander and then leave to soak while frying the other vegetables.

Heat oil or *ghee* in a heavy saucepan. Add the mustard seeds and fry until they begin to pop and jump. Add the onion, garlic and ginger and fry gently until golden. Add the *garam masala* and turmeric and fry gently for 1 minute. Drain the lentils and stir into the spices. Add the remaining ingredients, bring to the boil, and simmer, covered, until the lentils are soft.

For a thick *dahl*, the lentils should be cooked until almost all the liquid has evaporated so that a purée is left. A thinner *dahl* can be almost like a soup, with plenty of liquid and each lentil more or less intact. Adjust the amount of water and the cooking time accordingly.

NOTE

A garnish of fried onions is excellent with *dahl*. For this, double the amount of onion and fry until brown but not burnt. Reserve half and scatter over the *dahl* before serving.

Indian Chickpeas
Channa Dahl

Make this with canned chickpeas and tomatoes for convenience.

SERVES 6

- 1 tablespoon oil, butter or *ghee**
- 1 medium onion, finely chopped
- 1 tablespoon finely chopped fresh ginger
- 3 cloves garlic, finely chopped
- 1 fresh green chilli, deseeded and finely chopped
- a 200 g/7 oz can tomatoes, mashed with juice
- 5 cm/2 in cinnamon stick
- 1½ teaspoons *garam masala**
- ½ teaspoon salt
- a 500 g/1 lb can cooked chickpeas, drained
- 2 tablespoons finely chopped parsley or coriander leaves

Heat the oil, butter or *ghee* in a large heavy saucepan and fry the onion, ginger and garlic until golden. Add the chilli, tomatoes, cinnamon, *garam masala* and salt and bring to the boil. Add the chickpeas and parsley or coriander. Mix well and simmer for 10 minutes.

East African Beans in Coconut Milk

SERVES 4

- 250 g/8 oz red kidney beans, soaked overnight
- 2 tablespoons oil
- 2 medium onions, finely sliced
- 3 cloves garlic, finely chopped
- 4 fresh red or green chillies, deseeded and finely chopped
- 1 teaspoon ground turmeric
- ½ teaspoon ground cumin
- ⅛ teaspoon ground black pepper
- 3 tomatoes, chopped
- 500 ml/17 fl oz coconut milk (p. 32)
- 1 teaspoon salt

Drain the beans and boil in plenty of *unsalted* water until tender. Drain.

Heat the oil in a heavy saucepan and gently fry the onions, garlic and chillies for 5 minutes. Stir in the turmeric and cumin and fry for 30 seconds. Add all the remaining ingredients and the beans. Bring to the boil, stirring constantly to prevent the coconut milk curdling. Simmer, uncovered, for about 15 minutes until the sauce has thickened.

Falafel

Made of chickpeas and/or dried broad beans, these spicy fried rissoles appear all over the Middle East, though they are believed to have originated in Egypt where the Christian Copts ate them during Lent when meat was forbidden. Today they are sold in little take-away shops on every street corner. For easy snack eating, they can be stuffed into *pitta* bread and garnished with salad. They are also often served as part of the *mezzeh* table; try them with *Hummus* (p. 48) used as a dip and, of course, warm *pitta* bread.

MAKES ABOUT 3 DOZEN

- 500 g/1 lb chickpeas, soaked overnight
- 1 medium onion, chopped
- 2 cloves garlic, chopped
- 1 egg, beaten
- ¼ teaspoon ground black pepper
- ½ teaspoon ground turmeric
- ½ teaspoon ground cumin
- ½ teaspoon ground chilli
- ½ teaspoon salt
- 2 tablespoons chopped parsley or coriander leaves
- fresh white breadcrumbs
- oil for deep-frying

Drain the chickpeas and boil in plenty of *unsalted* water until tender. This could take up to 4 hours. Alternatively, use drained canned chickpeas.

Put the drained chickpeas into the container of an electric blender or food processor (in two or more batches if necessary) with all the other ingredients except the breadcrumbs and oil. Blend to a paste. If additional liquid is needed to allow the blades to work properly, add a little olive oil or water. Transfer to a bowl and mix in enough breadcrumbs to give a firm consistency – the actual amount will depend upon how much liquid was added. Shape into 2.5 cm/1 in balls and deep-fry – a few at a time – in medium-hot oil for about 3 minutes until golden. Drain on paper towels and eat hot.

NOTE

Tamia are similar to *falafel* but can be made from dried broad beans (skinned) or a mixture of broad beans and chickpeas.

Burmese Split Pea Balls

- 250 g/8 oz split green or yellow peas, soaked overnight
- 1 medium onion, chopped
- ½ teaspoon ground chilli
- ½ teaspoon ground turmeric
- ½ teaspoon salt
- oil for deep-frying

Drain the split peas and boil for 30 minutes in fresh water. Drain, then use a pestle and mortar to pound the peas, onion, chilli, turmeric and salt to a stiff paste. Shape into walnut-size balls and flatten slightly to form small patties. Deep-fry in medium-hot oil for about 3 minutes until golden. Drain on paper towels.

Serve with curries, or on cocktail sticks with a dipping sauce as an appetizer with drinks.

Salads

A salad has an essential role to play in a chilli meal. It acts as a foil. Cool and light, it balances the aggressive pungency of highly spiced food by cleansing the palate and sharpening the taste buds. Crisp and crunchy, it complements the softer textures of main dish ingredients such as fish, eggs, poultry and braised meats.

A salad has visual importance, too. With a wide range of colourful vegetables to choose from, the clever cook can paint a table-top picture with salads that are pale and delicate, brash and bright, or fresh and clean. For example, cucumber in yoghurt provides a creamy contrast to a fiery red chilli sauce, in both looks and taste. A multi-hued riot of Mexican peppers, avocados and tomatoes brightens up bland and beige *tacos, tortillas* and mushy refried beans. Crisp green lettuce can add sparkle to a basically brown dish of meat and gravy.

The following salads make perfect partners for chilli-hot main dishes.

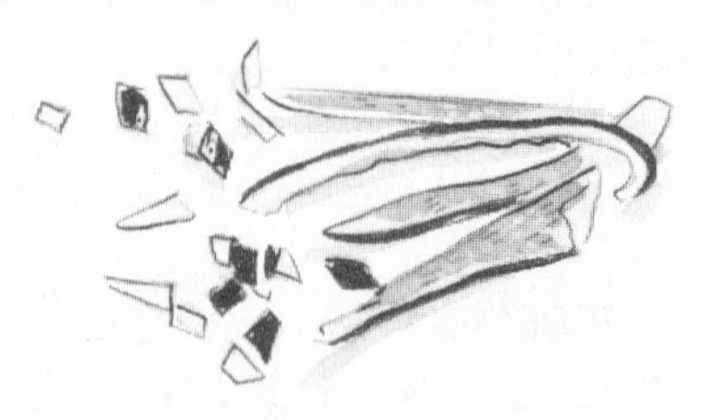

Moroccan Carrot Salad

A brilliant Moroccan carrot combination, with carrots that are under-cooked and crisp and a paprika-red and parsley-green dressing.

SERVES 4–6

- 500 g/1 lb carrots, peeled and sliced in rounds
- 1½ teaspoons salt
- 6 cloves garlic, chopped
- 1 teaspoon ground cumin
- ½ teaspoon *harissa**
- 1 tablespoon paprika
- 4 tablespoons oil
- 3 tablespoons finely chopped parsley
- 2 tablespoons lemon juice

Boil the carrots in enough water to cover, with 1 teaspoon of the salt, for a bare 10 minutes until tender but still crisp. Allow them to cool in their liquid.

In a mortar, pound the garlic, cumin, *harissa* and paprika with the remaining ½ teaspoon of salt. Heat the oil in a frying-pan and gently fry the paste for 1 minute. Add 250 ml/8 fl oz of the carrot cooking liquid and bring to the boil, stirring constantly. Remove from the heat.

Drain the remaining liquid from the carrots. Pour the spice dressing over the drained carrots. Add the parsley and lemon juice. Toss gently and chill.

Will keep for 3 or 4 days, covered with aluminium foil in the fridge.

Carrot Pachadi

One of South India's many imaginative and original vegetarian side dishes. Serve it with curries or as part of a Western-style salad.

SERVES 4–6

- 3 medium carrots, grated
- 1 small onion, grated or very finely chopped
- 1 fresh red chilli, deseeded and finely chopped
- ½ teaspoon salt or more to taste
- 1 tablespoon oil
- 2 teaspoons black mustard seeds*
- 3 tablespoons desiccated coconut
- 150 ml/¼ pint yoghurt

Mix the carrots, onion, chilli and salt together and set aside.

Heat the oil in a heavy frying-pan and fry the mustard seeds until they pop and jump. Take the pan off the heat and allow them to cool for a minute. Add the desiccated coconut and return the pan to a low heat. Fry the coconut, stirring constantly, until golden. Watch it all the time, as it burns very easily. Add the carrot mixture, then turn off the heat, leaving the pan on the stove for 1 minute.

Transfer to a bowl and cool for 5 minutes. Stir in the yoghurt and check the salt seasoning.

Caribbean Cucumber Salad

SERVES 4–6

- 1 large cucumber
- 1 teaspoon salt
- 1 tablespoon lemon or lime juice
- 1 clove garlic, very finely chopped
- 1 fresh red or green chilli, deseeded and finely chopped
- few grindings of black pepper
- pinch ground allspice*

Top and tail the cucumber. Peel and cut in quarters lengthwise. Scoop out the seeds and chop the cucumber into small chunks. Sprinkle with salt and leave for 30 minutes, then rinse, drain and dry on paper towels. Mix with all the other ingredients and chill for 30 minutes before serving.

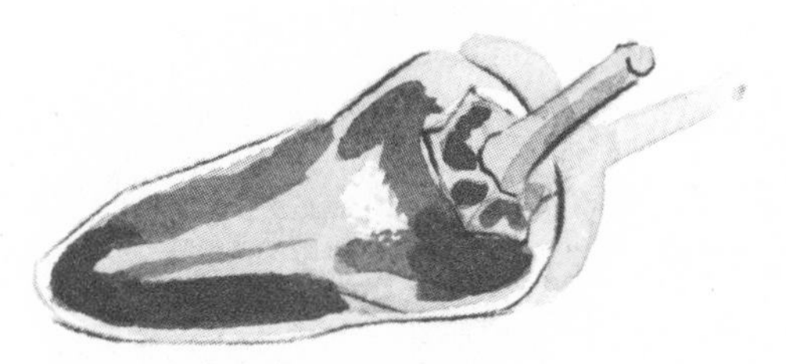

Thai Cucumber Salad

SERVES 4–6

- 2 tablespoons dried prawns*
- 2 medium cucumbers, peeled and diced
- 1 small onion, very finely chopped
- 2 fresh red chillies, deseeded and finely chopped
- 2 tablespoons fish sauce*
- 1 tablespoon lemon juice
- ½ teaspoon sugar

Grind the dried prawns to a powder in an electric coffee grinder. Mix all the ingredients together and chill for 10 minutes before serving.

Beetroot Salad

SERVES 4–6

- 500 g/1 lb cooked beetroots, peeled and thinly sliced horizontally
- 1 tablespoon olive oil
- 4 tablespoons red wine vinegar
- ½ teaspoon sugar
- ½ teaspoon cayenne pepper
- ¼ teaspoon salt
- 3 tablespoons finely chopped onion
- 1 clove garlic, finely chopped
- 1 tablespoon finely chopped parsley or coriander
- a few thinly cut onion rings for garnish
- red chilli flowers (p. 223) for garnish

Put the beetroot in a bowl. Make a dressing with the oil, vinegar, sugar, cayenne pepper, salt, onion and garlic. Pour over the beetroot and leave to marinate for at least 1 hour. Stir in the chopped herbs just before serving, and arrange on a shallow dish or platter. Garnish with onion rings and chilli flowers.

Yemeni Tomato Salad

SERVES 4–6

- 4 tomatoes, peeled and cut into segments
- ground chilli to taste
- 3 tablespoons finely chopped coriander leaves
- 3 tablespoons olive oil
- 1 tablespoon lemon juice
- salt

Sprinkle the tomatoes with the ground chilli and coriander leaves. Make a dressing with the olive oil, lemon juice and salt. Pour over and allow to stand for 30 minutes before serving.

Tunisian Grilled Tomato and Pepper Salad
Meshwia

Grilling the tomatoes and sweet peppers in order to loosen their skins gives the vegetables an unmistakable smoky flavour that combines beautifully with chilli.

SERVES 4

- 2 large sweet red or green peppers
- 5 tomatoes
- ½ teaspoon ground chilli
- ½ teaspoon salt
- ¼ teaspoon ground black pepper
- 2 tablespoons finely chopped onion
- 2 cloves garlic, finely chopped
- 2 tablespoons lemon juice
- 1 tablespoon finely chopped parsley
- 2 tablespoons olive oil
- black olives for garnish

Roast the peppers and tomatoes in a very hot oven, or place under a hot grill, for about 15 minutes until the skins are black and charred. Turn frequently. Plunge immediately into cold water to loosen the skins, and peel off all the skin that comes away easily. Chop the flesh fairly finely and mix with the remaining ingredients except the black olives, which are used as a garnish.

The salad can be puréed in a blender or food processor, but I prefer it chopped.

Serve at room temperature with grilled or roast meats, or with flat bread as a starter or as part of the *mezzeh* table.

Green Pepper Salad

SERVES 4–6

- 2 medium sweet green peppers, deseeded and coarsely chopped
- 1 cucumber, peeled and diced
- 2 sticks celery, coarsely chopped
- 1 small onion, finely sliced
- 1 fresh red chilli, deseeded and finely chopped
- salt and black pepper to taste
- $\frac{1}{4}$ teaspoon sugar
- 1 tablespoon lemon juice

Put the first 5 ingredients in a bowl and season with salt and pepper. Dissolve the sugar in the lemon juice and pour over. Chill for 15 minutes, then toss and serve.

Red Pepper Salad

SERVES 4–6

- 2 medium sweet red peppers, deseeded and coarsely chopped
- 2 tomatoes, diced
- 1 cucumber, peeled and diced
- 1 small onion, finely sliced
- 1 fresh green chilli, deseeded and finely chopped
- 1 tablespoon finely chopped mint, parsley or coriander
- salt and pepper to taste
- 1 tablespoon lemon juice

Put the first 6 ingredients in a bowl and season to taste. Pour on the lemon juice. Chill for 15 minutes, then toss and serve.

Gado Gado Salad

An Indonesian salad of cooked and raw vegetables, served with a chilli peanut sauce.

SERVES 4–6

Prepare a selection of cool cooked and raw vegetables from the following:

potatoes, boiled and sliced
sliced green beans, boiled in salt water until barely tender, then rinsed in cold water
shredded white cabbage, blanched
fresh beansprouts, blanched
onion rings
spring onions, sliced vertically
tomatoes, cut into wedges
cucumber, cut into chunks

Arrange in individual portions on crisp lettuce leaves and garnish with:

hard-boiled eggs, sliced
shredded omelette, made by pouring a thin layer of beaten egg into an oiled omelette pan and cooking until firm then cutting into thin ribbons
pineapple chunks, fresh or tinned
watercress
krupuk (prawn crackers)

Serve with a separate bowl of Gado Gado sauce (p. 276).

Nam Prik Salad

The Thais love fresh, crispy salads pepped up by a pungent *Nam Prik* sauce (p. 264). I like to serve individual bowls of salad with individual side dishes of the sauce and roughly torn mint leaves. If you are unsure that your guests can cope with *Nam Prik*, you could serve some curry-flavoured mayonnaise as well.

SERVES 4–6

Choose salad ingredients from the following:
- blanched beansprouts
- lightly cooked green beans
- sliced radishes
- shredded cabbage
- diced cucumber
- watercress
- carrot matchsticks
- celery chunks
- sweet pepper strips
- tinned bamboo shoots
- tomato wedges
- pineapple wedges

Chinese Pickled Salad

SERVES 4–6

- 1 cucumber
- 3 sticks celery
- ¼ white cabbage
- 2 teaspoons salt
- 1 tablespoon vinegar
- 1 tablespoon light soy sauce*
- 2 tablespoons sesame oil*
- ½ teaspoon sugar
- 1 fresh red chilli, deseeded and very finely chopped
- 2 cloves garlic, very finely chopped

Peel the cucumber and cut off the ends. Cut in quarters length-wise and then into 1.5 cm/½ in pieces. Cut the celery into 1.5 cm/½ in slices horizontally. Remove the core of the cabbage then shred the leaves finely. Put the vegetables in a bowl, sprinkle with salt and leave for 3 hours, then rinse and drain well.

Mix the remaining ingredients together to make a dressing. Pour over the vegetables and mix well. Refrigerate for 3 hours, stirring occasionally.

This salad looks attractive served on a bed of crisp lettuce, and you could sprinkle it with toasted sesame seeds, if liked. It makes an excellent accompaniment to Sichuan dishes.

Melon and Watercress Salad with Salsa Roja

A crazy mixture . . . but unbelievably good!

SERVES 2–3

- 1 medium-sized, ripe melon
- 1 small bunch watercress
- 1 tablespoon oil
- 1 tablespoon lemon juice
- salt and pepper to taste

FOR THE SALSA ROJA (RED SAUCE)

- 2 medium tomatoes, chopped
- 1 small sweet red pepper, deseeded and chopped
- 1 small onion, chopped
- 1 clove garlic, chopped
- ½ teaspoon dried oregano
- 1 tablespoon lemon juice
- chillies to taste (preferably *serranos*)
- salt

Use a melon scoop to make melon flesh into balls or cut in 2.5 cm/1 in cubes. Take the leaves off the watercress, discarding any tough stems. Mix the melon and watercress together in a glass bowl (to show off the colours to best advantage). Make a vinaigrette of oil and lemon juice. Season to taste and pour over the salad. Chill for at least 30 minutes and serve with a bowl of *salsa roja*.

To make the *salsa roja*, put all the ingredients into the container of an electric blender or food processor and blend to a purée. If additional liquid is required, use a little extra lemon juice or, if tinned chillies are used, some of the chilli juice. For some tastes, a touch of sugar may be needed.

NOTE

Salsa roja is very light and refreshing. It makes an excellent accompaniment to most vegetables and salads. It is especially successful with avocado slices, pineapple cubes, lightly cooked cauliflower florets and blanched tender green beans. It is also an ideal contrast to creamy mayonnaise. Try serving a bowl of each with a salad of mixed cooked vegetables, tossed in vinaigrette.

Cactus Leaf Salad
Ensalada de Nopalitos

Fresh cactus leaves in a vinaigrette dressing make one of Mexico's favourite salads. It was discovered some years ago that cactus leaves are particularly high in nutrients. In Mexico, where they are cheap and plentiful, the fleshy leaves are blanched or quickly grilled before being cut into bite-sized pieces and dressed. Canned cactus leaves are a reasonable substitute and have a delicious juicy freshness that is an excellent contrast to chilli tastes. Either prepare the salad without chillies or add finely chopped green chillies (preferably *jalapeños* or *serranos*) to taste. Either way, this is a very pretty salad – a multi-coloured mosaic of red, green and white.

- a 300 g/10 oz tin chopped *nopalitos* (cactus leaves), rinsed and drained
- 2 medium tomatoes, coarsely chopped
- 1 small onion, finely chopped
- 1 tablespoon finely chopped coriander leaves
- 3 tablespoons oil
- 1 tablespoon vinegar
- salt and pepper to taste
- 1 tablespoon lemon juice

Put the first 4 ingredients into a serving bowl and gently mix together. Make a dressing of oil, vinegar, salt and pepper. Pour over the salad and chill for at least 30 minutes. Just before serving, add the lemon juice and carefully turn the salad so that the dressing is evenly distributed.

VARIATION
Serve the salad on a platter on a bed of shredded lettuce. Slice the tomatoes and arrange on the lettuce. Scatter the chopped cactus leaves on top and sprinkle with a little finely chopped oregano. Slice the onion in very fine rings and arrange on the salad with about 75 g/3 oz crumbly white cheese such as feta. Pour on vinaigrette dressing and chill.

Sophie's Mexican Salad

. . . as created by my step-daughter after three months in Mexico. It is a riot of colour with an interesting contrast of textures. Make it as hot as you like!

- 1 large sweet red pepper
- 1 large sweet green pepper
- a 400 g/13 oz tin red kidney beans, rinsed and drained
- a 400 g/13 oz tin sweetcorn, rinsed and drained
- finely chopped chillies (preferably *jalapeños*) to taste
- 1 small onion, cut in fine rings
- 50 g/2 oz olives, either black or pimento stuffed, or mixed

FOR THE VINAIGRETTE DRESSING

- 6 tablespoons olive oil
- 1 tablespoon red wine vinegar
- 1 tablespoon lemon juice
- ½ teaspoon mild French mustard
- 1 clove garlic, finely chopped
- salt and freshly ground black pepper to taste

Remove stem, pithy core and seeds from peppers. Cut flesh into narrow strips. Mix with all other salad ingredients in a large bowl.

Make dressing and pour over. Serve with a bowl of *Salsa Cruda* (p. 268).

VARIATION
To make a main course, add cubed boiled potatoes, chopped celery and quartered hard-boiled eggs.

RICE

Rice is one of the oldest grains known to man and is the natural accompaniment to chilli cooking in many parts of the world. Even in countries where other cereals provide the main staple food, rice is invariably eaten as well.

For people who eat rice every day of their lives – and that is more than half the world's population – its preparation is of almost ritual importance, but what is regarded as perfect rice varies considerably. Should it be long, medium or short grain? Dry and fluffy? Soft and moist? Sticky and glutinous? Is it best brown and nutty or polished and pearly? No one type of rice can possibly satisfy the demands of every national cuisine, but probably the most universally acceptable is plain boiled white long grain rice. Yet this is something that European cooks have traditionally found frustratingly difficult to prepare. It is, in fact, very easy and straightforward to cook if the absorption method is used.

How much rice to allow per person?

For non-habitual rice-eaters, 1 teacup (approx 175 g/6 oz) of dry rice will be ample for 2–3 people. In rice-eating countries, however, rice is consumed in enormous quantities by that standard. Most Asians, for example, will happily eat twice that amount at one sitting, accompanied by a relatively small portion of meat. This is not necessarily a result of poverty or food shortage. They simply enjoy their rice so much that they eat a lot of it . . . without drowning it with too much richer food.

To wash or not to wash?

Rice that has been specially treated to be non-stick needs no washing. Other rice should be rinsed to remove dust and dirt and also to wash out some of the surface starch. However, many cooks believe that excessive washing takes out valuable minerals. Put the grains in a fine sieve or wicker basket and run under fresh water for a few seconds. Allow to drain before transferring to the cooking pot.

If the rice is going to be fried before the cooking liquid is added – for Indian *pilaus* and *birianis*, for example – allow at least 1 hour after washing so that it dries out completely before cooking and is able to absorb the frying medium.

How much water?
Allow double the amount of water for the first cupful of rice, and 1½ times the amount for all subsequent cups. Therefore –

1 cup rice – 2 cups water
2 cups rice – 3½ cups water
3 cups rice – 5 cups water

Add a pinch of salt (or more to taste) for each cup of rice and be sure that the cooking pot has a good heavy bottom and is large enough for the rice to double in volume.

How long to cook?
Having added the correct amount of water, the aim is for this liquid to be totally absorbed by the rice so that at the moment when the rice becomes tender, it is also dry. To achieve this, bring the rice to the boil over a high heat, stirring once or twice to prevent sticking. When boiling, lower the heat slightly to produce a steady rolling boil. Cover and cook for 15 minutes, by which time the water should have been absorbed and there will be crater-like holes on the surface. Take the pan off the heat but do *not* stir. Leave the pan covered and undisturbed for 10 minutes, then fluff up the rice with a fork before serving either directly from the cooking pot or from a pre-warmed dish.

Rice Cookers
For anyone who cooks rice regularly – and that is most committed chilli cooks – the acquisition of an electric rice cooker is worth serious consideration. Apart from guaranteeing infallible boiled rice every time, the rice cooker has two other enormous advantages. First, it requires absolutely no attention once it has been filled and switched on because it automatically turns itself off when the rice is cooked. Secondly, when it turns off, it then switches to 'keep' so that the rice stays warm and in perfect condition for up to 3 hours.

Rice cookers are available in various sizes, ranging from something suitable for 2 or 3 people to those of banquet proportions. I have two – one for family meals and one for parties. They are composed of an outer container that houses an electric element in the bottom; an inner pan that holds the rice and liquid; a lid; and a lead similar to that on an electric kettle. The element heats up the contents of the pan to boiling point and maintains that heat until the rice is cooked and all the liquid has been absorbed. Depending on size, this will take from about 20 minutes to over 1 hour, at which time the cooker automatically switches to 'keep'.

A rice cooker is great, too, for heating up left-over rice. Just add a minimal amount of water to prevent sticking, and switch on. I also use mine for many of the composite rice dishes that appear on the following pages.

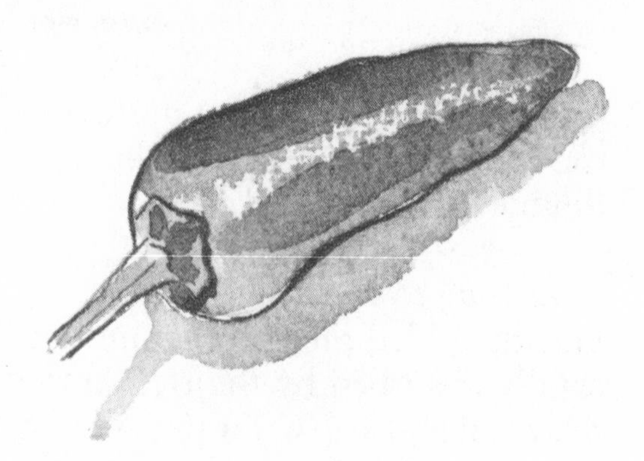

Simple Rice Recipes to Accompany Chilli Dishes

Sweet Yellow Rice

Although the idea of sweet rice with chilli dishes may sound strange at first, it can be surprisingly good, especially with very hot curries. It also makes an excellent accompaniment to non-spiced dishes which are traditionally served with fruit, such as duck and goose.

SERVES 4–5

- good pinch of saffron threads or powdered saffron*
- 2 tablespoons warm water
- 50 g/2 oz butter or *ghee**
- 250 g/8 oz long grain rice
- 2.5 cm/1 in cinnamon stick
- 3 cardamom pods,* bruised
- 500 ml/17 fl oz water
- ½ teaspoon salt
- 50 g/2 oz sugar
- dash of yellow food colouring
- 1 tablespoon raisins or sultanas
- 1 tablespoon slivered almonds, lightly fried in butter

Soak the saffron in warm water for at least 10 minutes.

Heat the butter or *ghee* in a large heavy pan and fry the rice very gently for 2 minutes. Stir constantly and do not allow the rice to colour. Add all the other ingredients except the almonds. Stir in the saffron and its soaking liquid, bring to the boil, and simmer, covered, for 20 minutes. Turn off the heat and allow the rice to stand for 10 minutes. Stir in the almonds and serve.

Muhammar

This sweet rice is a speciality of the island of Bahrain in the Persian Gulf. It was traditionally eaten by the island's pearl divers, who needed to maintain high sugar levels in their bodies in order to survive long periods underwater. They descended rapidly to a depth of 40 metres (130 feet) and were able to remain there for an incredible length of time without the aid of any breathing equipment. The best divers could stay down for 10–15 minutes, during which time they grabbed every oyster in sight. Today's divers use scuba gear but the Bahrainis still enjoy *Muhammar*. It is delicious with roast and grilled lamb dishes and with fish.

SERVES 6–8

- 2 tablespoons rose water*
- good pinch of saffron threads or powdered saffron*
- seeds from 4 cardamom pods*
- 50 g/2 oz butter or *ghee**
- 375 g/12 oz long grain rice, preferably Basmati
- 800 ml/27 fl oz water
- 1 teaspoon salt
- 75 ml/3 fl oz runny honey

Put the rose water, saffron and cardamom seeds in a cup and set aside.

Heat the butter or *ghee* in a large heavy saucepan and fry the rice gently for 2 minutes. Stir constantly, and do not allow the rice to colour. Add the remaining ingredients, bring to the boil, and simmer for 25 minutes. Turn off the heat. Sprinkle the rose water mixture over the rice, replace the lid, and allow to stand for 10 minutes. Fluff up the rice and serve.

Mexican White Rice
Arroz Blanco

SERVES 6–8

- 2 tablespoons oil
- 1 tablespoon butter
- 375 g/12 oz long grain rice
- 800 ml/27 fl oz water
- ½ teaspoon salt
- 1 chicken stock cube
- 2 tablespoons finely chopped onion
- 1 whole fresh green chilli
- 1 clove garlic
- 1 spring parsley or coriander

(the last three tied together in a muslin bag)

Heat the oil and butter in a large heavy saucepan. Fry the rice gently for 3 minutes, stirring constantly. Do not allow to brown. Add all the other ingredients. Bring to the boil and simmer, covered, for 25 minutes, then turn off the heat and allow rice to stand for 10 minutes. Discard the bag of seasonings. Fluff up the rice and serve.

VARIATION

Omit the bag of seasonings. Fry the onion in oil and butter together with a chopped garlic clove and ½ a sweet red or green pepper, finely chopped.

Tomato Rice

This red rice is found in various forms all over Latin America.

SERVES 6–8
2 tablespoons oil
1 tablespoon lard
1 small onion, finely chopped
2 cloves garlic, finely chopped
375 g/12 oz long grain rice
800 ml/27 fl oz water
6 tablespoons tomato purée
1 chicken stock cube
2 whole fresh green chillies
½ teaspoon salt

Heat the oil and lard in a large heavy saucepan and fry the onion and garlic until soft. Add the rice and fry for 3 minutes, stirring constantly. Do not allow to brown. Add all the remaining ingredients and proceed as for *Arroz Blanco* (p. 217). Remove the whole chillies before serving.

Green Rice

Arroz Verde

In Mexico, *poblano* peppers are used for *Arroz Verde* but they are not available in Europe. I use a mixture of sweet green peppers and fresh green chillies. Traditionally the *poblano* peppers are charred and peeled, but this is not necessary if using sweet peppers.

SERVES 6–8
4 *poblano* chillies, charred and peeled, or 3 sweet green peppers and 2 fresh green chillies
2 tablespoons chopped parsley
2 tablespoons finely chopped onion
2 cloves garlic, finely chopped
800 ml/27 fl oz chicken stock or water+stock cube
2 tablespoons oil
1 tablespoon olive oil
375 g/12 oz long grain rice
½ teaspoon salt
freshly ground black pepper to taste

Deseed the peppers, and remove the stems and inner ribs. Chop them coarsely and put them into the container of an electric blender or food processor with the parsley, onion and garlic. Add enough stock to allow the blades to work properly and blend to a paste. This will probably have to be done in two or three batches.

Heat the oils in a large heavy frying-pan and gently fry the rice for 3 minutes, stirring constantly so that each grain is coated in oil. Do not allow to colour. Add the chilli paste and fry for 4 minutes, stirring constantly. Add the remaining stock, salt and black pepper. Bring to the boil and simmer, covered, for 20 minutes. Turn off the heat and allow to stand for 10 minutes. Fluff up before serving.

Rice with Dates

Versions of Rice and Dates are found throughout the Arab countries from the Gulf across the Middle East to North Africa. This one is beautifully fragrant with aromatic spices and orange blossom water.

SERVES 6

- 75 g/3 oz butter or *ghee**
- 350 g/11 oz long grain rice
- 850 ml/28 fl oz water
- 1 teaspoon salt
- 75 g/3 oz stoned dates, chopped
- 2 tablespoons flaked almonds, gently fried in butter
- 3 tablespoons raisins
- generous pinch each of ground cinnamon, cloves and cardamom*
- 1 teaspoon orange blossom water*

Heat the butter or *ghee* in a large heavy saucepan and gently fry the rice for about 4 minutes until it is starting to turn golden (this is a different technique to the other rice dishes mentioned here, where the rice should *not* colour). Add the water and salt, bring to the boil, and simmer, covered, for 20 minutes. Stir in the remaining ingredients, using a fork. Replace the lid and leave rice to stand for 15 minutes before serving.

Pilau

An Indian rice dish that is a favourite all over Asia. For *very* special occasions, top with *vark* (edible silver paper).

SERVES 6–8

- good pinch of saffron threads or powdered saffron*
- 2 tablespoons warm water
- 75 g/3 oz butter or *ghee**
- 1 medium onion, finely chopped
- 1 clove garlic, finely chopped
- ½ teaspoon chopped fresh ginger
- 4 cm/1½ in cinnamon stick
- 4 cardamom pods,* bruised
- 4 cloves
- 375 g/12 oz Basmati rice
- 800 ml/27 fl oz chicken stock, or water+stock cube
- 1 teaspoon salt
- 2 tablespoons raisins or sultanas
- 2 tablespoons flaked almonds, fried in butter until pale brown

Soak the saffron in the warm water for at least 10 minutes.

Heat the butter or *ghee* in a large heavy saucepan and gently fry the onions, garlic and ginger for about 3 minutes, until soft but not coloured. Add the cinnamon, cardamoms and cloves and fry for 30 seconds. Add the rice and fry for 3 minutes, stirring constantly so that each grain is coated. Do not allow to brown. Add the stock, salt, raisins and the saffron with its soaking liquid. Bring to the boil and simmer, covered, for 20 minutes. Turn off the heat and allow rice to stand for 10 minutes. Serve garnished with almonds.

Pilau is especially good with lamb dishes.

Rice with Peas
Mattar Pilau

Proceed as for the above recipe but omit the saffron, raisins and almonds. Add 375 g/12 oz of raw shelled peas with the stock.

Mushroom Pilau

Proceed as for the *Pilau* recipe on p. 220 but omit the saffron, raisins and almonds. With the stock, add 175 g/6 oz of sliced button mushrooms that have been lightly fried in butter, and ½ teaspoon *garam masala.**

Pilaff

The Near and Middle Eastern version of *Pilau* invariably includes nuts and dried fruits. Chicken stock is a good simmering liquid for general use, but if accompanying meat, use a light meat stock or water and a beef stock cube.

SERVES 6–8

- good pinch of saffron threads or powdered saffron*
- 2 teaspoons warm water
- 2 tablespooons olive oil
- 1 medium onion, finely chopped
- 375 g/12 oz long grain rice
- 800 ml/27 fl oz stock (see above)
- 1 teaspoon salt
- 3 generous tablespoons pine nuts
- 2 generous tablespoons raisins or sultanas
- 2 tablespoons finely chopped parsley

Soak the saffron in warm water for at least 10 minutes.

Heat the olive oil in a large heavy saucepan and gently fry the onion until just turning golden. Add the rice and cook for 3 minutes, stirring constantly. Do not allow to colour. Add the stock, salt and the saffron with its soaking liquid. Bring to the boil and simmer, covered, for 20 minutes. Stir in the nuts, dried fruit and parsley. Replace the lid and allow the rice to stand for 10 minutes.

Rice and Peas

Almost every Caribbean island has its own Rice and Peas dish – which can, in fact, be made with red kidney beans (locally called peas), pigeon peas, black-eyed peas or black beans.

SERVES 8

- 250 g/8 oz red kidney beans, soaked overnight
- 1 clove garlic, finely chopped

Drain the beans. Put them in a large saucepan with fresh water to cover by about 5 cm/2 in. Bring to the boil and simmer, covered, until tender. This can take anything from 45 minutes

- 1 spring thyme or ¼ teaspoon dried thyme
- 2 spring onions, finely chopped
- 375 g/12 oz long grain rice
- salt and black pepper

to over 2 hours, depending on the age of the beans. Check from time to time and add more water if too dry. Add all the remaining ingredients, and pour in extra water to cover the beans and rice by 2.5 cm/1 in. Bring to the boil and simmer, covered, for about 20 minutes until the rice is tender and all the liquid has been absorbed. Stir before serving to ensure that the beans are evenly dispersed.

Chilli Dishes with Left-over Rice

In countries where rice is an essential part of the daily diet, cooks have devised all kinds of delicious ways of dealing with the inevitable left-over rice. Many of these dishes are so popular that it is a good idea to cook more rice than is needed for main meals. Additional ingredients are flexible but often include chillies and other local seasonings.

I usually allow approximately 1–1½ generous teacups of cooked rice per person. For dishes that are to be fried, you will need a big frying-pan or wok that allows enough room to stir and turn the ingredients comfortably.

Arroz Poblano

In this Mexican dish, left-over rice is baked with peppers, cheese and cream. Authentically one of the milder *poblano* chilli peppers would be used, but as these are not easily available outside Mexico, a mixture of sweet peppers and chilli peppers is a perfectly good substitute.

SERVES 6

- 6 cups cold boiled rice or *Arroz Blanco* (p. 217)
- 125 ml/4 fl oz sour cream thinned with a little milk
- 1 large sweet pepper, deseeded and shredded (or 1 small red pepper and 1 small green pepper)
- 2 fresh chilli (red or green) peppers, deseeded and finely sliced
- 75 g/3 oz grated Cheddar cheese
- 25 g/1 oz butter

Put about a quarter of the rice in the bottom of a fairly deep ovenproof dish. Cover with a quarter of the cream, then the peppers, then the cheese. Repeat, ending with a layer of cheese. Dot with butter and bake for about 30 minutes in a preheated oven at 180°C/350°F/gas 4. Serve immediately.

Nasi Goreng

This well-known fried rice dish is popular in Indonesia, Malaysia and Singapore. It almost always includes prawns (frozen ones are ideal) and sometimes pork, although not for Muslims, who may add a little tender beef.

SERVES 4–6

- 2 eggs, beaten
- 4 tablespoons oil
- 1 medium onion or 6 shallots, finely chopped
- 2 cloves garlic, finely chopped
- 2–4 fresh red chillies, deseeded and finely chopped, or 1–2 teaspoons *sambal ulek**
- 6 cups cold boiled rice, stirred with a fork to break up lumps
- 2 tablespoons light soy sauce*
- 4 spring onions, finely sliced
- 250 g/8 oz ready-cooked frozen prawns

Use the beaten eggs to make 3 or 4 paper-thin omelettes. Use a little of the oil to grease the pan. Roll the omelettes up and cut them into narrow strips horizontally. Set aside.

Heat the remaining oil in a large heavy frying-pan or wok and fry the onion and garlic over a gentle heat for about 5 minutes, until just turning golden. Add the chillies or *sambal ulek* and fry for 1 minute. Add the rice and turn up the heat slightly. Add the soy sauce and cook for 5 minutes, stirring and turning the rice frequently. Stir in the spring onions, prawns and shredded omelette.

Serve on a large heated platter with side dishes of soy sauce, *Sambal Blachan* (p. 262) or Chilli and Ginger Sambal (p. 264).

VARIATIONS

Nasi Goreng is often served with the shredded omelette laid in a criss-cross pattern on top of the rice, rather than stirred in. Alternatively, a fried egg can be served on top. As extra garnishes, add a handful of seedless raisins or Crispy Fried Onions (p. 260) just before serving. If beef or pork are being included, cut them into small dice and fry with the onions.

Chinese Fried Rice
Chow Fan

SERVES 4

- 3 tablespoons oil
- 1 medium onion, finely chopped
- 1 clove garlic, finely chopped
- ½ teaspoon finely chopped fresh ginger
- 1 stick celery, finely chopped
- 2 fresh red chillies, deseeded and finely chopped
- 250 g/8 oz of the following, or a selection: cooked, diced chicken, diced cooked ham, sliced Chinese sausage, diced red barbecued pork (*char siu*), raw or cooked prawns
- 2 dried black Chinese mushrooms, soaked in warm water for 30 minutes and shredded
- 2 eggs } beaten together
- 2 teaspoons soy sauce } beaten together
- 5 cups cold boiled rice, stirred with a fork to break up lumps
- 3 tablespoons cold cooked peas (optional)
- 4 spring onions, finely chopped
- 4 fresh red chillies to garnish

Heat the oil in a large frying-pan or wok and fry the onion, garlic, ginger, celery and chillies over a gentle heat for 5 minutes, stirring constantly. Add the meats, raw prawns (cooked prawns should be added just before serving) and shredded mushrooms, and fry for 1 minute. Turn up the heat to medium, add the beaten eggs and soy sauce and cook for a few seconds, stirring vigorously, until the egg sets. Add the rice and cook over a medium heat for 2 minutes, stirring constantly. Stir in the cooked peas and half the spring onions and cook for 30 seconds. Garnish with the remaining spring onions and red chilli flowers (see below).

Serve with additional soy sauce.

TO MAKE RED CHILLI FLOWERS

Leave the stem on fresh chillies and carefully cut 4 or 5 vertical slits from the pointed end to within about 2 cm/1 in of the stem end. Put in a bowl of iced water and leave in the fridge for 30 minutes, during which time the vertical strips will curl up to form petals.

Chinese Vegetarian Fried Rice
Chai Chow Fan

SERVES 4

- 3 tablespoons oil
- 1 tablespoon sesame oil
- 1 tablespoon finely chopped fresh ginger
- 4 cloves garlic, finely chopped
- 3 fresh green chillies, deseeded and finely chopped
- 2 leeks (white part and 5 cm/2 in green), finely sliced
- 4 sticks celery, finely chopped
- 4 tender young carrots, peeled and finely chopped
- 10 dried Chinese mushrooms, soaked in warm water for 30 minutes and shredded
- 200 g/7 oz green beans, cut into 2.5 cm/1 in lengths
- 1 small tin bamboo shoots, drained
- 125 g/4 oz beansprouts, washed and picked over
- 10 spring onions, finely sliced
- 5 cups cold boiled rice
- 3 tablespoons light soy sauce*
- chilli oil*

Heat the two oils in a large frying-pan or wok. Add the ginger, garlic, chillies, leeks, celery, carrots, mushrooms, and green beans. Stir-fry over a high heat for 3 minutes. Add the bamboo shoots, beansprouts and spring onions and stir-fry for 30 seconds. Lower the heat slowly, add the rice and soy sauce, and stir constantly until heated through. Sprinkle with chilli oil.

Serve with additional soy sauce and chilli and ginger sauce (p. 274).

Thai Chilli Fried Rice

SERVES 4

- 3 fresh red chillies, chopped
- 1 clove garlic, chopped
- ½ teaspoon chopped lemon rind
- ½ teaspoon ground coriander
- ¼ teaspoon ground cumin
- ¼ teaspoon ground turmeric
- ½ teaspoon paprika

Put the first 10 ingredients into the container of an electric blender or food processor. Add enough of the oil to allow the blades to work properly, and blend to a paste.

Put the remaining oil in a large frying-pan or wok, and fry the onion for about 5 minutes until golden. Add the chilli paste and fry for a further 5 minutes, stirring constantly to prevent sticking. Add a little more oil if necessary. Add the pork

¼ teaspoon salt
1 teaspoon chopped coriander or parsley leaves
1 teaspoon water
4 tablespoons oil
1 large onion, finely chopped
125 g/4 oz lean pork, diced
250 g/8 oz shelled prawns (frozen ones are all right)
2 eggs, beaten with a little salt
5 cups cold boiled rice
3 tablespoons fish sauce*
5 spring onions, sliced
finely chopped coriander leaves and chilli flowers (p. 223) to garnish

and prawns and fry for 3 minutes. Turn up the heat, add the beaten eggs and stir vigorously for 1 minute. Add the rice and stir until it is heated through and all the ingredients are well mixed. Turn off the heat and stir in the fish sauce and spring onions.

Garnish with chopped coriander leaves and chilli flowers (p. 223). Serve with extra fish sauce.

Main Meal Rice and Chilli Dishes

Birianis are acknowledged as the ultimate masterpieces of North Indian cuisine. In olden days in the court kitchens of the maharajas, the *biriani* chef was considered to have reached the zenith of his art.

Birianis are the traditional festive dish – a subtle blend of rice, meats and spices. They are time-consuming to prepare, involving three separate processes – making a meat and spice sauce, pre-cooking the spiced rice, and the final assembly and baking. However, as most of the preparation can be done in advance, this makes an ideal dish for entertaining.

Chicken Biriani

This is my favourite recipe. It is very aromatic with fragrant spices and has a lovely perfume from the rose water. For special occasions I use boned chicken breasts, cut into about 3 pieces. They should be removed from the sauce after about 5 minutes simmering, or else they can become over-cooked and dry.

SERVES 6

FOR THE CHICKEN AND SAUCE

a 1.5 kg/3 lb chicken, cut into about 12 pieces and skinned
2 tablespoons oil
3 tablespoons butter or *ghee**
1 large onion, finely chopped
4 cloves garlic, finely chopped
2 teaspoons finely chopped fresh ginger
1 teaspoon ground coriander
1 teaspoon ground cumin
½ teaspoon ground turmeric
¼ teaspoon ground black pepper
1½ teaspoons ground chilli
3 tomatoes, chopped
125 ml/4 fl oz yoghurt
4 tablespoons water
2 tablespoons finely chopped mint or coriander or both
1 teaspoon salt
2.5 cm/1 in cinnamon stick } ground together
6 cardamoms* } ground together
6 cloves } ground together

Dry the chicken pieces on kitchen paper. Heat the oil in a large heavy pan and gently fry the chicken pieces a few at a time until golden. Transfer to a bowl as each batch is cooked.

Add the butter or *ghee* to the remaining oil and gently fry the onion, garlic and ginger for about 5 minutes until golden. Add the ground coriander, cumin, turmeric, black pepper and chilli and fry for 3 minutes, stirring to prevent sticking. If too dry, add a little more butter, *ghee* or oil. Add the tomatoes and cook for 1 minute. Remove the pan from the heat and add the yoghurt a little at a time, stirring constantly to prevent curdling. Return to the heat and add the water, chopped herbs and salt. Return the chicken to the pan, bring to the boil and simmer covered for about 30 minutes until the chicken is just tender (it will be baked again before serving) and the sauce has reduced. Stir in the ground spices.

NOTE

If boneless chicken is being used, add only 1 tablespoon of water and simmer the sauce for 15 minutes.

FOR THE RICE

2 tablespoons oil
2 tablespoons butter or *ghee**
1 medium onion, finely chopped
2 cloves garlic, finely chopped
1 teaspoon finely chopped ginger
400 g/13 oz Basmati rice, washed and drained 1 hour in advance
2 tablespoons rose water*
chicken stock cube (optional)
1 teaspoon salt

Heat the oil and butter or *ghee* in a large heavy saucepan and fry the onion, garlic and ginger for 5 minutes until just turning golden. Add the rice and stir well so that each grain is coated in oil. Stir in the rose water and add enough water to cover the rice by 2 cm/¾ in, dissolving the stock cube in the water if using. Add the salt, bring to the boil, and simmer covered for about 12 minutes until rice is barely tender but the liquid has been absorbed.

TO ASSEMBLE

- 2 tablespoons flaked almonds that have been gently fried in butter
- 2 tablespoons raisins
- good pinch of saffron threads or powdered saffron*
- 125 ml/4 fl oz milk with a dash of yellow food colouring
- 25 g/1 oz butter

Spread alternate layers of rice and chicken mixture in a large greased casserole. Distribute the almonds and raisins among the layers. The top layer should be rice.

Dissolve the saffron threads or powder in the milk, with a dash of yellow food colouring for additional colour. Dribble over the rice so that it soaks through to give a streaky effect (this is much nicer than a uniform yellow). Dot with butter and bake for 30 minutes in a slow oven 150°C/300°F/gas 2.

Serve from the casserole or on a large ceremonial platter. It can be garnished with segments of hard-boiled egg, tomato wedges and cucumber slices. I usually serve this *biriani* with sweet mango chutney and a salad.

VARIATIONS

Lamb Biriani is best made with tender lean meat cut into 2 cm/¾ in chunks. Proceed as for the chicken recipe, but it may be necessary to add extra liquid to the sauce to allow for a longer cooking time. The sauce should still reduce to a thick gravy. With lamb, I also add a few potatoes. Peel about 4 medium potatoes and cut into chunks about the same size as the lamb. Fry in oil or butter to brown and cook with the rice. Make sure the potatoes are not too floury a variety or they will disintegrate.

For a large party dish, make one chicken mixture, one lamb mixture and assemble together with a double quantity of rice . . . you will need a very big casserole, though!

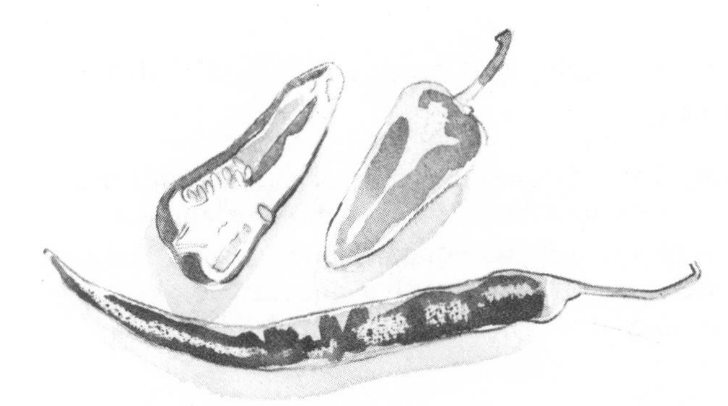

Rice and Duck
Arroz con Pato

An unusual combination of ingredients in this popular Peruvian dish produces a delicious and distinctive taste.

SERVES 4

- 1 teaspoon oil
- 4 duck portions
- 1 medium onion, finely chopped
- 4 cloves garlic, finely chopped
- 2 fresh green chillies, deseeded and finely chopped
- ½ teaspoon coriander
- ½ teaspoon ground cumin
- 1 chicken stock cube
- ¾ teaspoon salt
- ¼ teaspoon ground black pepper
- 1 bay leaf
- 250 g/8 oz long grain rice
- 1 medium sweet green pepper, deseeded and chopped
- 2 tablespoons finely chopped parsley or coriander leaves
- 1 teaspoon finely grated orange peel
- 300 ml/½ pint brown ale

Heat the oil in a large heavy saucepan and gently fry the duck portions for about 10 minutes until they have shed some of their fat and are nicely browned all over. Remove from the pan and pour off all but 2 tablespoons of the fat. Add the onion and garlic to the fat remaining in the pan and gently fry until golden. Stir in the chillies, ground coriander and cumin. Return the duck to the pan and add enough water barely to cover. Crumble in the stock cube. Add the salt, pepper and bay leaf. Bring to the boil and simmer, covered, for 40 minutes. Drain off the liquid and reserve.

Add the rice, sweet green pepper, parsley or coriander leaves and orange peel to the duck. Add enough cooking stock to the brown ale to make it up to 600 ml/1 pint. If there is insufficient stock, add water. Add this liquid to the pan and bring to the boil. Simmer, covered, for about 15 minutes until the rice and duck are tender and all the liquid has been absorbed. Allow to stand for 10 minutes before serving.

Serve with *Pebre* (p. 271) and salad.

VARIATION

Use chicken instead of duck (with 1 tablespoon of oil for frying in place of the 1 teaspoon specified here). Substitute lager or white wine for the brown ale.

Machbous

This is a popular dish in the Gulf States, where the prawns are absolutely superb – big, flavoursome and plentiful.

SERVES 4

- 1 kg/2 lb raw prawns
- 3 tablespoons butter or *ghee**
- 3 cloves garlic, finely chopped
- 1 large onion, finely chopped

Shell and devein the prawns. Heat half the butter or *ghee* in a large heavy saucepan and fry the prawns over a moderate heat for about 30 seconds until they stiffen and turn pink. They should not be cooked through. Remove the

- 3 teaspoons *baharat**
- 1 teaspoon ground turmeric
- ½ teaspoon ground chilli
- ½ teaspoon paprika
- 1 small can tomatoes (about 200 g/7 oz)
- 1 teaspoon salt
- 1 tablespoon finely chopped parsley or coriander
- 400 g/13 oz long grain rice
- 600 ml/1 pint water
- freshly ground black pepper

prawns and set aside. Add the remaining butter or *ghee* and gently fry the garlic and onion until just turning golden. Add the *baharat*, ground turmeric, ground chilli and paprika. Fry for 1 minute, stirring constantly to prevent burning. Add all the remaining ingredients except the black pepper. Bring to the boil, cover the pan, and simmer very gently for 20 minutes. Stir in the black pepper and prawns. Cover and cook very gently for 5 minutes. Turn off the heat and allow to stand for a further 5 minutes.

Serve with *pitta* bread and a salad.

Riz au Poisson à la Tunisienne

In typical North African fashion, this rice and fish dish is highly spiced with *harissa*. Serve extra *harissa*, thinned with a little water, with the meal. Any fish fillets or cutlets or sardines could be used.

SERVES 4

- 750 g/1½ lb fish fillets or steaks
- 5 tablespoons oil
- 3 tablespoons finely chopped onion
- 2 cloves garlic, finely chopped
- 1 tablespoon tomato purée
- 1 teaspoon *harissa*,* mixed with 1 tablespoon water
- salt and black pepper to taste
- 300 g/10 oz long grain rice
- 25 g/1 oz butter

Dry the fish on kitchen paper. Heat the oil in a large pan big enough to take the fish in a single layer. Add the fish and fry until nicely browned on all sides. Remove from the pan. Add the onion and garlic to the remaining oil and fry gently until golden. Stir in the tomato purée and *harissa*. Return the fish to the pan and add enough water just to cover the fish. Season with salt and black pepper. Cover and simmer for about 8 minutes until the fish is cooked. Remove the fish from the pan and keep warm.

Measure the liquid remaining in the pan and make up to 750 ml/1¼ pints with water. Return to the pan with the rice. Bring to the boil and simmer, covered, for about 20 minutes until the rice is tender and the liquid has been absorbed. Stir in the butter and pile the rice on to a warm serving dish with the fish on top.

Serve with lemon slices, or a cucumber salad made as follows: peel and thinly slice a cucumber and soak it in salt water for 10 minutes. Drain thoroughly. Mix with 2 tablespoons of finely chopped mint, parsley or coriander, salt, black pepper and 125 ml/4 oz single cream.

Jollof Rice

Jollof rice is a West African version of *Pilau*. It is an anything-goes sort of dish which includes a selection of vegetables with chilli, tomato purée and rice. It can also include a variety of meats and/or chicken and/or shellfish.

SERVES 6–8

- 1 large chicken or chicken portions (about 2 kg/4 lb), skinned and cut into pieces
- 8 tablespoons oil
- 2 large onions, finely chopped
- 3 cloves garlic, chopped
- 3 sweet red and/or green peppers, deseeded and coarsely chopped
- about 500 g/1 lb prepared vegetables cut into chunks: choose from carrots, celery, green beans, cauliflower florets, aubergines, courgettes, shelled peas and sweetcorn
- 4 tomatoes, chopped
- 2 teaspoons ground chilli
- 1 teaspoon dried thyme
- 1½ teaspoons salt
- ½ teaspoon ground black pepper
- 500 g/1 lb long grain rice
- 3 tablespoons tomato purée
- 250 g/8 oz ready-cooked prawns

Dry the chicken on kitchen paper. Heat the oil in a heavy pan large enough to hold all the ingredients and fry the chicken, a few pieces at a time, until golden. Remove all the chicken pieces and add the onions, garlic and sweet peppers. Fry over a moderate heat for 5 minutes, stirring frequently. Add the vegetables and cook for 3 minutes, stirring constantly. (Peas and sweetcorn need less cooking so can be added for the last 30 seconds only.) Add the tomatoes, ground chilli, thyme, salt, pepper and rice. Stir gently and add enough water to cover by 2 cm/¾ in. Stir in the tomato purée and return the chicken pieces to the pan. Bring to the boil, cover, and simmer for 10 minutes. Remove the lid and stir carefully. Replace the lid and simmer for a further 10 minutes. Take the pan off the heat. Stir in the prawns and allow to stand for 5 minutes.

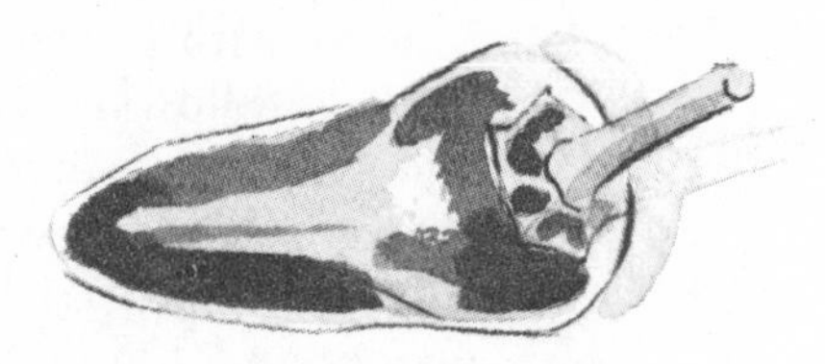

Caribbean Shrimp and Rice

SERVES 3

- 1 rasher streaky bacon, diced
- 2 tablespoons oil
- 3 tablespoons finely chopped onion
- 2 cloves garlic, finely chopped
- 750 g/1½ lb prawns, peeled (weight before peeling, but see note below)
- 1 sweet red pepper, diced
- 1 fresh green chilli, diced
- 1 tomato, chopped
- ⅛ teaspoon dried marjoram
- 300 g/10 oz long grain rice
- 375 ml/13 fl oz water
- 2 tablespoons white wine
- salt and pepper to taste
- few dashes Tabasco or other hot pepper sauce* (optional)

Put the bacon in a large heavy saucepan with a little of the oil and fry until starting to crisp. Add the remaining oil, and the onion and garlic. Fry gently until soft. Add the prawns and fry for 30 seconds. Add the remaining ingredients, bring to the boil and simmer covered for 20 minutes or until the rice is tender and the liquid has been absorbed.

Serve with an all-green salad made from lettuce leaves, sliced spring onions, cucumber and avocado slices in a dressing of oil and lemon juice. Remember not to prepare the avocado until the last minute, as it turns black if exposed to the air for too long. Offer a dish of hot chilli sauce, from the selection on pp. 226–8.

NOTE

I usually make this with ready-cooked frozen prawns. Just add 200 g/7 oz prawns (still frozen) for the final 5 minutes cooking time.

VARIATIONS

There are many versions of this dish among the West Indian islands. Crabmeat – fresh, canned or frozen – can be substituted for prawns; try using thyme instead of marjoram; add some finely chopped chives or parsley for extra flavour and colour; 2 teaspoons of fresh lemon or lime juice can be stirred in just before serving; some people like to sprinkle a little parmesan cheese and/or crumbled crisp fried bacon on top.

COUSCOUS, NOODLES AND TORTILLAS

Couscous is the staple cereal of the North African countries and is served at most meals, although rice and – to a lesser extent – noodles are also popular.

A type of semolina or dried granulated flour, *couscous* is commonly sold as fine or medium grains (I would recommend using medium) and is traditionally cooked by steaming. This is done in a *couscousier* – a double pan, the lower part of which contains a liquid that can simply be seasoned water or may be a soupy stew. A perforated steamer containing the *couscous* grains fits on top. The water or stew is brought to boiling point and then reduced to a gentle simmer which steams the *couscous* above, imparting flavour to the grains during cooking.

Confusingly, the term *couscous* can refer to the grains alone (which might accompany, for example, a *tajine*) or it can equally refer to a complete dish i.e. *couscous* grains *and* the stew cooked with them in the *couscousier*.

In either case, the grains need to be dampened before steaming, which is a rather tedious and time-consuming affair. Increasingly, therefore, modern cooks prefer to use specially treated fast-cooking *couscous* grains. These are easily available and can be prepared without a *couscousier*. Purists may feel they are inferior to traditional grains but they are today widely accepted and I have to admit that I always use them. The following recipes, therefore, are intended for these fast-cooking grains. Instructions are given on the pack but they may only be in French and Arabic. This is the method that I use.

Measure out the amount of grains needed, allowing 1 teacup per person. Put in a heavy-bottomed saucepan large enough for the *couscous* to double in volume. Add an equal volume of hot water and a little salt. Place over a very low heat and cook for 5 minutes, stirring constantly. The grains will then be tender but may be a bit clogged (perfectly cooked *couscous* should be light and fluffy, with every grain separate). I find that 10 minutes steaming in addition to this initial cooking makes them just right. To do this, transfer the *couscous* to a colander lined with a dampened napkin. Place the colander over a pan no more than a quarter full of simmering water and steam, covered, for up to 10 minutes. Stir in 1 tablespoon of butter or *ghee* for every 250 g/8 oz *couscous* before serving. Ground spices may also be added at this time. For the above quantity, try ¼ teaspoon of ground chilli and/or ¼ teaspoon of ground coriander and/or ¼ teaspoon of ground cinnamon.

Whichever method of preparation is used, presentation is always the same.

The *couscous* grains are piled up like a volcano with a crater in the top, in a large shallow serving dish. If solid chunks of meat, fish or vegetables are part of the meal, these are arranged in the crater with a little of their gravy ladled on, too. Any remaining gravy is served separately in a bowl. *Harissa* (the indispensable North African chilli condiment) is always at hand so that everyone can adjust the chilli seasoning to personal taste. Extra *harissa* may also be added to the gravy just before serving.

The stew that accompanies *couscous* grains usually has an abundance of rather thin gravy. This is because the grains tend to soak up liquid, even after they have absorbed water during cooking. Do not be alarmed, therefore, if the two dishes below seem to be floating in sauce – that's the way they are intended to be and it is quite normal to keep ladling on extra sauce during the meal.

The *couscous* grains also seem to have the effect of diminishing accompanying seasonings. For this reason, North African dishes are often very highly spiced with what may appear to be excessive amounts of the fragrant spices and paprika, as well as chilli. When tasting the following dishes, therefore, they could seem to be over-seasoned. They aren't. When blended on the plate with the *couscous* grains, the flavourings become less dominant.

Party Couscous

This special *couscous* makes an easy and exotic party dish that can be prepared in advance. If a few more vegetables are added, the chicken and lamb can be stretched to serve even more people.

SERVES 8–10

- 6 tablespoons oil
- 1 kg/2 lb boneless lamb, cut into 2.5 cm/1 in chunks
- 4 litres/6½ pints water
- 3 large onions, finely sliced
- 2 tablespoons *harissa**
- 2 tablespoons paprika
- generous pinch of saffron threads or 2 mini-tubs ground saffron*
- 2 tablespoons ground coriander
- 2 teaspoons ground black pepper
- 2 teaspoons ground ginger
- ½ teaspoon ground nutmeg
- 2 large cinnamon sticks
- 4 tablespoons finely chopped coriander or parsley leaves
- 1 tablespoon salt
- 4 tablespoons tomato purée
- a 1.5 kg/3 lb chicken, cut into serving pieces
- 8 carrots, peeled and cut into chunks
- 4 medium potatoes, peeled and quartered
- 6 courgettes, topped, tailed and cut into chunks
- two 400 g/13 oz cans chickpeas
- 750 g/1½ lb *couscous* grains prepared on p. 234 with 1 teaspoon each ground cinnamon and cumin and 125 g/4 oz raisins added

Heat the oil in a very large pan and fry the lamb until nicely browned. Pour off the oil and reserve. Add the water, onions, *harissa*, paprika, saffron, ground coriander, black pepper, ginger, nutmeg, cinnamon, parsley or coriander leaves, salt and tomato purée. Bring to the boil and simmer, covered, for 40 minutes.

Meanwhile heat the reserved oil in another pan and gently fry the chicken pieces until golden. Add to the main pan and continue simmering for 20 minutes. Add the carrots and continue simmering for 10 minutes. Add all the remaining vegetables and cook for 15 minutes.

Serve with *couscous* as described on p. 235.

Vegetarian Couscous

SERVES 4–6

- 2 litres/3½ pints water
- 3 medium onions, finely sliced
- 3 cloves garlic, finely chopped
- 1 tablespoon tomato purée
- 2 teaspoons *harissa**
- 2 whole fresh red or green chillies
- 2 tablespoons *ras-el-hanout** or curry powder
- 1 tablespoon paprika
- ½ teaspoon ground black pepper
- 2 teaspoons salt
- 2 bay leaves
- 2 tablespoons finely chopped parsley or coriander leaves
- 3 carrots, peeled and cut into chunks
- 2 turnips, peeled and cut into chunks
- 1 large aubergine, topped, tailed and cut into chunks
- 4 medium potatoes, peeled and quartered
- ¼ cabbage, finely shredded
- 3 courgettes, topped, tailed and cut into chunks
- 4 tomatoes, quartered
- 4 hard-boiled eggs, shelled and quartered, for garnish
- 400 g/13 oz *couscous* grains, prepared as on p. 234 with 75 g/3 oz grated Cheddar cheese or crumbled *feta* cheese stirred in + ¼ teaspoon ground chilli and 50 g/2 oz pine nuts

Put the first 12 ingredients into a large pan and bring to the boil. Add the carrots and turnips and simmer, covered, for 10 minutes. Add the aubergine, potatoes and cabbage and simmer, covered, for 10 minutes. Add the courgettes and tomatoes and simmer for 5 minutes. Remove the bay leaves and whole chillies before serving.

Serve as described on p. 235, garnished with the hard-boiled eggs.

Noodles

Noodles are generally believed to be a Chinese invention introduced into Italy by Marco Polo after his oriental travels in the thirteenth century. From Italy they passed to the rest of the Western world.

The blandness and smoothness of noodles makes them an ideal contrast for aggressive chilli flavourings, as the following recipes reveal.

Char Mee

This dish is Chinese fried noodles Singapore-style, with the inevitable addition of plenty of chillies. It is a complete and economical meal in itself, and is a spiced-up version of the bland *chow mein* served in every Chinese restaurant.

SERVES 6

- 350 g/11 oz dried Chinese wheat noodles
- 4 tablespoons oil
- 1 medium onion, finely chopped
- 4 cloves garlic, finely chopped
- 1 teaspoon finely chopped fresh ginger
- 4 fresh red or green chillies, deseeded and finely chopped
- 1 chicken breast, cut into 1 cm/½ in dice
- 75 g/3 oz *char siu* (Chinese barbecued pork) or pork fillet, cut into 1 cm/½ in dice
- 2 teaspoons oyster sauce*
- 2 tablespoons light soy sauce*
- 200 g/7 oz beansprouts
- 125 g/4 oz cooked prawns
- 3 spring onions, finely sliced

Bring a large saucepan of salted water to the boil. Add the noodles and boil for 4 minutes, untangling them with a fork as they cook. Drain and stir in 1 tablespoon of oil to prevent sticking. Set aside.

Heat the oil in a very large frying-pan or wok. Add the onion, garlic, ginger, chillies, chicken and pork. Stir-fry over a fairly high heat for 3 minutes. Add the oyster sauce and the soy sauce, then the noodles. Mix well and fry for 1 minute. Add the beansprouts and fry for 3 minutes, stirring frequently. Mix in the prawns and spring onions, cook for a further 2 minutes, and serve immediately, straight from the pan, with a bowl of Chilli and Ginger Sauce (p. 274).

Thai Crispy Noodles
Mee Krob

Crispy noodles with pork, chicken, prawns and crabmeat in a hot-sour sauce.

SERVES 6

- 300 g/10 oz Chinese vermicelli noodles
- oil for deep frying
- 3 tablespoons oil
- 1 medium onion, finely chopped
- 4 cloves garlic, finely chopped
- 4 fresh red chillies, deseeded and finely chopped
- 250 g/8 oz pork fillet, cut into 1.5 cm/½ in cubes
- 250 g/8 oz boneless chicken breast, cut into 1.5 cm/½ in cubes
- 4 tablespoons light soy sauce*
- 3 tablespoons lemon juice
- 2 tablespoons vinegar
- 2 tablespoons fish sauce*
- 1 tablespoon sugar
- 250 g/8 oz beansprouts
- 125 g/4 oz cooked prawns
- 125 g/4 oz cooked crabmeat
- 6 spring onions, sliced
- 3 tablespoons finely chopped coriander leaves

Fry the vermicelli, a couple of handfuls at a time, in hot oil until crispy and golden. Drain on kitchen paper and set aside.

Heat the 3 tablespoons of oil in a large heavy frying-pan or wok. Add the onion, garlic, chillies and pork fillet and stir-fry for 3 minutes. Add the chicken and stir-fry for a further 3 minutes. Add the soy sauce, lemon juice, vinegar, fish sauce and sugar. Bring to the boil and add the beansprouts. Cook for 1 minute, tossing and turning the beansprouts. Stir in the prawns, crabmeat, spring onions and coriander. Add the crispy noodles and mix in well. Serve immediately, garnished, if you like, with red chilli flowers (p. 223) and Crispy Fried Onions (p. 260).

Libyan Noodles

The Italian influence in Libya has resulted in pasta – especially spaghetti – becoming an accepted part of the diet. The spaghetti is often cooked in a *couscousier* in a similar way to that in which *couscous* is traditionally cooked (see p. 234), with the meat stew underneath and the pasta steaming in a perforated pan above. However, the spaghetti can just as well be cooked in the normal way in boiling salted water. The stew recipe given below is sufficient to accompany 500 g/1 lb dry spaghetti.

SERVES 6

- 2 tablespoons butter
- 1 large onion, finely chopped
- 2 cloves garlic, finely chopped
- 1 kg/2 lb boneless lamb, cut into 2 cm/¾ in cubes
- a 400 g/13 oz can tomatoes, with juice
- 2 tablespoons tomato purée
- 1 teaspoon ground chilli
- 1 teaspoon paprika
- 1 teaspoon *ras-el-hanout**
- 1 teaspoon salt
- ½ teaspoon black pepper
- 1 carrot, diced
- a 400 g/13 oz can chickpeas, drained

Heat the butter in a large heavy saucepan and gently fry the onion and garlic until soft. Add the meat and fry until nicely browned. Add all the remaining ingredients except the chickpeas, and enough water barely to cover. Bring to the boil and simmer, covered, for about 1¼ hours until the meat is tender. Add the chickpeas for the last 10 minutes.

Serve with spaghetti.

Mexican Dry Vermicelli Soup
Sopa Seca de Fideos

Like the Spaniards, Mexicans serve a 'dry soup' – which is usually based on rice or pasta, sometimes *tortillas* – as a separate course in a meal. A dry soup is not really a soup at all but a fairly substantial dish which – in Mexico at any rate – is frequently seasoned with chillies and is similar to the typical Italian pasta course traditionally served after the *antipasto* and before the fish or meat course.

In this *sopa seca*, vermicelli noodles are fried until crisp in the same way as in Thai *Mee Krob* (p. 239). The flavourings, however, are very different.

SERVES 4

- 125 ml/4 fl oz oil
- 175 g/6 oz vermicelli
- 1 small onion, finely chopped
- 1 clove garlic, finely chopped
- 3 fresh green chillies, deseeded and finely chopped
- a 200 g/7 oz can tomatoes, mashed with their juice
- 1 tablespoon finely chopped parsley or coriander leaves

Heat the oil in a large heavy frying-pan. When fairly hot, add the dry vermicelli and fry for about 30 seconds until golden. Remove immediately (it can burn very quickly) and drain on kitchen paper. Pour off all but about 2 tablespoons of the oil. Add the onion and garlic to the pan and fry gently until soft. Return the vermicelli to the pan and add all the remaining ingredients except the parmesan. Bring to the boil, then simmer, uncovered, for about 30 minutes until almost all the liquid has been absorbed. Serve immediately, sprinkled with parmesan cheese.

salt and freshly ground black pepper to taste

¼ teaspoon dried oregano

600 ml/1 pint chicken stock, or water+stock cube

2 tablespoons grated parmesan cheese

Tortillas

Mexican Flat Bread
Tortillas

Of all the breads that accompany chilli cooking, the Mexican *tortilla* indisputedly reigns supreme. *Tortillas* and chillies together provide the basis for an unequalled repertoire of imaginative dishes that range from cocktail nibbles to informal snacks and substantial meals.

One of the most ancient breads known to man, *tortillas* have been cooked and eaten since the earliest times of Latin American civilization. The most common form of *tortilla* is made from *masa harina* – a distinctive cornmeal prepared from corn that has been soaked in lime water. Ordinary cornmeal is not suitable for making *tortillas*.

In the north of Mexico, which is a wheat-growing region, *tortillas* are made from wheat flour. Both kinds of *tortilla* are simply made by mixing the flour with water and then kneading to give a soft dough. Corn *tortillas* are shaped by hand or by flattening a ball of dough in a purpose-designed press, which can often be bought from shops selling *masa harina*. Wheat *tortillas* – which are larger – are rolled into shape. The *tortillas* are dry-cooked on a heavy griddle for about a minute on each side.

Tortillas – served soft and warm – may be eaten with meat or poultry dishes in much the same way as any other bread but, in addition, they can be combined with shredded cooked meat, chilli sauces and other complementary ingredients to produce a tantalizing array of so-called *antojitos*. An exact translation of *antojitos* is difficult, but they could be termed as little whims and fancies or on-the-spur-of-the-moment desires. They can be eaten at any time of day (Mexicans are great in-between-meal eaters) and are absolutely tailor-made for the modern trend of casual easy-to-eat snack foods rather than formal meals.

Corn Tortillas

The normal size for corn *tortillas* is 15 cm/6 in in diameter, but smaller 10 cm/4 in ones are more suitable for some dishes. Tiny 5 cm/2 in *tortillas* are used for appetizers.

Tortillas stick together when stacked in their uncooked state, so a supply of greaseproof paper (about 20 cm/8 in squares for the largest size) is necessary.

If 2 tablespoons of plain flour is substituted for 2 tablespoons of *masa harina* in the following quantities, the dough becomes easier to handle.

MAKES 12 TORTILLAS
15 CM/6 IN IN DIAMETER

275 g/9 oz *masa harina** + extra for kneading

pinch salt

300 ml/½ pint warm water

Mix the *masa harina* and salt together in a bowl. Add the water and mix to a soft dough. Transfer to a board and knead for at least 10 minutes. Test that the dough is of the correct consistency by dropping a marble-sized ball into cold water. If it does not dissolve, the dough is ready.

Divide the dough into 12 portions and roll each into a ball. Place a paper square on the base of an open *tortilla* press and put a dough ball on top, then another paper square. Close the press and apply pressure on the handle. If the press is difficult to close, or if the *tortilla* comes out with torn edges, the dough is too dry. If the *tortilla* sticks to the paper, the dough is too wet. It is impossible to over-work the dough, so add more water or *masa harina* to the remaining dough and try again.

Continue as for wheat *tortillas*, but cook for about 1½ minutes on each side. Remove the paper from one side and place dough-side down on the griddle. Remove the second sheet before turning the *tortilla* over.

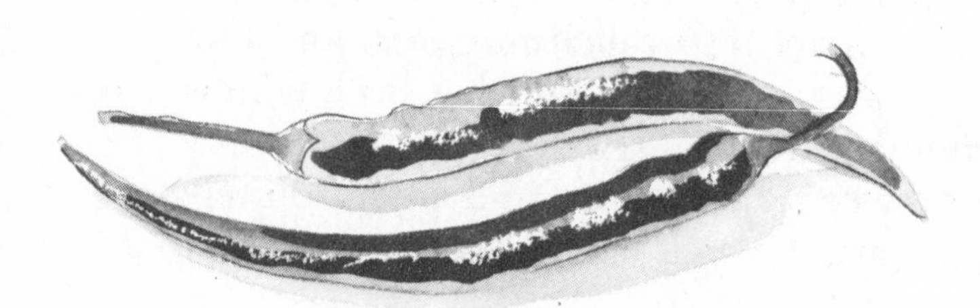

Wheat Tortillas

These are thought to have first been made by Spanish settlers who moved into the sparsely populated northern part of Mexico. They cooked the traditional *tortillas* using their own type of flour and eventually cultivated wheat in this area.

MAKES ABOUT 18
500 g/1 lb plain flour+extra for rolling out
2 teaspoons salt
75 g/3 oz lard
300 ml/½ pint warm water

Sift the flour and salt into a mixing bowl. Rub in the lard as in making pastry. Add about three-quarters of the water and mix to a soft dough. If necessary, add the remaining water. Transfer to a floured board and knead for about 5 minutes until no longer sticky. Return to the bowl and cover with a damp tea towel.

Pull off walnut-sized lumps of dough and roll out on a floured board to give a thin disc about 24 cm/9 in in diameter. For a neater shape, cut around a dinner plate. Cook on an ungreased medium hot griddle for 1 minute, using a rolling pin to transfer the tortilla from the rolling-out board. Turn over and cook for 30 seconds on the other side. Eat immediately or stack in a tea towel to keep warm.

For freezing, stack the *tortillas*, separated with sheets of cling film or greaseproof paper, and wrap in kitchen foil or a plastic freezer bag. To reheat, cook *unthawed* on a medium hot griddle for 30 seconds on each side.

Tostados

Tostados are crisp-fried corn *tortillas* that are garnished, pyramid-like, with assorted goodies. They are absolutely impossible to eat elegantly – but it's fun trying. Tiny bite-sized *tostados* make excellent appetizers with drinks, and they are easier to handle!

There are no rules concerning the combination of ingredients that make up *tostados* – use any assortment, including left-over cooked meat. Allow 2 *tostados* per person for a light lunch or supper.

Deep-fry corn *tortillas* in hot oil or fat for about 1 minute until golden and crisp. Drain on kitchen towels. Spread each with about 2 tablespoons of Refried Beans (p. 198) and 1 teaspoon of *Salsa Cruda* (p. 268). Pile on a mini-salad of shredded lettuce, chopped tomato, chopped spring onion and sliced avocado. Sprinkle with shredded cooked chicken or pork and finely chopped *serrano* chillies. Top with grated cheese and/or a dollop of sour cream. Decorate with sliced radish and pitted olives.

Serve immediately with extra chilli sauce (see Mexican chilli sauce recipes, pp. 268–71).

Alternatively lay out all the garnishes so that everyone can make up their own mixture.

Tacos

Tacos are an American derivation of a Mexican *tortilla* that has been stuffed, rolled and then fried. In the updated American version, the *tortilla* is first fried in a horseshoe shape until crisp and the cavity is then filled with assorted ingredients.

Taco shells can be bought ready fried but they are quick and easy to make at home. You will need a deep frying-pan and a pair of kitchen tongs. Heat at least 10 cm/4 in oil or lard until medium hot. Fold a corn *tortilla* in half and hold with the tongs so that the open edges are about 5 cm/2 in apart. Fry for 1 minute, continuing to hold the *tortilla* in shape with the tongs. After this time, the *taco* should retain its shape. Fry for a little longer until evenly golden. Drain on kitchen paper and store in an airtight container when cool.

To make cocktail *tacos*, cut *tortillas* into small circles with a pastry or cookie cutter and fry as explained above.

Tacos can be filled with practically anything – left-over chopped meat, chopped chillies, refried beans, shredded lettuce, grated cheese and a variety of chilli sauces. Here are a few tried-and-tested combinations:

1 Spread 2 tablespoons of Refried Beans (p. 198) in the bottom of the *taco* shell. Add *Salsa Cruda* (p. 268) and scatter shredded cooked chicken over. Spoon on a generous portion of *Guacamole* (p. 50) and top with shredded lettuce, finely chopped onion and more *Salsa Cruda*.
2 Beat 125 g/4 oz of cream cheese with a little milk, cream or sour cream to make it softer. Stir in 50 g/2 oz of chopped cooked ham, 2 tablespoons of finely chopped onion, 2 medium tomatoes, finely chopped, and finely chopped fresh green chillies to taste. Put a generous portion in the bottom of a *taco* shell. Top with shredded lettuce and *Guacamole* (p. 50) or *Salsa de Jitomate* (p. 269).
3 Heat up left-over *Chili con Carne* (p. 115) and spoon into the *taco* shells. Top with shredded lettuce, finely chopped onion and *Guacamole* (p. 50) or grated cheese.

4 Make up a quantity of *Picadillo* (p. 140). Spoon into the *taco* shells and top with shredded lettuce, finely chopped onion, *Salsa Cruda* (p. 268) and halved pitted olives.

5 Fry *chorizo* meat mixture (p. 135) in a little oil. Alternatively skin and crumble ready-made *chorizo* sausages and fry. Just before serving, stir in 175 g/6 oz Cheddar cheese cut into small dice. Spoon into *taco* shells and top with *Guacamole* (p. 50), shredded lettuce, finely chopped onion and *Salsa Cruda* (p. 268).

Chilaquiles

This popular Mexican breakfast dish is made with *tortillas* which are cut into pieces, fried and then coated in chilli and tomato sauce. It is an ideal way of using up yesterday's left-over *tortillas*.

SERVES 4–6

- oil or lard for deep-frying
- 10–12 corn *tortillas*, cut into 1 cm/½ in strips or triangular segments
- double quantity *Salsa de Jitomate* (p. 269)
- 50 g/2 oz grated Cheddar cheese or parmesan
- finely chopped fresh green chillies (optional)
- 3 tablespoons finely chopped onion

Heat the oil or lard to medium hot and fry the *tortilla* pieces for about 30 seconds until lightly browned but still soft and not crispy. Do this in 2 or more batches if necessary. Drain on kitchen towels and keep warm. Bring the *salsa* to the boil. Put the fried *tortilla* pieces in a warm shallow dish, pour the *salsa* over, and sprinkle the remaining ingredients on top. Serve immediately with, if you like, fried eggs on the side.

VARIATIONS

Fry 250 g/8 oz *chorizo* (p. 135) and add to the sauce. Top with 4 tablespoons of sour cream and avocado slices in addition to the garnishes above.

A more substantial lunch or supper dish of *chilaquiles* can be made by adding 500 g/1 lb of shredded cooked chicken and 250 ml/8 fl oz of thick or sour cream to the basic recipe. Spread a layer of *salsa* in the bottom of an ovenproof dish, and add a layer of fried *tortillas*, some of the chicken and a little cream. Repeat until all the ingredients have been used up, ending with a layer of cream. Sprinkle on chillies and onion and top with grated cheese. Bake for about 15 minutes in a moderate oven pre-heated to 190°C/375°F/gas 5 until the cheese is melted and golden and the dish has heated through. Serve with a salad.

Enchiladas

Enchiladas are a substantial dish of stuffed and rolled *tortillas*, coated in chilli sauce. Allow three *tortillas* per person for those with healthy appetites. Each helping of *enchiladas* can be served in an individual ovenproof dish, or use one large ovenproof dish that will hold all the *enchiladas*.

SERVES 6

- oil or lard for shallow frying
- 18 corn *tortillas*
- double quantity of *Salsa de Jitomate* (p. 269), warmed up
- 250 g/8 oz grated Cheddar cheese
- 250 g/8 oz shredded cooked chicken
- 1 large onion, finely chopped

Heat the oil or lard in a large heavy frying-pan until fairly hot. Fry the *tortillas*, one at a time, for a few seconds on each side so that they become limp and soft. Do not over-fry or the *tortillas* will crisp. Keep warm until all the *tortillas* have been fried.

Dip each *tortilla* in the *salsa*, place a little grated cheese, chicken and chopped onion on each, and roll up to make a cigar-shape. Lay the rolled-up *tortillas* side-by-side in a shallow ovenproof dish (rather like Italian cannelloni). Pour the remaining *salsa* over the top. Sprinkle with any remaining chopped onion and grated cheese. Bake for 5 minutes in a medium hot oven, preheated to 190°C/375°F/gas 5, for about 5 minutes until heated through. Serve immediately with salad and extra chilli sauce.

VARIATIONS

Make green *enchiladas* with *Salsa de Tomatillo* (p. 269) instead of *Salsa de Jitomate*, and substitute cooked pork for the cooked chicken.

Add 150 ml/¼ pint of thick cream to the *salsa* for a richer dish.

Use ready-made *chorizo* sausage, skinned, crumbled and fried with a little finely chopped onion and fresh chillies, or use a half quantity of the *chorizo* recipe (p. 135) and fry in a little oil or lard.

NOTE

Excellent after-Christmas *enchiladas* can be made with left-over turkey, and the *mole* sauce that is used for *Mole de Guajolote* (p. 168). Dip the *tortillas* into the warm *mole* sauce and roll up with a little shredded turkey and sauce inside. Pour the warmed sauce over and sprinkle on a few toasted sesame seeds.* Serve with shredded lettuce, sliced tomato and finely chopped onion.

Nachos

These are fried *tortilla* crisps topped with chillies, and make appropriate cocktail nibbles before a Mexican meal. The crisps alone – without their topping – are perfect for eating with *Guacamole* (p. 50) as a starter course.

- oil or lard for deep-frying
- 12 corn *tortillas*, each cut into 8 segments
- 200 g/7 oz grated Cheddar cheese
- finely chopped fresh green chillies to taste
- ½ medium onion, grated

Heat the oil or lard until medium hot. Fry the *tortilla* segments, in batches, for about 1 minute until crisp and golden. Drain on kitchen paper. Mix the cheese, chillies and onion together. Put a little of the mixture on each *tortilla* segment and place in a single layer on a baking sheet. Bake for 5–10 minutes in a moderate oven pre-heated to 180°C/350°F/gas 4 until the topping has melted. Serve warm.

ACCOMPANIMENTS

Curry Accompaniments

Indian-style curries, wherever in the world they might have been transposed, are traditionally accompanied by a selection of side dishes – chutneys, pickles and a wide variety of relishes that come under the general heading of *sambals*. Some are fiery hot and are eaten in minute amounts, others are intended as coolers. Some are as simple as a little grated coconut or sliced banana scattered over the main dishes, others are complex chutneys and pickles that need many months to allow the flavours to mature and blend. The choice is endless, and there is enormous scope for experimentation and invention. Those included here – most of which contain chilli – are representative of many of the most popular and well known, including quite a few of my favourites.

Unlike the Indian chutneys, which are preserves intended for storing (pp. 253–8), fresh chutneys are made up just before serving or will keep for 2 days at the most in a refrigerator. They are at their best if chilled for 30 minutes before serving. They can be very hot or quite mild, so adjust the chilli content to suit the other dishes being served. It is usual for at least one fresh chutney to be served as part of a Indian meal.

Fresh Mint Chutney

- 1 teacup firmly packed mint leaves
- 6 spring onions or 1 medium onion, chopped
- 1 clove garlic, chopped
- 2 fresh green chillies, deseeded and chopped
- 3 tablespoons vinegar
- 1 teaspoon salt
- ½ teaspoon sugar

Put all the ingredients into the container of an electric food processor or blender and blend to a purée. Taste, and adjust the salt and sugar seasoning if necessary.

NOTE

½ teaspoon of *garam masala** can be added.

Fresh Coriander Chutney

If coriander is not available, use parsley. The flavour will, of course, be different, although it will still give the taste of fresh herbs.

- 1 teacup firmly packed coriander leaves
- 8 shallots or 1 medium onion, chopped
- 1 teaspoon chopped fresh ginger
- 2 fresh green chillies, deseeded and chopped
- 3 tablespoons lemon juice
- 1 tablespoon water
- 1 teaspoon salt
- 1½ teaspoons sugar

Follow the method of the previous recipe.

NOTE

1 tablespoon of desiccated coconut can be added with 1 tablespoon of extra water.

Peanut and Mint Chutney

The East African adaptation of mint chutney contains – of course – peanuts.

- 2 teacups closely packed mint leaves, or half mint and half coriander leaves
- ½ teacup fresh peanuts (not salted)
- 3 cloves garlic, chopped
- 2 spring onions, chopped
- 1 fresh green chilli, deseeded and chopped
- ½ teaspoon ground coriander
- ¼ teaspoon salt
- 4 tablespoons lime or lemon juice
- 1 teaspoon sugar or to taste

Put all the ingredients in the container of an electric blender or food processor and blend to a coarse purée.

Fresh Coconut Chutney

Make this with freshly grated coconut or desiccated coconut.

- 1 teacup desiccated coconut
- 1 teaspoon chopped lemon rind (without pith)
- 1 fresh green chilli, deseeded and chopped
- ½ teaspoon chopped fresh ginger
- 2 shallots or spring onions, chopped
- 1 tablespoon chopped coriander or mint leaves
- 1 teaspoon salt
- 2 teaspoons oil
- ½ teaspoon black mustard seeds*
- 1 teaspoon cumin seeds
- 1 teaspoon sesame seeds*

Put the first 7 ingredients into the container of an electric blender or food processor with just enough water to allow the blades to operate (try 2–3 tablespoons to begin with). Blend to a thick paste, then transfer to a bowl.

Heat the oil in a saucepan and fry the mustard seeds until they jump and pop. Add the cumin and sesame seeds and gently fry until golden. Do not allow to burn. Stir into the coconut paste.

Fresh Tomato Chutney

- 500 g/1 lb tomatoes, peeled and chopped
- 1 medium onion, chopped
- 1 clove garlic, chopped
- 1 teaspoon chopped fresh ginger
- 1 tablespoon chopped coriander or parsley leaves
- 1 tablespoon chopped basil leaves
- ½ teaspoon ground chilli
- ½ teaspoon *garam masala**
- ½ teaspoon salt
- 2 tablespoons lemon juice
- sugar to taste

Put all the ingredients except the sugar into the container of an electric blender or food processor. Blend to a purée and add sugar to taste. Extra salt may be needed, too. Chill for 30 minutes before serving.

Fresh Carrot Chutney

- 250 g/8 oz carrots, grated
- 1 tablespoon very finely chopped or grated fresh ginger

Mix all the ingredients together and chill for 30 minutes before serving.

2 fresh green chillies, deseeded and finely chopped

2 tablespoons finely chopped onion

2 tablespoons finely chopped coriander or parsley leaves

3 tablespoons lemon juice

1 teaspoon salt

sugar to taste

Chutney and Pickles for Conservation

I was taught to make chutneys and pickles by the sister of my Indian cook, who was the acknowledged expert of the family. I have never bought a ready-made one since. There are many commercially prepared conserves available but – as with jams and Western-style chutneys – they lack the freshness and individuality of those made at home. However, making conserves is a fairly time-consuming business and, more and more, modern housewives are opting for bought varieties. It could well be that my cook's sister will be the last generation of specialists in her family but for me, at any rate, it is still very much worth the effort. Home-made pickles and chutneys do have a special flavour, and there is an undeniable feeling of satisfaction in having a cupboard full of pots and jars made in one's own kitchen.

Making Indian pickles can be a powerfully pungent affair, so be prepared. The effect of chillies simmering for an hour or more with lots of onions, garlic and spices can be stultifying. Work with a window open and keep very young children out of the kitchen. Use only enamel or stainless steel cooking pots – the traditional copper preserving pan is not suitable – and wear a cover-up apron, as the splatters will stain.

Most of the following recipes are for conserves that improve with keeping. The oil-based pickles will keep for years if there is always a thin layer of oil covering the pickle, and the flavour will continue to improve with the years. Remember to use a dry spoon to remove pickles from the jar.

Where the recipe is not one that is intended for long storage, it has been clearly stated.

Lime or Lemon Oil Pickle

A most delicious pickle, best made with thin-skinned fruit. In tropical climates the fruit would be left in the sun to dry out during daylight hours, being brought in every evening. Instead of two or three days' sunshine, place the fruit in an oven set at the lowest possible heat for a couple of hours and then leave in an airing cupboard or warm place for 48 hours. The oven or cupboard door should be ajar to allow some ventilation.

- 750 g/1½ lb limes or lemons
- coarse salt
- 1 teaspoon fenugreek seeds*
- 250 ml/8 fl oz vinegar
- 10 cloves garlic, chopped
- 3 tablespoons chopped fresh ginger
- 500 ml/17 fl oz oil
- 1 tablespoon black mustard seeds*
- 3 tablespoons ground cumin
- 3 tablespoons ground coriander
- 1 tablespoon fennel seeds*
- 1 teaspoon ground turmeric
- 1 teaspoon ground chilli
- 15 fresh red or green chillies, stems removed, cut into shreds
- salt to taste

Cut the limes or lemons into quarters. Sprinkle with salt (about 5 tablespoons) and leave for 48 hours, by which time the salt will have absorbed much of the fruit juice and the segments will start to look dry.

Soak the fenugreek seeds overnight in 3 tablespoons of the vinegar, during which time they will swell and become gelatinous. Put the fenugreek seeds, plus their soaking vinegar, garlic and ginger, into the container of an electric blender or food processor. Add extra vinegar if necessary and blend to a purée.

Pour off the juice and excess salt from the limes or lemons and chop each segment into 2 or 3 pieces.

Heat the oil in a large heavy saucepan (stainless steel or enamel, because the high acidity will tarnish other metals) and fry the mustard seeds until they jump and pop. Add the cumin, coriander, fennel, turmeric and ground chilli and fry gently for 30 seconds, stirring constantly. Add the blended mixture and fry for 2 minutes, stirring constantly. Add the remaining vinegar, the limes or lemons and the fresh chillies. Bring to the boil and simmer, uncovered, for about 30 minutes until the fruit is tender and the oil has separated. Stir frequently and gently so that the fruit does not break up. Add more salt if necessary. The taste should be hot, sour and salty.

Allow to cool slightly and bottle in warm jars. There should be a film of oil over the surface of the pickle. Add more oil to the jar if necessary. It improves with age and will last for 2 or 3 years.

Sweet Pineapple Oil Pickle

- 2 teaspoons fenugreek seeds*
- 250 ml/8 fl oz white wine vinegar
- 2 tablespoons chopped fresh ginger
- 1 head garlic, peeled and chopped
- 500 ml/17 fl oz oil
- 1 tablespoon ground turmeric
- 2 tablespoons ground cumin
- 2 teaspoons ground fennel
- 20 fresh green chillies, stems removed, cut into shreds
- 75 g/3 oz sugar
- 2 fresh barely ripe pineapples, peeled, cored, coarsely chopped and squeezed to remove juice
- 50 g/2 oz seedless raisins or sultanas
- 1 tablespoon salt
- ½ teaspoon ground black pepper
- 2 bay leaves

Soak the fenugreek seeds overnight in half the vinegar. They will swell and become gelatinous. Put them into the container of an electric blender or food processor with the ginger and garlic and blend to a paste.

Heat the oil in a large heavy saucepan and gently fry the turmeric, cumin and fennel for 30 seconds. Add the paste and fry for 3 minutes, stirring constantly. Add the remaining vinegar, the chillies and the sugar. Stir constantly until the sugar dissolves. Add all the remaining ingredients and simmer for 30 minutes. Check for salt and add more if necessary. Bottle and keep for 3 months before opening. It improves with age.

Tomato Oil Pickle

- 75 g/3 oz fresh ginger, peeled and chopped
- 1 head garlic, cloves peeled and chopped
- 1 tablespoon black mustard seeds*
- 350 ml/12 fl oz vinegar
- 300 ml/½ pint oil
- 1 tablespoon turmeric
- 4 tablespoons ground cumin
- 2 tablespoons ground chilli
- 2 kg/4 lb tomatoes, peeled and chopped
- 1 tablespoon salt
- 2 tablespoons sugar
- 10 fresh green chillies, stems removed, cut into long shreds

Put the ginger, garlic and mustard seeds into the container of an electric blender or food processor. Add about a third of the vinegar and liquidize.

Heat the oil in a large heavy saucepan and fry the turmeric, cumin and chilli over a gentle heat for 30 seconds. Add all the remaining ingredients, the vinegar and the vinegar purée. Bring to the boil and simmer, uncovered, for about 45 minutes until the mixture is thick and pulpy with oil floating on top. Cool slightly and put into warm jars. Seal when cold. It improves with age.

Green Chilli Oil Pickle

For addicts only!

- 1 kg/2 lb fresh green chillies
- 1 litre/1¾ pints oil
- 4 tablespoons cumin seeds
- 4 tablespoons black mustard seeds*
- 1 teaspoon cloves
- 1 tablespoon paprika
- 2 tablespoons salt
- 8 bay leaves
- 4 cloves garlic, halved

Leave the stems on the chillies. Carefully make a slit on one side and remove the seeds. Wash, drain and allow to dry completely.

Heat the oil over a low heat for 2 minutes. Add the cumin, mustard seeds and cloves. Fry for 30 seconds and remove from heat. Stir in the paprika and salt and allow to cool.

Pack the chillies into a large clean jar or smaller jars. Disperse the bay leaves and garlic among them and fill up with oil to cover. It may be necessary to add a little extra oil. Seal and leave 2 weeks before using.

Indian Mango Chutney

A mild sweet mango chutney, similar to the popular commercial brands. It should be made with fairly hard under-ripe fruit.

- 8 unripe mangoes
- 4 dried red chillies, soaked in a little vinegar
- 3 cloves garlic, chopped
- 1 tablespoon chopped fresh ginger
- 500 ml/17 fl oz vinegar
- 500 g/1 lb sugar
- 1 tablespoon salt
- 1 teaspoon ground cumin
- ½ teaspoon ground turmeric

Peel the mangoes and grate or finely chop the flesh. Discard the stones.

Tear the chillies into pieces and put them in the container of an electric blender or food processor with their soaking vinegar and the garlic and ginger. Add extra vinegar if necessary and blend to a coarse paste. Transfer to a large heavy saucepan and add the remaining vinegar with the sugar, salt, cumin and turmeric. Bring to the boil, stirring until the sugar has dissolved. Add the mangoes and simmer until the fruit is soft and the sauce is thick and pulpy. Pour into warm jars and seal when cold.

Peach Chutney

Making mango chutney – the previous recipe, for example – is expensive because mangoes have to be imported into Europe and thus become a luxury ingredient. I live in a peach-growing area, however, and peaches are therefore cheap when they are in season. Inevitably, I began using under-ripe peaches instead of under-ripe mangoes for my annual stock of Indian-style 'mango' chutney. The results were delicious, but peeling hard peaches proved to be difficult. Now I use ripe (not over-ripe) fruit with great success. To peel them, plunge the peaches – a few at a time – into a large pan of boiling water. Remove after 1 minute and cool under running cold water. The skins will then slip off easily.

The recipe below produces a hot, sweetish chutney with a pronounced taste of ginger. If preferred, cut down on the ginger and add 2 teaspoons of concentrated tamarind extract* to balance the sweetness.

- 2 kg/4 lb peaches, skinned, stoned and chopped
- 2 cloves garlic, chopped
- 3 tablespoons finely chopped fresh ginger
- 500 g/1 lb brown or white sugar
- 350 ml/11 fl oz vinegar
- 1 teaspoon *garam masala**
- 1 teaspoon ground chilli
- 3 fresh chillies, finely shredded
- 2 teaspoons salt

Put all the ingredients in a large heavy saucepan and bring to the boil, stirring constantly until the sugar has dissolved. Simmer for 30–40 minutes until thick, checking frequently for signs of burning and sticking. Pour into warm jars and seal when cold. This chutney improves with keeping for up to 2 years.

Serve with Indian dishes or cold meat.

Caribbean Peach Chutney

- 2 kg/4 lb peaches, skinned, stoned and chopped
- 500 ml/17 fl oz vinegar
- 150 g/5 oz seedless raisins
- 1 teaspoon ground ginger
- 1 teaspoon crushed allspice berries*
- 6 fresh chillies, finely chopped
- 2 cloves garlic, chopped
- 200 g/7 oz brown sugar
- juice of 1 lemon
- 1 tablespoon salt

Put all the ingredients in a large heavy pan and bring to the boil, stirring constantly until the sugar has dissolved. Simmer for about 30 minutes until thick. Pour into warm jars and seal when cold.

South African Apricot Chutney

This is not a chutney for long storage. Keep in the refrigerator and eat within 4 weeks. Serve with curries.

- 250 g/8 oz dried apricots, halved
- 125 g/4 oz seedless raisins
- 1 small onion, finely chopped
- 2 tablespoons sugar
- 250 ml/8 fl oz vinegar
- 2 tablespoons finely chopped fresh ginger
- 5 cloves garlic, chopped
- 1 teaspoon ground chilli
- 2 teaspoons ground coriander
- 1½ teaspoons salt
- 6 tablespoons flaked almonds

Put the apricots, raisins, onion, sugar and vinegar in a heavy saucepan with 250 ml/8 fl oz of water. Bring to the boil, stirring constantly until the sugar has dissolved. Simmer for about 10 minutes, until the fruit is soft and the liquid is syrupy. Meanwhile pound the ginger and garlic to a paste, using a pestle and mortar or a food processor. Add the paste, chilli, coriander and salt to the pan. Simmer for 5 minutes, then stir in the almonds and pack into warm jars. Seal when cold.

Assorted Side Dishes and Sambal

Onion Sambal

Crisp vegetable sambals are traditional side dishes to accompany curries and other hot dishes in South East Asia. They should be served fresh.

- 2 medium onions
- 1 teaspoon salt
- ¼ teaspoon paprika
- ¼ teaspoon ground chilli
- 2 tablespoons lemon juice

The onions for this *sambal* are finely sliced, but traditionally the slices are not in rings. Cut the onions in half vertically and place on a board, cut side down. Now slice very finely, starting on the rounded side of the onion, not the top or bottom.

Put the sliced onions in a bowl and mix in the salt. Add enough water just to cover and chill for 1 hour.

Drain and gently squeeze out all the excess moisture from the onions. Stir in the paprika and chilli so that the onions turn pink. Sprinkle with lemon juice.

A small tomato, diced, could be scattered over the top.

Pineapple and Cucumber Sambal

Use either fresh or tinned pineapple for this *sambal*. If using fresh pineapple, you may want to add a little sugar to the dressing.

- 1 teacup chopped pineapple
- 1 medium cucumber, peeled, deseeded and chopped
- 2 tablespoons finely chopped onion or shallots
- 1 fresh red chilli, deseeded and finely chopped
- 1½ tablespoons colourless vinegar
- ½ teaspoon salt
- ½ teaspoon very finely chopped fresh ginger

Mix all the ingredients together and chill for 30 minutes before serving.

Fresh Prawn Sambal

This can be made very successfully with frozen cooked prawns which have been thoroughly thawed and dried on kitchen paper.

- 2 tablespoons *sambal ulek** or 6 fresh red chillies, chopped
- 1 medium onion, chopped
- 2 cloves garlic, chopped
- 1 tablespoon oil
- 1 tablespoon brown sugar
- ½ teaspoon salt
- 2 tablespoons lemon juice
- 2 tablespoons chopped prawns

Using a pestle and mortar or a food processor, pound the *sambal ulek* or chillies, onion and garlic to a paste. Heat the oil in a heavy frying-pan and gently fry the chilli paste until the onion smells cooked (about 5 minutes). Stir in the sugar, salt and lemon juice. Add the prawns and gently fry for 1 minute or until the prawns are pink. Serve at room temperature.

Quince or Cucumber Sambal

- 3 quinces or 2 large cucumbers
- 1 teaspoon salt
- 1 fresh chilli, deseeded and finely chopped
- 1 teaspoon sugar
- 3 tablespoons vinegar

Peel and core the quinces or peel and deseed the cucumbers. Chop into small dice, sprinkle with salt and leave for 30 minutes. Drain and dry on kitchen paper. Mix with all the other ingredients and chill for 30 minutes.

This can also be made with tart apples. More sugar might be needed.

Fresh Fruit Sambals

Fresh fruit can be sprinkled with salt and ground chilli to accompany curries. Try fresh pineapple, coarsely chopped; hard unripe mangoes, peeled and sliced; tart eating apples such as Granny Smith, peeled, cored, chopped and sprinkled with lemon juice to prevent discolouring.

Crispy Fried Onions

Scatter these over curry dishes before serving. They are also almost essential with *Dahl* (Indian lentils, p. 201) and any rice dishes.

Peel and finely slice shallots or onions. If the onions are large, first cut them in quarters so that the slices are smaller. Dry on kitchen paper and then put out in the sun for about 1 hour to dry off even more. Alternatively, place them in a cool oven. Deep-fry them in medium-hot oil for a few minutes until dark gold in colour. Do not allow to burn. Drain and leave until cold, when they will become crisp. Store in an airtight jar.

NOTE

Commercially prepared dried chopped onion is ideal for frying in this way.

Yoghurt is frequently served as a contrast to highly spiced dishes. The yoghurt may be simply beaten until smooth and served in a bowl, or combined with fruit, vegetables and spices.

Cucumbers in Yoghurt
Raita

- 1 large cucumber, peeled and thinly sliced
- 1 teaspoon salt
- 125 ml/4 fl oz yoghurt
- 1 fresh green chilli, deseeded and finely chopped
- ¼ teaspoon finely grated ginger
- 1 teaspoon lemon juice or more to taste

Put the cucumber in a colander and sprinkle with the salt. Leave for 1 hour. Gently squeeze out all the excess moisture. Beat the yoghurt until smooth and mix with all the remaining ingredients. Add the cucumber and taste to see if more salt is required. Chill for 30 minutes before serving.

NOTE

For extra freshness, stir in 1 tablespoon of freshly chopped mint leaves before chilling.

Bananas in Yoghurt

- 125 ml/4 fl oz yoghurt
- 1 tablespoon desiccated coconut, moistened with 1 teaspoon milk
- pinch of ground chilli or to taste
- 1 tablespoon lemon juice
- 1 teaspoon sugar
- ¼ teaspoon salt
- 2 ripe bananas, thinly sliced

Beat the yoghurt until smooth and mix with the coconut, chilli, lemon juice, sugar and salt. Stir in the bananas and chill for 30 minutes before serving.

Spinach with Yoghurt

Make this with frozen spinach for convenience.

- 2 teaspoons oil or *ghee**
- 1 teaspoon black mustard seeds*
- 1 teaspoon cumin seeds
- ¼ teaspoon fenugreek seeds*
- 125 ml/4 fl oz yoghurt
- ⅛ teaspoon ground chilli
- 250 g/8 oz frozen spinach, thawed and squeezed dry
- salt to taste

Heat the oil or *ghee* in a small frying-pan and gently fry the mustard seeds until they pop and jump. Add the cumin and fenugreek seeds and fry for 30 seconds. Allow to cool.

Beat the yoghurt until smooth. Stir in the fried spices and ground chilli. Mix with the spinach and add salt to taste. Serve chilled or at room temperature.

Yoghurt with Herbs and Nuts

- 250 ml/8 fl oz yoghurt
- 1 tablespoon finely chopped mint
- 1 tablespoon finely chopped coriander or parsley
- 1 teaspoon finely chopped fresh green chilli
- 1 spring onion, finely sliced
- salt and ground black pepper to taste
- 2 tablespoons coarsely chopped nuts

Beat the yoghurt until smooth and mix with all the other ingredients. Chill before serving.

South-East Asian Shrimp Paste Sambals

The combination of chillies and fermented shrimp paste is a familiar and indispensable theme throughout South-East Asia. Bright red in colour, aggressively hot and pungent, they are eaten in very small quantities, as a side dish or relish, with practically every meal. Asians abroad claim to be unable to survive without them, and I can tell you from personal experience that expatriates suffer from the same problem when they return home. So, be warned – for anyone who has crossed the '*blachan** barrier' (and many foreigners find it an alien taste that is impossible to acquire) these fiery concoctions become compulsive eating, not only in their traditional role but in sandwiches, on toast, with cheese and salad vegetables, on their own even. Leave a dish of *Chilli Sambal* in the fridge at my house and it is as if the mice get at it. Bit by bit, it disappears every time the refrigerator door opens!

The following recipes demonstrate regional variations of the basic chilli/*blachan* mix. Chilli is incorporated in various forms – fresh, dried and powdered, although I tend to prefer *sambal ulek*.* The actual ratio of chilli to *blachan* and salt is very much a personal affair. The proportions given here are those that suit my taste. They are all very hot, pungent and salty, but the amounts of chilli and *blachan* could be almost doubled for some tastes. However, there is no such thing as a mild chilli *sambal*, so there is no point in making them with a drastically reduced chilli or *blachan* content.

NOTE

Uncooked *blachan* has an unpleasant raw taste which prevents it blending with other ingredients. If it is not going to be cooked in the *sambal*, it should be flattened to about 80 mm/¼ in thickness, wrapped in a double layer of kitchen foil, and grilled or dry fried for 3–4 minutes.

These *sambals* will keep for up to 2 weeks in the refrigerator. Store them in an airtight container, though, or everything in the fridge will be *blachan*-flavoured.

Sambal Blachan (Malaysia and Singapore)

- 1 teaspoon *blachan**
- 6 fresh red chillies or 2 teaspoons *sambal ulek**
- 2 teaspoons lemon juice
- salt

Prepare the *blachan* as explained above. Pound the *blachan* and chillies to a paste, using a pestle and mortar. Add the lemon juice and a pinch of salt to taste.

Balachuang (Burma)

- 3 tablespoons oil
- 1 onion, finely chopped
- 6 cloves garlic, finely chopped
- 4 tablespoons dried prawn powder*
- 1 teaspoon ground chilli
- ½ teaspoon *blachan*
- 1½ teaspoons vinegar
- salt to taste

Heat the oil in a heavy frying-pan and gently fry the onion and garlic to a rich golden brown. Remove from the pan and set aside to cool, when they will become crisp.

Add the prawn powder to the pan and gently fry for 4 minutes. Add all the remaining ingredients and fry for 2 minutes.

When cold, mix with the fried onions and serve at room temperature.

NOTE

This is a very oily *sambal* but the greasiness is not a problem when it is eaten with mounds of dry boiled rice. However, some of the oil could be drained off before serving if preferred.

Sri Lankan Fried Onion Sambal

- 3 tablespoons oil
- 1 large onion, finely sliced
- 1 teaspoon *sambal ulek** or ground chilli
- 1 teaspon *blachan**
- ½ teaspoon paprika
- 1 tablespoon lemon juice
- salt to taste

Heat the oil in a heavy frying-pan and gently fry the onion until golden. Add the *sambal ulek*, *blachan* and paprika and fry gently for 5–10 minutes, stirring constantly until the oil separates. Stir in the lemon juice and add salt to taste.

Sambal Bajak (Indonesia)

- 1 teaspoon *sambal ulek** or 3 fresh red chillies, chopped
- 1 medium onion, chopped
- 4 cloves garlic, chopped
- 2 tablespoons oil
- 1 teaspoon *blachan**
- 1 tablespoon ground cashews or peanuts
- ½ teaspoon salt
- 2 tablespoons lemon juice
- 1 tablespoon brown sugar

Put the first 3 ingredients into the container of an electric blender or food processor with 1 tablespoon of the oil. Blend to a paste. Heat the remaining 1 tablespoon of oil in a heavy frying-pan and gently fry the chilli paste for 5 minutes, stirring constantly. Add the *blachan* and mash with a fork to break it up. Add the nuts and salt and fry for 2 minutes. Add the lemon juice and sugar, stirring until the sugar has dissolved and the lemon juice is blended in. Serve at room temperature.

Nam Prik

The classic Thai version of a *blachan* and chilli *sambal.*

- 2 tablespoons dried shrimps, soaked in warm water for 30 minutes
- 1 teaspoon *blachan,** prepared as directed on p. 262
- 2 cloves garlic, chopped
- 2 teaspoons *sambal ulek** or 5 fresh red chillies, chopped
- 2 tablespoons lemon juice
- 2 tablespoons fish sauce*
- 2 teaspoons sugar

Drain the dried shrimps and put them in the container of an electric blender or food processor. Blend to a purée with the other ingredients. For a thinner consistency, add 2 tablespoons of water.

English-Style Chutneys

English-style chutneys are a direct adaptation of the traditional Indian chutneys featured on pp. 256–8. In fact, the word chutney is taken from the Indian *chatni.* Make them as hot or as mild as you like. They will usually improve with keeping for up to 12 months.

Serve with grills, roasts, cold meats and salads. Spicy chutneys are also an easy way to add interest to vegetarian dishes.

Chilli and Apple Chutney

- 1.2 litres/2 pints vinegar
- 500 g/1 lb brown sugar
- 1.5 kg/3 lb apples, peeled, cored and chopped
- 2 tablespoons finely chopped garlic
- 125 g/4 oz seedless raisins
- 6 fresh green chillies, deseeded and finely chopped
- 3 tablespoons black mustard seeds*
- 1 tablespoon salt

Put the vinegar and brown sugar in a heavy saucepan and heat gently until the sugar dissolves. Add all the other ingredients and slowly bring to the boil. Simmer until thick, stirring frequently. Allow to cool slightly and pack into warm jars.

Apricot Chutney

- 2.5 kg/5 lb dried apricots
- 3 large onions, chopped
- 500 g/1 lb seedless raisins
- 1 kg/2 lb brown sugar
- 900 ml/1½ pints vinegar
- grated rind and juice of 2 oranges and 2 lemons
- 1 teaspoon ground turmeric
- 1 teaspoon mixed spice
- ½ teaspoon ground chilli
- 6 fresh red chillies, deseeded and finely chopped
- 1 tablespoon salt
- 1 tablespoon orange blossom water*
- 125 g/4 oz walnuts, coarsely chopped

Put all the ingredients except the last two into a large heavy saucepan. Bring to the boil and simmer until the mixture is thick and the apricots are soft. Stir in the orange blossom water and walnuts and bottle in warm jars.

Green Tomato Chutney

- 1.5 kg/3 lb green tomatoes, peeled and chopped
- 750 ml/1½ pints vinegar
- 500 g/1 lb brown sugar
- 1 teaspoon salt
- 1 teaspoon black mustard seeds*
- 1 teaspoon ground allspice*
- ½ teaspoon ground cloves
- 1 medium onion, chopped
- 125 g/4 oz seedless raisins
- 1 teaspoon ground ginger
- ½ teaspoon ground chilli
- 6 fresh green chillies, deseeded and finely chopped

Put all the ingredients in a large heavy saucepan and simmer for about 1½ hours until thick and pulpy. Stir frequently. Cool slightly and pack into warm jars. Seal when cold.

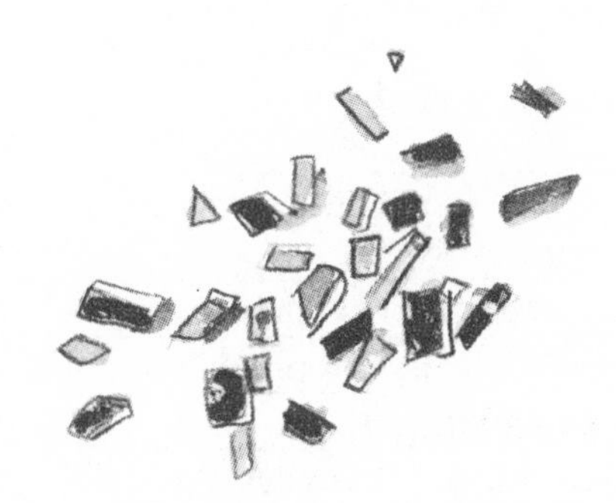

Red Tomato Chutney

- 2 kg/4 lb ripe tomatoes, skinned and chopped
- 1 kg/2 lb onions, chopped
- 6 cloves garlic, chopped
- 2 teaspoons ground ginger
- 500 g/1 lb sugar
- 2 teaspoons salt
- 600 ml/1 pint vinegar
- 2 teaspoons ground chilli
- 5 cm/2 in stick cinnamon

Put all the ingredients into a large heavy saucepan and simmer, uncovered, until almost all the liquid has been absorbed. Remove the cinnamon stick and allow to cool slightly before bottling.

Chilli Sauces

The world-wide range of sauces that can broadly be classed as predominantly chilli-seasoned is enormous. The selection of commercially bottled chilli sauces alone would, if all displayed together, fill the shelves of a whole shop. In addition to these, there is a plethora of home-made sauces. In the West Indies, for example, every island has its own favourite hot pepper sauce, which appears on every table for every meal. As each cook has his own particular version, the result is a vast repertoire of fiery sauces and relishes that are pure delight for the chilli enthusiast to discover.

Trinidad Hot Pepper Sauce

- 2 tablespoons grated unripe papaya
- 10 fresh chillies, deseeded and finely chopped
- 1 medium onion, finely chopped
- 1 clove garlic, finely chopped
- 4 tablespoons vinegar
- 1 teaspoon mustard powder
- ½ teaspoon salt

Put all the ingredients in a pan with enough water just to cover. Bring to the boil and simmer for 15 minutes. Cool and bottle. Can be kept in the refrigerator for 3 weeks.

VARIATION
Add ½ teaspoon of curry powder.

Sauce Ti-Malice (Haiti)

- 2 medium onions, finely chopped
- 2 cloves garlic, finely chopped
- 4 tablespoons lemon or lime juice
- 4 fresh chillies, finely chopped
- 1 tablespoon oil
- salt and freshly ground black pepper to taste

Put the first 3 ingredients in a bowl and leave for 1 hour. Put in a saucepan with the remaining ingredients and bring to the boil. Simmer for 10 minutes and allow to cool. Will keep in the refrigerator for 1 week.

Puerto Rican Pepper Sauce

- 1 large sweet red pepper, deseeded and chopped
- 2 fresh red chillies, deseeded and chopped
- 1 small onion, chopped
- 3 cloves garlic, chopped
- 4 tablespoons lime or lemon juice
- 3 tablespoons olive oil
- ½ teaspoon salt
- ¼ teaspoon freshly ground black pepper

Put all the ingredients into the container of an electric blender or food processor and blend to a purée.

Chilli Seafood Sauce

- 1 medium onion, finely chopped
- 6 tablespoons lemon or lime juice
- 2 cloves garlic, finely chopped
- 3 fresh red chillies, deseeded and finely chopped
- 25 g/1 oz butter
- salt and freshly ground black pepper to taste

Marinate the onion in the juice for 1 hour. Drain, reserving the marinade. Gently fry the onion, garlic and chillies in the butter for 5 minutes. Add the reserved marinade, season to taste, and simmer for 10 minutes.

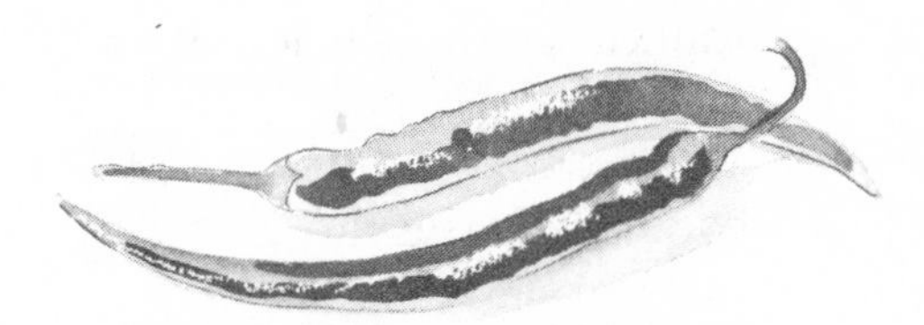

Sauce Piquante

Associated particularly with the French-speaking islands, the sauce is based on a vinaigrette and is flavoured with chillies, capers and gherkins.

- 5 tablespoons olive oil
- 3 tablespoons red or white wine vinegar
- 1 fresh red chilli, deseeded and finely chopped
- 1 clove garlic, finely chopped
- 2 shallots, finely chopped
- 1 tablespoon finely chopped parsley
- 1 tablespoon capers, chopped
- 1 tablespoon gherkins, chopped
- salt and freshly ground black pepper to taste

Mix all the ingredients together and allow to stand for 1 hour at room temperature.

The early Spanish colonizers recorded the array of hot chilli sauces that were used in local Aztec, Inca and Maya cooking. Today there is still an infinite number of variations on the same theme – many of them combining chillies and tomatoes.

Mexican Uncooked Tomato Sauce
Salsa Cruda

This is the everyday Mexican condiment, eaten with cooked meat, poultry, fish, eggs and beans. It is also an essential addition to many *tortilla*-based dishes (see p. 241). It does not keep well and is best immediately served.

- 2 large ripe tomatoes, finely chopped
- 1 small onion, finely chopped
- 2 or more fresh green chillies or canned *serrano* chillies, deseeded and finely chopped
- 1 tablespoon finely chopped coriander leaves
- salt and sugar to taste

Mix all the ingredients together and serve at room temperature.

Mexican Green Tomato Sauce
Salsa de Tomatillo

This should be made with canned Mexican green tomatoes and not green under-ripe tomatoes. Although they are in the same family, the two species are quite different.

- a 300 g/10 oz can Mexican green tomatoes,* drained
- 1 tablespoon finely chopped onion
- 2 or more fresh green chillies or canned *serrano* chillies, deseeded and finely chopped
- ½ clove garlic, finely chopped
- 1 tablespoon finely chopped coriander leaves
- salt to taste

Mix all the ingredients together or blend briefly in an electric blender or food processor.

NOTE
If preferred, the onion and garlic could be omitted and the amount of coriander leaves increased.

Mexican Cooked Tomato Sauce
Salsa de Jitomate

- 1 medium onion, chopped
- 1 clove garlic, chopped
- 3 large tomatoes, peeled and chopped
- 2 fresh green chillies or 2 tinned *serrano* chillies, deseeded and chopped
- salt and sugar to taste
- 2 tablespoons oil
- 1 tablespoon finely chopped coriander leaves

Put the onion, garlic, tomatoes and chillies in the container of an electric blender or food processor and blend briefly. The texture should not be too smooth. Season with salt and sugar. Heat the oil in a heavy pan and cook the purée over a moderate heat for about 5 minutes until it is thick. Stir in the coriander and serve hot or cold.

Mexican Red Chilli Sauce
Salsa de Chile Rojo

This is the classic Mexican red chilli sauce. It is mild. For a hotter sauce, add 6 crumbled *pequin* chillies or ground chilli.

- 4 *ancho* chillies
- 2 large tomatoes, peeled, deseeded and chopped
- 1 large onion, chopped
- 1 clove garlic, chopped
- 1 tablespoon oil
- 1 tablespoon finely chopped parsley
- salt and freshly ground black pepper to taste
- ½ teaspoon sugar
- 3 tablespoons olive oil
- 1 tablespoon wine vinegar

Wash the chillies and remove the stems, ribs and seeds. Tear the pods into pieces and soak in warm water for 1 hour, then drain.

Put the chillies, tomatoes, onion, garlic (and *pequin* chillies or ground chilli, if used) into the container of an electric blender or food processor and blend to a purée. Heat the oil in a heavy pan and cook the purée for 5 minutes, stirring constantly. Stir in the parsley, salt, pepper and sugar. When cool, stir in the olive oil and vinegar. Serve at room temperature.

Mexican Red Almond Sauce
Salsa de Almendra Roja

A rich sauce which is good with hot vegetables such as peas and green beans. Serve it also with fish, pork or chicken.

- 3 tablespoons olive oil
- 1 slice white bread
- 1 small onion, finely chopped
- 1 clove garlic, finely chopped
- 50 g/2 oz blanched almonds
- ½ teaspoon crumbled *pequin* chillies or ground chilli
- ½ teaspoon dried oregano
- 1 tomato, peeled, deseeded and chopped
- 375 ml/13 fl oz chicken stock, or water+stock cube
- salt and freshly ground black pepper to taste
- pinch of sugar

Heat 2 tablespoons of olive oil in a heavy pan and fry the bread until golden on both sides. Drain on kitchen towels and chop coarsely.

Add the remaining oil to the pan and gently fry the onion, garlic and almonds until the almonds are golden and the onion is soft but not coloured. Stir in the chilli. Transfer to the container of an electric blender or food processor and add the fried bread, oregano, tomato and 125 ml/4 fl oz of the stock. Blend to a purée.

Transfer to a saucepan and stir in the remaining stock and the seasonings. Simmer for 10–15 minutes. Serve hot.

Will keep for 1 week in the refrigerator.

Mexican Pasilla Chilli Sauce
Salsa de Chile Pasilla

- 4 *pasilla* chillies
- 1 teaspoon dried oregano
- salt and freshly ground black pepper to taste
- 1 tablespoon oil
- 3 tablespoons olive oil
- 1 tablespoon wine vinegar

Prepare the chillies as described in the previous recipe, but reserve their soaking liquid.

Put the chillies in the container of an electric blender or food processor with the minimum amount of soaking liquid necessary to make the blades operate properly. Blend to a purée and stir in the dried oregano, salt and pepper. Heat the oil in a heavy saucepan and cook the purée over a moderate heat for 5 minutes. Cool and stir in the olive oil and vinegar.

Serve at room temperature.

Ixni-Pec

This is the chilli sauce commonly associated with the Yucatan peninsula of Mexico, but it is also found in the Caribbean. Traditionally the yellow *habanero* chilli is used, but any hot pepper can be substituted, or you can use tinned Caribbean peppers. The bitterness of the juice from Seville oranges gives this sauce a characteristic flavour. If Seville oranges are not available, use two-thirds sweet orange juice with one-third lime juice.

Mix together equal quantities of finely chopped onion, finely chopped fresh or tinned chillies, chopped tomato and freshly squeezed Seville orange juice. Add salt to taste. Use within 24 hours.

Chilean Hot Pepper Sauce
Pebre

- 1 medium onion, finely chopped
- 1 clove garlic, finely chopped
- 2 tablespoons finely chopped parsley or coriander
- 1–8 fresh green chillies, deseeded and finely chopped
- 3 tablespoons olive oil
- 1 tablespoon lemon or lime juice
- salt to taste

Mix all the ingredients and leave to stand for 1 hour.

Brazilian Chilli and Lemon Sauce
Molho de Pimenta e Limeo

- 4 fresh red chillies
- 1 small onion, chopped
- 2 cloves garlic, chopped
- juice of 2 lemons
- ¼ teaspoon salt

Liquidize all the ingredients in an electric blender or food processor. Allow to stand at least 2 hours for the flavours to blend.

Brazilian Chilli and Tomato Sauce
Molho ao Tomate

- 3 fresh red chillies, chopped
- 4 canned tomatoes+4 tablespoons juice
- 2 tablespoons vinegar
- 2 tablespoons olive oil
- 2 tablespoons chopped parsley
- 1 teaspoon lemon juice
- a few fresh basil leaves
- ½ teaspoon salt
- ¼ teaspoon ground black pepper
- ¼ teaspoon sugar

Follow previous recipe.

Argentinian Parsley Sauce
Chimichurri

Serve with barbecued, grilled and roast meats.

- 6 tablespoons olive oil
- 6 tablespoons wine vinegar
- 2 cloves garlic, finely chopped
- 2 tablespoons finely chopped onion
- 1 teaspoon ground chilli
- ½ teaspoon dried oregano
- 3 tablespoons finely chopped parsley

Mix all the ingredients and allow to stand for 1 hour. Serve at room temperature.

- ½ teaspoon salt
- ¼ teaspoon freshly ground black pepper

Brazilian Hot Peppers in Olive Oil

In Brazil a tiny, ferociously hot birdseye chilli is used, but any fresh red or green chilli can be substituted.

Put whole chillies in a bowl with enough olive oil to cover. Leave to stand for several hours, by which time the oil will be chilli-hot.

Venezuelan Hot Peppers in Milk

Put 6 fresh chillies, halved lengthwise, in a glass jar with an onion slice, a clove of garlic and a sprig of mint leaves. Bring 300 ml/½ pint of milk and ½ teaspoon of salt to boil. Take off the heat immediately and allow to cool slightly. Pour over the chillies and leave overnight. Serve as a sauce with meat, poultry or fish.

Chilean Red Pepper Sauce
Salsa de Aji

- 24 fresh red chillies, deseeded and coarsely chopped
- 300 ml/½ pint wine vinegar
- 1 clove garlic, chopped
- 1 teaspoon salt
- 150 ml/¼ pint oil

Marinate the chillies in vinegar for at least 8 hours. Drain and reserve the vinegar. Put the chillies into the container of an electric blender or food processor with the garlic and enough of the reserved vinegar to blend to a purée. Add the salt and oil and blend for a little longer to produce a mayonnaise-type sauce. Thin with more reserved vinegar if necessary. For a milder sauce, discard the marinade vinegar and add fresh vinegar.

NOTE
Do not use the marinating chillies directly from the refrigerator. Chillies and oil should be at room temperature for processing.

Assorted Chilli Sauces

Chilli Sauce 1

- 8 fresh red chillies, stems removed, coarsely chopped
- 2 cloves garlic, chopped
- 1 teaspoon chopped fresh ginger
- 1 teaspoon sugar
- vinegar

Put the chillies, garlic, ginger and sugar into the container of an electric blender or food processor. Add enough vinegar to make the blades work properly, and blend to a purée. Add extra vinegar to give a thick pouring consistency. Bottle and keep in the refrigerator.

Chilli Sauce 2

- 300 g/10 oz fresh red chillies, stems removed, coarsely chopped
- 10 dried red chillies, stems removed, soaked, chopped
- 5 cloves garlic, chopped
- 1 teaspoon chopped fresh ginger
- 250 g/8 oz sugar
- 2 tablespoons salt
- 3 tablespoons vinegar

Put the fresh and dried chillies, garlic and ginger into the container of an electric blender or food processor. Measure out 450 ml/¾ pint of water and add as much as required to blend the chillies to a purée.

Transfer the purée to a heavy saucepan. Add the remaining water, sugar and salt. Bring to the boil, stirring constantly until the sugar has dissolved. Simmer over a very low heat for about 1¼ hours until thick, stirring occasionally. Stir in the vinegar and simmer for 5 minutes. Cool and bottle.

Chilli Sauce 3

- 3 tablespoons ground chilli
- 600 ml/1 pint vinegar
- 375 g/12 oz seedless sultanas
- 2 tablespoons chopped fresh ginger
- 6 cloves garlic, chopped
- 3 teaspoons salt
- 200 g/7 oz sugar
- 3 tablespoons tomato purée

Put all the ingredients except the tomato purée in a saucepan and bring to the boil, stirring constantly until the sugar has dissolved. Simmer, uncovered, for about 30 minutes until thick. Liquidize. Stir in the tomato purée. Bottle.

Chilli and Ginger Sauce

This is a Chinese Singaporean relish that is one of my favourites. It goes with almost anything but is particularly good with fried rice and noodle dishes.

- 1 tablespoon chopped fresh ginger
- 2 cloves garlic
- 1 tablespoon *sambal ulek** or 8 fresh red chillies, deseeded and chopped
- 1 tablespoon chicken stock
- 1 tablespoon lime or lemon juice
- salt to taste

Using a pestle and mortar, pound the first 3 ingredients to a paste. Stir in remaining ingredients. Taste and adjust the amounts of stock and juice as desired. A pinch of sugar can also be added.

Nuoc Mam

This is the classic Vietnamese chilli condiment, served at every meal. If preferred, use light soy sauce* instead of fish sauce for a less pungent flavour.

- 3 cloves garlic, chopped
- 2 fresh red chillies, deseeded and chopped, or 1 teaspoon *sambal ulek**
- 2 tablespoons lemon juice
- 2 tablespoons water
- 6 tablespoons fish sauce
- 2 teaspoons sugar

Use a pestle and mortar to pound the garlic and chillies to a paste. Mix in all the other ingredients, taste, and adjust the seasonings if necessary.

Sichuan Sauce

- 1 tablespoon vinegar
- 2 tablespoons sesame paste* or smooth peanut butter
- 3 tablespoons water
- 1 teaspoon chilli oil*
- 1 tablespoon sesame oil*
- 4 tablespoons light soy sauce*
- 2 cloves garlic, finely chopped
- 1 teaspoon very finely chopped fresh ginger
- 1 fresh red or green chilli, deseeded and very finely chopped
- 3 spring onions (white and some green), finely sliced
- 1 teaspoon sugar
- ½ teaspoon Sichuan peppercorns,* crushed

Mix all the ingredients together well. Serve with hot, warm or cold cooked chicken, fish or shellfish.

Thai Chilli Sauce

- 12 long dried red chillies, stems removed
- 3 cloves garlic, chopped
- 1 small onion, chopped
- 2 tablespoons fish sauce*
- 1 teaspoon sugar
- ½ teaspoon salt
- ¼ teaspoon ground black pepper

Tear the dried chillies into quarters and put them in a saucepan with just enough water to cover. Boil for 5 minutes. Drain and liquidize with all the other ingredients.

Thai Garlic and Vinegar Sauce

- 4 very finely chopped fresh red chillies
- 4 very finely chopped cloves garlic
- 1 tablespoon sugar
- ½ teaspoon salt
- a little ground black pepper
- 4 tablespoons of vinegar

Mix all the ingredients together.

Indonesian Gado Gado Sauce

- 6 long dried red chillies, stems and seeds removed, soaked
- 1 medium onion, chopped
- 2 cloves garlic, chopped
- ½ teaspoon *blachan** or more to taste (optional)
- 2 tablespoons oil
- 375 ml/13 fl oz coconut milk (p. 32)
- 6 tablespoons crunchy peanut butter
- 1 teaspoon brown sugar (or more to taste)
- 3 tablespoons water
- 2 teaspoons lemon juice
- salt to taste

Drain the soaked chillies, rip into pieces, and put in the container of an electric blender or food processor with the onion, garlic, *blachan* and 1 tablespoon of the oil. If additional liquid is needed to make the blades work properly, add a little of the chilli soaking water. Blend to a thick purée.

Heat the remaining 1 tablespoon of oil in a heavy saucepan and fry the purée over a medium heat for 4 minutes, stirring all the time to prevent burning. Add the coconut milk a little at a time, stirring constantly to prevent curdling. Add all the remaining ingredients and simmer for about 3 minutes until the sauce thickens. Cool and serve with Gado Gado Salad (p. 209).

NOTE

This sauce can be made in advance but must be kept in a refrigerator as coconut milk turns sour in warm temperatures.

Romesco Sauce

The classic Spanish sauce containing chilli, which is clearly related to the Mexican sauces thickened with nuts (p. 270). Romesco Sauce can either be served as a condiment or added to braised dishes to give extra piquancy.

- olive oil for frying
- 1 slice white bread, crusts removed
- 2 tablespoons flaked almonds
- 3 cloves garlic, chopped
- 2 dried red chillies, deseeded and soaked in warm water for 30 minutes
- 1 tablespoon chopped parsley
- 2 tablespoons chicken stock
- 2 tablespoons dry sherry
- 1 tablespoon wine vinegar
- salt to taste

Heat about 80 mm/¼ in of olive oil in a heavy frying-pan and gently fry the bread until golden on both sides. Remove and drain on kitchen paper. Chop coarsely. Add the almonds and garlic to the oil in the pan and gently fry until pale gold. Remove and drain on kitchen paper.

Put the bread, almonds and garlic into the container of an electric blender or food processor. Add all the remaining ingredients and blend to a purée.

Rouille

The southern French version of a chilli-flavoured sauce can be made in a similar way to Romesco Sauce, i.e. thickened with bread, although nuts are not usually used. The alternative method is based on a mayonnaise sauce, as in this recipe. *Rouille* is traditionally served with *bourride* (fish stew) or fish soup. For the latter, toasted French bread is spread with *rouille*, topped with grated cheese and dunked in the soup. It can also be served with boiled potatoes or poached fish.

- 2 cloves garlic
- 2 egg yolks at room temperature
- 250 ml/8 fl oz olive oil at room temperature
- ½ teaspoon ground chilli
- ½ teaspoon paprika

Using a pestle and mortar, pound the garlic until crushed. Add the egg yolks and stir to break up. Continue stirring the egg yolks briskly, always in the same direction, and gradually dribble in the olive oil to make a mayonnaise. Once the sauce has begun to thicken, the oil can be added a little less sparsely. When all the oil has been absorbed and the sauce is really thick, stir in the chilli and paprika. Chill and use within 24 hours.

Chilli Soup Sauce

8 dried red chillies
300 ml/½ pint vodka

Put the dried red chillies in a colander and pour a kettle of boiling water over them. Drain them thoroughly and put them in a bottle. Top up with vodka.

Use a few drops to pep up soups and salad dressings.

Chilli Sherry

Follow the previous recipe exactly but use sherry instead of vodka. Put in a bottle with a sprinkler or a cork with a hole and keep topping up with sherry . . . for years! Use a few drops in soups and stews.

Pepper Wine

Yet another Caribbean version uses fresh red chillies – preferably the fragrant Scotch Bonnets – with light rum. Use for flavouring local soups such as Callaloo (recipe p. 73).

Chinese Chilli Oil

Take an empty wine bottle, wash and dry thoroughly. Loosely pack with dried red chillies. Fill with oil. Pierce a hole through the cork (to act as a sprinkler) and replace. Cover with a small glass or kitchen foil so that the air cannot penetrate. Leave for one week before using. Will keep for months in a cool place, getting stronger all the time. Sprinkle a little on Chinese dishes just before serving.

Pizza Oil

Take an empty wine bottle, wash and dry thoroughly. Push in a large sprig of rosemary, a small bunch of thyme, a bay leaf and dried red chillies to taste. Fill up with good quality olive oil and proceed as above. Serve with pizzas, to be sprinkled on to individual taste.

Glossary

ALLSPICE
A dried black berry native to the New World. Popular with Caribbean cooks and used extensively in the Middle East. It is usually ground and has a musty fragrance similar to nutmeg and cloves.

BAHARAT
A spice mixture used in Middle Eastern cookery. A recipe appears on p. 40.

BEANCURD, FRESH
Also called *tofu*. Available from Chinese food shops. It can be kept in the refrigerator for up to 3 days if covered with water. Change the water daily. Cut into small dice and use in Chinese soups.

BESAN
A flour made from ground chickpeas. It can be bought in specialist Asian food shops. Alternatively, grind dried chickpeas in an electric coffee grinder. Wheat flour is not a suitable substitute.

BLACHAN
Blachan is the Malay name for the dried fermented shrimp paste which is used throughout South-East Asia, where it is known by various names, e.g. *ngapi* in Burma, *trasi* in Indonesia, *kapi* in Thailand. For the sake of convenience, it is always referred to as *blachan* in this book. *Blachan* is sold as a soft brown block or in powder form. When raw it has a strong, rather unpleasant smell. It should be wrapped in plastic and stored in an airtight jar so that its smell does not affect other foodstuffs. It keeps indefinitely.

Blachan is always cooked before being eaten. It is usually ground to a purée with other ingredients such as onions, ginger and garlic before being fried to form the basis for a rich sauce. However, if it is being mixed with ingredients that will be eaten raw it should be wrapped in foil and either grilled or fried in a dry pan for 2 or 3 minutes.

BLACK MUSTARD SEED
Tiny brownish-black seeds with a hot nutty flavour that are used in southern Indian cooking. European yellow mustard seeds cannot be substituted.

BLACK GRAM
A lentil used in southern Indian dishes. It can be bought ready husked from specialist shops. It does not need soaking before cooking.

CANDLENUTS
Rich, creamy nuts that are ground to thicken Malaysian and Indonesian curries. Almonds or macadamias can be used instead.

CARDAMOM
One of the world's most expensive spices, with a lovely lemony fragrance. The finest cardamoms have a straw-coloured pod which should be slit or 'bruised' to release the full flavour of the small black seeds inside. A coarser type of cardamom has a tough black pod which should be discarded.

CASAREEP
A bitter-sweet thickening agent made from the juice of cassava root. Used in West Indian cooking. No substitute.

CHICKPEA FLOUR
See *besan*.

CHORIZO
A spicy sausage used in Spanish and Mexican cooking.

COCONUT MILK AND COCONUT CREAM
See pp. 32–3.

CURRY LEAVES
Dark green leaves rather like bay leaves, though with a different flavour, which are used in southern Indian, Sri Lankan and Malaysian curries. They are sometimes available fresh or dried in specialist shops. Fresh are better than dried. Substitute a bay leaf for a sprig of curry leaves.

DRIED BLACK MUSHROOMS
Available from Chinese food stores. Soak in warm water for 30 minutes before using.

DRIED PRAWNS
Small sun-dried prawns or shrimps. They should be soaked in warm water for about 10 minutes before using. Store in a screwtop jar. Fresh prawns cannot be substituted.

DRIED PRAWN POWDER
Ground dried prawns which can be bought in packets from specialist shops. Alternatively, grind dried prawns (without soaking) in a coffee grinder.

DRIED SHRIMP PASTE
See *blachan*.

FENNEL
A dried seed, similar in appearance to cumin. It is often used in conjunction with cumin in curries from Malaysia, Sri Lanka and southern India. It is sometimes confused with aniseed but the flavour of fennel is less pronounced. Aniseed can be substituted, but use half quantities.

FENUGREEK
Small, hard, pale brown, flat-sided seeds which are an essential ingredient (though in small quantities) in Indian curries, particularly fish curries. Fenugreek is also used in Middle

Eastern cooking and is a main ingredient in the fiery Yemeni chilli paste – *hilba* (p. 42). In fact, *hilba* is the Arab name for fenugreek. If the whole seeds are soaked in water, they swell up and become slightly gelatinous.

Note: Dried fenugreek leaves may also be sold as 'fenugreek'. They are used in Indian and Middle Eastern cooking but are not included in any recipes in this book.

FISH SAUCE
A thin, brown sauce with a pronounced salty fish flavour which is a basic ingredient in Thai, Burmese and Vietnamese cooking. It looks rather like thin soy sauce, but is in fact the liquid residue of fish and salt packed into wooden barrels. It is an acquired taste. Thin soy sauce may be substituted, though, of course, the taste will be different.

FIVE SPICE POWDER
A Chinese mixed spice seasoning made from ground star anise, fennel, cloves, cinnamon and Sichuan pepper.

GARAM MASALA
A fragrant spice mixture used in Indian cooking. It can be bought ready-mixed from specialist shops. A recipe appears on p. 39.

GHEE
Clarified butter, used in Indian and Arabic cooking. It imparts a special flavour and can be heated to high temperatures without burning.

GINGER
A succulent root with a pungent flavour that is an essential ingredient in Chinese, Indian and South-East Asian cooking. Fresh ginger should be peeled and finely chopped or grated. It will keep for several weeks if wrapped in a plastic bag and stored in the fridge. It can also be peeled, put in a jar, immersed in dry sherry and kept in the fridge. The sherry can then be used as a substitute for rice wine in Chinese recipes.

Note: Dried, powdered ginger cannot be substituted for fresh ginger, but in some parts of the world (e.g. North Africa, the Middle East and the Caribbean) dried ginger is preferred to fresh ginger root. In the recipes in this book, it is clearly stated whether fresh or dried ginger should be used.

HARISSA
A red chilli paste used extensively in North African cooking. It is also diluted with water and used as a condiment. Available from specialist shops.

HILBA
A chilli paste from the Gulf. A recipe appears on p. 42.

HOISIN SAUCE
A thick sweetish brown sauce used in Chinese cooking and available from specialist shops. It will keep for several months in the refrigerator.

LAOS POWDER
See *Lengkuas*.

LEMON GRASS

A lemon-scented plant that looks like a spring onion. Only the fleshy part at the bottom of the stem is used in cooking, and this is either pounded to a paste or bruised and added whole.

Dried and powdered lemon grass is sold in plastic pots as *serai* or *sereh* powder. Use 1 teaspoon in place of a stalk of fresh lemon grass. Alternatively use ½ teaspoon of grated lemon rind.

LENGKUAS

The root of the greater galangal, which looks rather like ginger. It is popular with South-East Asian cooks and has an unmistakable delicate fragrance. Fresh *lengkuas* is thinly sliced and one or two slices are added to fish and chicken dishes. It is rarely found outside the region, though dried, powdered *lengkuas* is sometimes sold in specialist shops under its Indonesian name – *laos*. There is no substitute, and *laos* powder does not have the subtlety of fresh *lengkuas* root.

MASA HARINA

Mexican flour made from corn that has been soaked in lime water. Used for making *tortillas* (Mexican flat bread). From Mexican food shops.

MEXICAN GREEN TOMATOES

These are a special variety of tomato and are *not* under-ripe red tomatoes. They are available in cans from specialist shops.

ORANGE BLOSSOM WATER OR ORANGE FLOWER WATER

A fragrant distillation of orange blossom, available in Middle Eastern and Greek food stores. A concentrated version is also available.

OYSTER SAUCE

A thick sauce made from oysters and used in Chinese dishes to heighten other flavours. It is available bottled in specialist shops.

PINE NUTS

Small, oval nuts which are the kernels of the Mediterranean umbrella pine.

RAS-EL-HANOUT

A spice mixture used in North African cooking. A recipe appears on p. 39.

ROSE WATER

A distillation of rose petals used in Indian, Middle Eastern and North African cooking. Available from specialist shops and sometimes from chemists.

SAFFRON

The world's most expensive spice, made from stamens of the autumn crocus. It has a delicate fragrance and gives food a rich yellow colouring. Saffron threads should be soaked in a little warm water or milk for 10 minutes before using, then added to the other ingredients with the soaking liquid. Tiny pots of powdered saffron are also available. Use in minute quantities.

SAMBAL ULEK

Indonesian-style puréed red chillies which can be bought in specialist shops.

SERAI POWDER
See *Lemon grass.*

SESAME OIL
A rich golden oil extracted from toasted sesame seeds. It has an incomparable flavour and is used sparingly to season Chinese dishes. It is also used extensively in Korean and Burmese cooking.

SESAME PASTE
A thick paste made from ground sesame seeds. It looks rather like peanut butter and is an essential ingredient in Middle Eastern cooking. It is called *tahina* and is available in tins or plastic pots from specialist Middle Eastern shops. After opening, a *tahina* will keep for many months in a cool place.

Chinese sesame paste is made from toasted sesame seeds and has a different flavour. The two are not interchangeable.

SESAME SEEDS
Small, creamy-coloured seeds with a delightful nutty taste. They are widely used in the Middle East and are an essential ingredient in Burmese and Korean cooking. The seeds are sometimes lightly toasted to a pale golden brown, which intensifies their flavour.

SICHUAN PEPPERCORNS
Hot reddish-brown 'peppercorns' from Sichuan in China, which give a distinctive taste to regional cooking. Available from Chinese shops.

SMEN
See *Ghee.*

SOY SAUCE
A sauce made from salted soya beans, indispensable in Far Eastern cooking. Two types are mentioned in this book. Light soy sauce is thinner and lighter in flavour than some other types. It is used in cooking and as a condiment to sprinkle on food before eating. Dark soy sauce is thicker and stronger in flavour and is mainly used for cooking. Both add saltiness to food. Soy sauce will keep indefinitely without refrigeration.

TAHINA
See *Sesame paste.*

TAMARIND
The acidic fruit of the tamarind tree, found only in the tropics. It is usually used in a dried form. Soak 1 tablespoon of dried tamarind pulp in 4 tablespoons of hot water for 5–10 minutes, then strain and press the pulp to extract all the flavour. Discard the pulp and any stones.

Instant tamarind extract is sold in some Indian specialist shops. Use 1 teaspoon to replace the above quantity. If unavailable, use 1 tablespoon of lemon juice.

TAUCHEO PASTE
A salted soy bean paste, available from Chinese grocery shops.

Index